The Logic of Life

Uncovering the New Economics
of Everything

TIM HARFORD

Little, Brown

LITTLE, BROWN

First published in Great Britain in 2008 by Little, Brown

Copyright © Tim Harford 2008

Tim Harford has asserted his right to be identified as the author of this work.

A CIP catalogue record for this book
is available from the British Library

HB ISBN 978-0-316-02756-4
CF 978-0-316-02757-1

Typeset in Janson by M Rules
Printed and bound in Great Britain by
Clays Ltd, St Ives plc

Little, Brown
An imprint of
Little, Brown Book Group
100 Victoria Embankment
London EC4Y 0DY

An Hachette Livre UK Company

www.littlebrown.co.uk

To Adrian
and
Africa, who will get her turn in the buggy

Contents

Introduction

This morning, I strapped my two-year-old daughter into her buggy and walked her to the toddlers' art club at our local community centre. Our Hackney neighbourhood is rough around the edges. A town planner might raise an eyebrow at the mechanic's yard, piled high with wrecks, at the end of a row of terraced houses. A sociologist might draw your attention to the betting shops and massage parlours, or the pool of dried-up vomit in the gutter outside our local bar. A novelist might linger descriptively on the bunch of dead flowers, bleached and desiccated in the bright June sunshine; they were propped forlornly against the wall of a notorious nightclub, commemorating a young man who was recently shot dead.

But I am an economist. You might think that my mind would be elsewhere, thinking about stock markets or inflation figures, but if so, you'd be mistaken. I notice the gamblers and the prostitutes, the drinkers and the gangs. I just see them in a different light. Economists are always looking for the hidden logic behind life, the way it is shaped by countless unseen rational decisions. Sometimes these rational decisions make life better, sometimes they make it worse. But if we want to understand our world – or how to change it – then understanding the rational choices that shape it is a good place to start.

To get to our destination, my daughter and I have to cross a busy road. This is a lot harder than it should be, because the traffic lights that smoothly guide the traffic through the T-junction give neither sufficient time nor any signals to pedestrians. I scurried across to the central island, spun my daughter's stroller around so that I was pulling it behind me, walked in front of a stationary double-decker, and peered out across a second lane, looking for a chance to scamper to the other side.

The dangerous crossing is the result of a political failure. In affluent Stoke Newington, just a mile away, there are three freshly painted pedestrian crossings on the main street, even though that street was never difficult to cross. Both neighbourhoods are covered by the same local government. What can account for the disparity? If I wasn't looking for the rational incentives under the surface, I might simply grumble about the way that rich white areas find it easy to pull strings and make friends in government. Or, if my political biases were different, I could grumble that the poor residents are just incompetent and stupid.

But both of those views – like much of today's conventional wisdom – are shallow. The economist's way of thinking suggests a deeper answer. The typical resident of Stoke Newington Church Street owns his or her own house, plans to live there for years, and so has a lot to gain from improvements in the neighbourhood. The political influence of Stoke Newington is stronger only because the individuals there have a stronger incentive to be politically active. In my neck of the woods, by contrast, residents tend to come and go; time spent fighting for a pedestrian crossing would be, for many, time wasted on producing an amenity that would benefit neither absentee landlords nor their transient tenants.

That is just the hint of an answer, idly formed while pushing my daughter past the local corner shops and nail salons. Even that hint is more help to a reformer than simply railing against the injustices of life. But to be convinced, I hope you'd want to see a little less speculation and a little more evidence.

A new breed of economists is gathering just that kind of

evidence, peeling away layers of confusing complexity and revealing the surprising truth. How much do my neighbours and I really care about living with dangerous road crossings, night-club shootings, and rowdy bars? For an answer, don't ask the neighbours, who would (rationally) exaggerate. Ask an estate agent. Economists have applied this deceptively simple principle with startling results. By comparing public data on sex offenders with a map of house prices, for example, they can see that when a paedophile moves in, the price of nearby houses drops – but only by about 4 per cent.

Home prices are a tool the economist can use to uncover the truth, like the hero of a spy movie spraying an aerosol that reveals a hidden web of security lasers. The movie character uses the aerosol, but what really matters to him are the lasers. In the same way, the economist uses information about prices, but what he really cares about are the choices we make and the values we hold. Those values are often concealed: would you really admit to the authorities that your outrage about a paedophile moving in around the corner would be assuaged by a slightly cheaper mortgage?

The fact that some people will, indeed, make that kind of trade-off – in this case, perhaps, students or childless couples – is fundamental to the idea of rationality I explore in this book. Such trade-offs are not often discussed, especially in polite company. They may even be made unconsciously. Yet as long as they are made, the rational choice framework helps us understand the world.

The argument of this book is: first, that rational behaviour is much more widespread than you would expect and crops up in the most unexpected places – including the heads of oversexed teenagers; and second, that the economists' faith in rationality (faith is, I think, the right word) produces real insight. In fact, I believe that if you do not understand the rational choices that underlie much of our behaviour, you cannot understand the world in which we live.

xii   **The Logic of Life**

Drug addicts and teenage muggers can be rational. Suburban sprawl and inner-city decay are certainly rational. Those endless meetings at the office and the grotesque injustices of working life? Rational. In the hands of economists, 'rational choice theory' produces an x-ray image of human life. Like the x-ray, rational choice theory does not show everything. Nor is the picture necessarily very pretty. But it shows you something important, and something that you could not see before.

At our destination, my daughter wriggled out of her buggy and scampered off to daub her hands in bright blue poster paint. I sat in the corner, thinking about the rational reasons why only two of the thirty-one accompanying parents were fathers; we'll get to those reasons in Chapter Three. My daughter interrupted my musings by demanding a snack, so we shared a Garibaldi biscuit and then I held her hand as she climbed up the stairs and slid down the slide several times. I helped her bounce on the trampoline and then we stuck glow-in-the-dark pictures of rocket ships and astronauts on to a paper plate before covering them with blue glitter. After a while she turned her face up to mine and stuck out her tiny nose for an Eskimo kiss. It was a perfect half hour.

There is nothing irrational about love; indeed, without our passions and our principles, where would the motivation come from to make rational choices about anything? So a world explained by economics is not a world lacking love, hate, or any other emotion. Yet it is a world in which people can generally be expected to make rational decisions, and where those rational decisions suggest some astonishing explanations for many of life's mysteries. It is this world that I would like to show you.

One

Introducing the logic of life

The economics of sex, crime and Minnie Mouse

Harpo Studios, Chicago

'Parents, brace yourselves.' With those words, Oprah Winfrey introduced America to the shocking news of the teenage oral sex craze. In the *Atlantic*, Caitlin Flanagan wrote, 'The moms in my set are convinced – they're certain; they know for a *fact* – that all over the city, in the very best schools, in the nicest families, in the leafiest neighbourhoods, twelve- and thirteen-year-old girls are performing oral sex on as many boys as they can.' Flanagan poked a bit of fun, but she wasn't really laughing: she was convinced that the fears were largely justified. Indeed, the American 'blowjob epidemic' has now been addressed everywhere from PBS documentaries to the editorial page of the *New York Times*, sometimes with giddy and slightly voyeuristic horror, sometimes with calm reassurance that the epidemic is simply a myth.

The so-called epidemic is often exaggerated, but it's no myth. One recent study, conducted by researchers at Johns Hopkins Bayview Medical Center in Baltimore, found that between 1994 and 2004, young people between ages twelve and twenty-four became more than twice as likely to report that they'd recently had oral sex. (For boys the rate climbed from 16 per cent to 32 per cent; for girls, from 14 per cent to 38 per cent.) Anecdotal evidence from experts suggests that the true increase may be even higher. I sought advice from Professor Jonathan Zenilman, an expert at Johns Hopkins University on sexually transmitted diseases. He explained to me that in 1990, perhaps half the women and a quarter of the men who came to his clinic (both teenagers and adults) sometimes performed oral sex on their partners. He believes that oral sex is now more much more common: 'Now it's seventy-five to eighty per cent.' And while it's the blowjobs that predictably have caused the panic, oral sex is now much more equitably distributed between boys and girls than in 1990. 'Epidemic' might be putting it too strongly, but oral sex is definitely in vogue.

The question few people seem to have asked is 'Why?' Are kids really becoming more depraved – or are they just being smart? Might there not be such a thing as a rational blowjob?

I'll say more about exactly what 'rational' means later in this chapter, after we've dealt with those libidinous teenagers. But the basic idea is not complicated: rational people respond to trade-offs and to incentives. When the costs or benefits of something change, people change their behaviour. Rational people think – not always consciously – about the future as well as the present as they try to anticipate likely consequences of their actions in an uncertain world.

Armed with this basic definition of rationality, then, we can ask: what are the costs, benefits and likely consequences of a blowjob? Okay, perhaps the benefits are too obvious to be stated, particularly for the recipient. But it should also be obvious that the cost of a close substitute for oral sex has risen: regular sex is more costly than it used to be, because of the spread of HIV/Aids. HIV is much more likely to be spead by regular sex than oral sex. Many teenagers know that: one recent study of sex education concluded that it was more common for US kids to be taught about HIV/Aids than about preventing pregnancy. Teenagers may also know of other sexually transmitted diseases such as gonorrhoea, an infection that might make a girl infertile if transmitted through penetrative sex but when transmitted by oral sex may have much milder symptoms, such as a sore throat. The costs of oral sex are, quite simply, lower than the costs of regular sex.

If teenage girls really do weigh those costs and benefits before going down on their boyfriends, this is a straightforward explanation for the growing popularity of oral sex. Since regular sex is riskier than it used to be, and since teenagers are unlikely to have given up on the idea of having sex, the rest is basic economics. When the price of Coca-Cola rises, rational people drink more Pepsi. When the price of a flat in the city goes up, rational people move out to the suburbs. And when the price of penetrative sex rises, rational teenagers have more oral sex instead.

Certainly, the evidence suggests that teenagers are moving towards less risky sexual behaviour. The US Centers for Disease Control and Prevention report that since the beginning of the 1990s, the number of teenage virgins has risen by over 15 per cent. There are still a few million teenagers who haven't given up on sex, of course, but since the early 1990s they've switched to using birth control methods that will also protect them from sexually transmitted infections. Use of the contraceptive pill is down by nearly a fifth, but use of condoms is up by more than a third.

Perhaps Oprah shouldn't be quite so worried. Oral sex isn't a symptom of more promiscuous teenagers. In fact, it's a sign that teenagers are behaving *more* responsibly, in enthusiastically – and rationally – choosing an alternative to riskier sex.

This is all very cute – or horrifying, depending on your tastes. But it is also a glib explanation. Before blithely claiming that oral sex is more popular because rational teenagers know that regular sex is riskier, a real economist would want a tighter hypothesis and serious data to back it up.

That real economist might well be Thomas Stratmann, who with the law professor Jonathan Klick has pinned down the rationality of the teenage sex drive rather precisely. Rational teenagers would have less risky sex if the cost of risky sex rose, so the question is how to work out whether that is how teenagers behave. That requires some precisely measurable source of increased cost, something more quantifiable than a general increase in the amount of education about Aids.

The US Constitution has duly obliged, by providing a federal structure that allows states to determine their rules governing teenage abortion; some permit teenagers to have abortions without the notification or consent of their parents, and some do not. Such laws provide plenty of fodder for political controversy, but they also provide a natural experiment for researchers. Since abortion notification laws make it more difficult for teenagers – but not for adults – to get an abortion, they should discourage risky sex among teens, relative to adults. If, that is, teenagers are in fact rational.

It is not hard to see that abortion notification laws raise the cost of getting pregnant, at least for those teenagers who, given the choice, would have terminated an accidental pregnancy without telling their parents. If teenagers look ahead and work all this out, they should also take extra steps to prevent that accidental pregnancy – steps which, besides that of choosing oral sex over regular sex, are likely to include more use of condoms, or perhaps no sexual activity at all.

Sex is not a calculated act, and so that degree of foresight may sound implausible, but Klick and Stratmann found persuasive evidence that abortion notification laws really do discourage teenagers from having risky sex. Looking at statistics from sexual health clinics, they found that whenever and wherever parental notification laws are passed, gonorrhoea rates start to fall in the teenage population relative to the adult population – to whom, of course, the new laws do not apply. The only explanation for this would seem to be that an abortion notification law significantly raises the risk of unprotected sex, and that the teenagers rationally respond to that risk.

Sex, then, has a cost. The risk of Aids – along with intensive education about that risk – has probably encouraged teenagers to switch to a lower-cost substitute, oral sex. The threat to careless or unlucky girls that they will have to tell Mum or Dad that they accidentally got pregnant has done something similar.

A young economist named Andrew Francis has gone still further. If oral sex is a substitute for regular sex, he reasoned, isn't it at least possible that heterosexual sex is a substitute for homosexual sex? The rise of Aids has made it more risky than it used to be to have sex with men, making homosexuality more dangerous for men and heterosexuality more dangerous for women. If the cost of one sexual orientation is perceived to have gone up, wouldn't we expect rational people to respond to that?

Francis stumbled upon the possibility – it remains speculative – while trawling through a survey from the early 1990s that had asked nearly 3,500 people intimate questions about their sexual preference and sexual history. The survey also asked people whether they knew anyone with Aids. He then concentrated on people whose relatives suffered from Aids, because you can choose your friends but not your relatives: it would not be surprising, or informative, to discover that gay men knew more people with Aids than straight men.

Francis discovered that both men and women with a relative who had Aids were less likely to have sex with men, and less likely to say they were attracted to men. At first, that didn't seem to make much sense – the unfortunate relatives were quite likely to be gay men, but if anything, genetic theories suggest that people with gay relatives should be more likely to be gay, not less. Then he realised what was going on: 'Oh my God, they were scared of Aids!' he told Stephen Dubner and Steven Levitt for the *New York Times Magazine*.

With that insight, everything fits. People with a relative who had Aids were more likely to be aware of how terrible it is, especially back in the early 1990s, when treatments for Aids were very limited and the disease killed many people within two years.

Then what? Men who had a relative with Aids were less likely to say that they found the idea of sex with men appealing. Women who had a relative with Aids also seemed to be turned off the idea of sex with men: they were more likely to say they were homosexual or bisexual. Both men and women with an acute awareness of the risks of Aids were shifting away from an obvious way of catching it.

Francis found a couple of other curiosities in the data that backed up this interpretation. While people who had a relative with Aids did shy away from sex with men, their earlier sexual history didn't reflect that. They were just as likely to have had sex with men at some stage, but then – becoming aware of the risks – they stopped. Furthermore, people with a relative with Aids were more likely to be having oral sex and were less likely to have syphilis, which suggests their close experience of Aids had inspired safer sex practices.

And the oddest fact of all: while none of the men in the survey who had a relative with Aids called themselves homosexual or said the idea of sex with men was appealing, those men were more likely than other self-reportedly heterosexual men to be having anal sex – but with women. Perhaps, just perhaps, men who preferred sex with other men had decided that this was a reasonable – and safer – substitute.

You've just been reading a brief introduction to the economics of oral sex, underage abortions, Aids and homosexuality. A fair question at this point would be: 'What business do economists have poking around in such matters?'

A new breed of economists is discovering something new about sex, crime, gambling, war, marriage, ghettos, racism, politics and the last million years of human history. These economists are using the assumption of rational behaviour as a way of focusing on something important about all these subtle, complicated topics. This is not to dismiss the contributions of psychology, history, sociology and all the other ways we might seek to understand the world. But since we cannot apply all these disciplines at once, we have to simplify. Economists hope that their way of simplifying the world will provide more insight than it destroys. But why should you believe them, and why should you listen to what I have to say about them?

First, because it can be useful: the assumption that people are rational leads us to some clear and testable theories about the way the world works. It can help us to strip forbidding layers of complexity from intractable-seeming problems – for instance, inner-city deprivation – and guide us towards possible solutions. If crime rates are high in some areas, then rational choice theory says that crime must pay in those areas: we need to look for a way of raising the cost or lowering the benefit of committing crime. If inner-city teenagers don't have qualifications, then rational choice theory says that they must believe the benefits of getting the qualifications are outweighed by the costs: we need to work out if they're right, and see if we can change the incentives for them. And so on. A rigorously simplified view of the world can help even when it is oversimplified, because the simplicity makes it easier to spot the unexpected implications of your ideas, to uncover inconsistencies in your view of the world, and to test your ideas against the evidence.

Of course, there isn't much use in producing clear and testable theories if the theories are always wrong. But they aren't – economists' faith in people's rationality is usually about right. Now, I'm not claiming that people are always and everywhere rational – as we shall see, it is easy to find instances where that is not true – but I do hope to convince you that people are sufficiently rational often enough to make the assumption of rational choice a very useful one. Later in this chapter I'll say more about what it's useful for.

But rational choice theory is not merely useful – it's also fun. The new economics of everything – sex and crime, racism and office politics – offers us perspectives that are unexpected, counter-intuitive, and refreshingly disrespectful of the conventional wisdom. The economists behind these iconoclastic ideas are often fascinating characters, too, and we'll get to meet them throughout the book.

In the rest of this chapter, I aim to flesh out the concept of rationality with some more examples, from collectible sports cards to Mexican prostitutes. But before I get to that, it's time to say some more about what I mean – and don't mean – when I talk about rational behaviour, and why the idea is often seen as controversial.

Let me remind you of the simple definition of rationality I laid out earlier. Rational people respond to incentives: when it becomes more costly to do something, they will tend to do less; when it becomes easier, cheaper, or more beneficial, they will tend to do more. In weighing up their choices, they will bear in mind the overall constraints upon them: not just the costs and benefits of a specific choice, but their total budget. And they will also consider the future consequences of present choices. As far as my definition goes, that's pretty much it. (It is true that economists sometimes use the word *rationality* to encompass more shades of meanings than this, but the technical distinctions are not important for our purposes.)

The definition doesn't seem controversial when I put it down in black and white. It's so obvious. So true. If the price of a Toyota rises, you buy a Honda instead. (People respond to incentives.) When your income rises, you plump for a Ferrari. (People consider their budget.) You know that the loan to buy that Ferrari must eventually be repaid. (People are mindful of future consequences.) It's almost banal. But if it's so banal, why have some of the economists we'll meet in these pages prompted storms of invective by reasoning from these first principles?

The controversy comes only when people realise that economists are not restricting their brand of analysis to straightforward financial transactions, such as buying cars. Cost is not just about money. The cost of sex includes the risk of Aids and the risk of unwanted pregnancy; if that cost rises, you'll tend to choose a safer kind of sex. Your total 'budget' isn't just the cash in your bank account. It also encompasses your time, energy, talent and attention, and it determines not only what make of car you end up with, but what kind of spouse. You bear in mind the future costs of an addiction to cigarettes just as much as your loan repayments. It is when I make this kind of claim that you may stop feeling that my statement that 'people are rational' is not banal at all, and might even be a little dangerous.

If you've read some of the criticisms of economics, you may be starting to fear that you're reading a book about an infamous character by the name of *Homo economicus*, or 'economic man'. He's the caricature of what economists are generally supposed to assume about people. Homo economicus doesn't understand human emotions like love, friendship, or charity, or even envy, hate or anger – only selfishness and greed. He knows his own mind, never makes mistakes, and has unlimited willpower. And he's capable of performing impossibly complex financial calculations instantaneously and infallibly. Homo economicus is the kind of guy who would strangle his own grandmother for a quid – assuming it didn't take more than a quid's worth of time, of course.

   With the greed of an Enron executive, the cold brilliance of Mr Spock, and the emotional intelligence of an armchair, Homo economicus doesn't get invited to a lot of parties. He isn't invited to my book, either – when I say that 'people are rational', rest assured that Homo economicus isn't what I have in mind. There's a long history of heated debate over this odd creature's place in economics – Peter Drucker wrote *The End of Economic Man* as far back as 1939. And some of the criticisms do have merit, especially when applied to macroeconomics and finance theory – some economists do, indeed, make some unrealistic assumptions about the extent to which normal people consider the fiendishly complicated interaction of variables such as inflation rates and estimated future government spending when weighing up whether to agitate for a pay rise or buy a new refrigerator. Fortunately, for me as well as for you, that's not what this book is about.

But because Homo economicus lies behind many criticisms of economists and rational choice theory, I need to set out how this crude caricature differs from what I mean when I talk about people being rational.

First, I do not suggest that people are wholly self-interested or obsessed with money. People are motivated by all kinds of normal human emotions – a fear of Aids or parental disapproval, as we've seen, or, as we'll later see, romantic love or racial hatred. These motivations are not financial, and not always selfish – but our responses to them are rational. As any teenager will remind you, no less planning, calculating and strategising goes on about matters of the heart than about matters of the wallet. So, yes, you're mad about the boy – but if you weren't, you wouldn't be dreaming up all those clever strategies to get him.

Second, I do not argue that we have the consciously calculating mind of a Spock. We do make complex calculations of costs and benefits when we act rationally, but we often do it unconsciously, just as when someone throws a ball for us to catch, we aren't conscious of our brain solving differential equations to work out where it's going to land. Most of us couldn't work out the calculations behind catching the ball if you gave us a pen and paper, yet the brain carries them out unconsciously. It's often the same for the calculations behind a rational analysis of costs and benefits. Homo economicus might instantly tally up in his mind the cost of the monthly interest payments he'll forgo by dipping into his savings account for a new fridge – or the risk of having unprotected sex. The real people who fill this book do not – but neither do they ignore such costs, or carry on regardless when the costs change.

Third, I do not argue that we are blessed with omniscience or perfect self-control. Homo economicus never regrets ordering dessert – he has infallibly weighed the fleeting gustatory pleasure against the likely effects on his girth. In reality, there are clear limits to our ability to calculate, think ahead and see our way through certain cognitive traps. There are also limits to our willpower – we make resolutions and then we break them. I explore some of these frailties in the next chapter. And yet I will argue that we are often too quick to label behaviour as irrational. Take the dessert trade-off: bad for you, but tastes good. That it's bad for you is less of a worry if you've got access to advanced healthcare – and some careful economic studies suggest that we're fatter these days in part because we've rationally recognised that it has become safer to be obese and harder to exercise.

In contrast, we now know much more about the health risks of smoking, and medical progress has not greatly diminished those risks. The response? Smoking rates have fallen dramatically. Maybe our attitudes to cigarettes and desserts are more rational than they seem at first glance. Yet in the end, just how rational we are is a question to be settled by research, not armchair theorising. Throughout this book I will be looking at evidence of our capacity to look ahead and reason backwards. I'll find evidence of mistakes, but also evidence of sophistication from apparently unsophisticated people.

Fourth, I do not deny that humans, unlike our infallible friend Homo economicus, have irrational quirks and foibles. Take the behaviour that Andrew Francis seems to have discovered – it is incredible to find evidence that sexual orientation responds to incentives. But that is rational behaviour of a strange and limited kind, because having a relative with Aids does not actually increase one's chances of catching the disease: the true costs and benefits of risky sex don't change, only the perceptions of them. When a gay man responds to a relative's suffering from Aids by switching to sex with women, either he is overreacting to the danger or he had been underreacting before he was personally touched by experience of the disease. One of those reactions is an error. This is hardly a case study of perfect rationality.

Does this mean that rational choice theory is as much use as flat earth theory? No. It's more like a perfectly spherical-earth theory. The earth isn't a perfect sphere, as anyone who has climbed Mount Everest will tell you. But it's nearly a sphere, and for many purposes the simplification that the earth is spherical will do nicely.

I've claimed that we're smart, but I've admitted that we make mistakes. The laboratory work of psychologists and 'behavioural' economists has provided plenty of proof. One of the most famous examples was discovered by Daniel Kahneman and Amos Tversky: their experiments showed that people make different choices depending on how the choices are framed. (Although he is a psychologist, Kahneman won the Nobel Prize in economics in 2002; Tversky had died a few years earlier, or he would have shared it.)

To one group of subjects, Kahneman and Tversky offered this choice:

> Imagine that the US is preparing for the outbreak of an unusual Asian disease, which is expected to kill 600 people. Two alternative programs to combat the disease have been proposed. Assume that the exact scientific estimate of the consequences of the programs are as follows:
> If Program A is adopted, 200 people will be saved.
> If Program B is adopted, there is 1/3 probability that 600 people will be saved, and 2/3 probability that no people will be saved.
> Which of the two programs would you favour?

To the second group, they offered the same preamble and then this choice:

If Program C is adopted 400 people will die.

If Program D is adopted there is 1/3 probability that nobody will die, and 2/3 probability that 600 people will die.

Which of the two programs would you favour?

The choice between A and B is exactly the same as the choice between C and D. That is not hard to see once the two choices are laid out side by side. Yet which programme the subjects chose depended on how it was described. Most subjects preferred to save one-third of the people for certain (Programme A), rather than taking a gamble to save everyone (Programme B). But change the framing and the choice changed, too: most subjects would accept a two-thirds risk of killing everyone (Programme D) rather than be certain that two-thirds of victims would die (Programme C). This preference reversal is clearly irrational, because nothing about the costs and benefits of the two treatments changed, but people's choices did. Kahneman, Tversky and others have produced many other laboratory examples in which people can be proved to have acted irrationally: the proof usually comes when experimenters show that their subjects have made inconsistent choices.

What are we to make of these findings? I think we should treat them with respect – and with caution. This book will often refer to laboratory experiments, but we cannot extrapolate from a laboratory experiment unless we are confident that the conditions of the experiment – which are necessarily contrived – resemble the kind of situations we face in real life. That is far from certain, as an American economics professor called John List has been discovering. On several occasions, List has taken a deeper look at the laboratory discoveries of irrationality, and found that rational behaviour isn't far beneath the surface after all.

His trick is to make his experiments as much like real life as possible, using experience he built up from an early age. His family didn't have much money to spare, so he'd mow grass and shovel snow to earn a dollar here and there, which he used to buy collectible sports cards. He financed his way through college by trading his collection of cards, all the while developing a strong grasp of how people behaved when you offered them trades. 'I was a sports card dealer for five or ten years, all the way through graduate school,' he recalls. 'Looking back, I was doing these field experiments all the time without knowing it. And I came to realise that I could use the sports cards as part of my research programme.'

While teaching MBA classes to some middle managers at Disney, List heard about the huge pin-trading conventions at the Epcot Center in Walt Disney World. He persuaded his students to do him a cut-price deal on scores of collectible pins of Mickey and Minnie Mouse, some marking Valentine's Day and others Saint Patrick's Day. Then he went to the Epcot Center and set up an ordinary-looking stall, just as he had done for years with his sports cards as a graduate student. It was the perfect opportunity to take economic experiments out of the laboratory and into the 'field' – somewhere realistic.

List was trying to understand this puzzlingly irrational behaviour that other economists had shown in the lab: people suddenly value objects more highly simply because they own them. They won't trade even when logic suggests they should. Economists call this 'the endowment effect'.

You might recognise this behaviour in yourself. Let's say you have held on to a nice bottle of wine that has been growing in value, but that you would never have gone out and bought for the forty pounds it is now worth, even though you could easily have sold it on eBay for that amount. The wine was *yours*, and even though you would have had no interest in buying it for forty pounds, you were just as unwilling to sell it for that price. This isn't rational behaviour, because rationally you either prefer the wine or you prefer the money, but not both. Yet laboratory experiments have repeatedly revealed that people make this mistake.

John List didn't dispute the experimental results, but he didn't entirely trust them either. Laboratory experiments can be strange. People are given unusual goods in unusual settings and then asked to make unusual decisions. ('Now, we've just given you that decorative coffee mug. Would you like to exchange it for a bar of chocolate?') List suspected that a more realistic setting might produce a more rational response.

That's why Professor List set up his stall in a trading convention full of thousands of people who came to buy, sell and swap pins. He asked people to come to his stall and fill in a questionnaire in exchange for a collectible pin. Then, at the end of filling in the details, he offered them a trade: would they like to keep *their* pin, which they had just earned by filling in the form? Or would they like to trade it? Half the subjects had initially received a Valentine's Day pin and were offered a Saint Patrick's Day pin of roughly equivalent value; the other half, who had the Saint Patrick's Day pin, were offered the Valentine's Day pin.

Because each subject had only a fifty–fifty chance of receiving the pin he or she preferred, each subject would have a 50 per cent chance of wanting to trade – if he or she was rational. The endowment effect, though, might have been expected to dampen trades, leaving people clinging to whatever they had originally been given. That irrational clinginess is exactly what John List discovered from the inexperienced collectors. Fewer than one in five of them accepted his offer.

But List also discovered that experienced pin collectors were much more likely to trade than inexperienced ones. Each experienced collector (someone who traded more than four times a month) accepted Professor List's offer about half the time, as a rational person would. Nor did the experienced traders accept the offer because they simply saw the pins as a way of making money. According to their questionnaire answers, most planned to keep the pins for their own collections. Yet each took a cool, logical view of whether they preferred the Valentine's Day pin or the Saint Patrick's Day pin – that is, a view uncoloured by which pin happened to be in their hands when the trade was offered.

Just to prove the point, List unloaded his inventory of baseball memorabilia at a sports card convention and found exactly the same mistakes from rookies and exactly the same rationality from experienced collectors. The endowment effect is irrational, and it's real – but it does not influence experienced people in realistic situations.

On another occasion, List punctured some previously influential laboratory work that seemed to show a different sort of irrationality. Again, his technique was to try to repeat the laboratory experiment in a more natural setting. The original laboratory experiments had divided subjects into 'employers' and 'workers'. They asked the employers how much they were willing to pay to attract workers, and asked the workers how hard they would work in response. The experimenters discovered that employers were likely to offer more generous wages than were strictly necessary to fill a particular position, and in return the grateful employees would offer to work harder than the minimum effort required. The conclusion: giving people an unexpected pay rise would persuade them to work harder.

That seems irrational: rational employers have no incentive to pay wages above the market rate, and rational workers have no incentive to work harder even if they're fortunate enough to have such an irrationally generous boss. (I am oversimplifying here. There are some more sophisticated economic models of rational choice in which both higher wages and harder work are rational as responses to turnover or imperfect information. But they are not what was being tested in the laboratory.) List realised that the laboratory experiments were not an especially realistic setting for this demonstration of irrationality. 'Wages' were being offered in exchange for 'work', but all that was really happening was that experimental subjects were ticking boxes on a questionnaire and being paid small amounts based on their answers. It was just a laboratory-based game of 'let's pretend'.

List and his colleague Uri Gneezy extended this artificial experimental work to real life. They advertised for and hired people to do actual jobs, such as data entry or door-to-door collection for a charity. They paid some employees the advertised wage and gave others an unexpectedly high wage. As the laboratory work predicted, the grateful recipients of the higher wage worked extra hard. But in the real-life setting the warm, fuzzy feelings didn't last long: for the data-enterers, just ninety minutes; for the door-steppers, all the way until lunchtime on day one. Many of us would like to live in the cuddly world of unexpected gifts and counter-gifts. For better or worse, once we have a little time to learn the rules of the game, the harder-edged world of rationality is the one we inhabit.

John List has discovered something that had been hidden in plain sight: that whatever their merits, the laboratory experiments had created a bias towards irrational behaviour, because they had put ordinary people in extraordinary situations. He shows that, by contrast, when you ask an ordinary person to make the kind of decisions he or she makes every day, you will tend to see rational behaviour.

I don't want to minimise the odd behaviour psychologists have discovered in their experiments. People do make mistakes, and not only in the laboratory. Sometimes we have to make important decisions when the situation is unfamiliar: how much money to put into a pension fund, or how cautious to be when a new epidemic of sexually transmitted disease makes headlines. We get confused enough about those decisions to screw them up.

But I do want to point out that most people spend most of their time inside their comfort zone. For obvious reasons, most pin trading is done by people who trade a lot of pins. Similarly, most shopping is done by experienced shoppers. Most work is done by experienced workers. While people will make mistakes, they are less likely to do so when doing something familiar, and since we all do familiar things all the time, that's a point in favour of rational choice theory as a tool for understanding the world. It rarely pays to assume that any human being is incapable of weighing up pros and cons of the decision in front of him. Indeed, as we shall see in the next section, rational decision-makers needn't even be human at all.

College Station, Texas, 1990

On the surface, the six lab rats quaffing root beer and tonic water were resolving a famous but rather unimportant textbook problem. More profoundly, they were demonstrating the presence of economic rationality in a place where it had hitherto not been suspected: inside their tiny rat brains.

The rational rats were being assisted by Raymond Battalio and John Kagel, who in the early 1970s began to ask how intelligent animals really are. (Kagel and Battalio were no strangers to searching for rationality in unexpected places: their early work showed that patients in long-term mental institutions were perfectly able to earn and spend 'token' wages sensibly.) They used some well-established tools of experimental psychology but asked fresh questions, such as, 'Can rats plan, calculate and make choices given wages, prices and a budget?'

Kagel and Battalio put each rat into an experimental box, about the size of a picnic basket, equipped with a little vending machine with a pair of levers that dispensed different drinks. The rats quickly learned that they could earn drinks by pressing on the levers, and with a week or two of practice were familiar with all the details of how much each lever produced.

The researchers then changed 'prices' or 'income' to see how the rats responded. They changed relative prices by adjusting the machine to dispense less drink per press of one lever, while leaving the other lever unchanged; they set income by limiting the total number of lever presses in each session.

In case you are feeling sorry for the poor rats, be reassured that economists are the best possible experimenters. Instead of dissecting the rats or testing toxins on them, Kagel and Battalio plied them with root beer and regularly got a vet, Ray Battalio's neighbour, to check up on their well-being.

After satisfying themselves, and a growing number of once-sceptical economists, that the experiments were meaningful, Battalio, Kagel and their colleague Carl Kogut decided to try to unlock a hundred-year-old mystery. They gave their rats the choice of two drinks, each of which had its own lever. One was root beer, a longtime favourite with your average lab rat. The second was water flavoured with quinine – tonic water, in other words. Rats don't like its bitter taste, but the researchers had made the servings of quinine solution much more generous than the servings of root beer.

Think yourself into the rat's position for a moment. You're thirsty. The root beer is delicious but it's expensive, so you compromise, slaking your thirst on the nasty quinine solution but also enjoying some root beer. You don't press the lever at random.

Now, what happens when the price of quinine goes up a little – that is, when the servings become less generous? To an experimental psychologist, the answer is simple. You're getting less for your money from the quinine lever so you should press it less frequently. That seems sensible. But it happens to be irrational, as an economist could attest and a rat instinctively grasps.

As a smart rat, you drink more quinine when it gets more expensive, as long as the servings are still larger than those of the root beer. That's because you're responding to your budget as well as the price. The total consumption of liquid – root beer plus quinine water – is what's keeping you alive. Quinine water is still cheaper than root beer, and because the experimenters have made you poorer by raising the price of quinine, you are obliged to drink less of the expensive root beer and slake your thirst by consuming even more of the nasty quinine water, which remains relatively cheap.

Battalio, Kagel and Kogut showed, quite convincingly, that this is exactly what rats do. By consuming more quinine when the price of quinine rose, the rats had solved a conundrum that went back to 1895 – do 'Giffen goods' exist? A Giffen good is a good like the quinine water, one that is such a wretched necessity for the poor that when the price rises, demand rises too, because the price rise creates more poverty and the poverty creates more demand. As an impoverished economics student, I imagined my staple diet of baked potatoes might be Giffen goods: if the price of potatoes rose, I would not be able to afford the cheese or tuna fillings and would buy larger potatoes instead. Over the years, economists had suggested, but never proved, that foods ranging from potatoes during the Irish famine to noodles in rural China are Giffen goods. Battalio, Kagel, Kogut and the rats provided the first incontrovertible example: quinine water.

Yet the real significance of Kagel and Battalio's experiments was not to settle obscure Giffen goods wagers in economics departments across the world. It was to establish that the rats showed surprising intelligence and responded to their full range of options, including the way that their present choices would restrict their future choices. Given the chance, even rats can be rational.

This isn't really about the rats, of course. It is about the way that rational decisions can be made without conscious calculation. I've already drawn an analogy between rational decision-making and the fiendishly difficult differential equations that describe the trajectory of a ball in flight; ask a typical cricketer to solve them with pen and paper and he's not likely to do much better than your average rat. Yet give him a glimpse of a flying ball and he will turn, sprint and then twist round in just the right spot to make the catch; some part of him was solving the differential equations after all.

The teenage fellatrices were subconsciously calculating, too. Being rational is not the same as being intellectually brilliant;

evolutionary pressure has tended to produce organisms that often behave in rational ways, whether consciously or unconsciously. We won't always get it right – the ball is dropped occasionally – but you'd be unwise to bet against our intuitive ability to respond rationally to incentives. The rats can.

Experimenting on rats is all very well, but can rational choice theory produce the sort of analysis that really matters? Can it cut through confusion and help shape policy on a vital issue? In the hands of two of Chicago's most famous economists, it already has, as we are about to discover.

Chicago

The shopping mall's car park is packed. The white-haired grandfather simply pulls into a space with a thirty-minute limit, not nearly long enough for the leisurely lunch we have planned. 'We should be fine here. I don't think they check that carefully,' he explains in gentle but distinctively Brooklynesque tones. I look across at him. 'Was that a rational crime?' He doesn't hesitate for a second. 'Yes it was.'

Gary Becker is a rational criminal. He is also a Nobel laureate in economics, in part because of the success of his theory of rational crime. The idea struck Becker forty years ago, when he was running late to examine a doctoral student. Without time to find a free space, he quickly weighed the cost of paying for parking against the risk of being fined for parking illegally. By the time he arrived at the examination, the then-unfashionable idea that criminals would respond to the risks and costs of punishment was taking shape in his mind. The unfortunate student was immediately asked to discuss. (He passed, and Becker did not get a ticket.)

Parking violations are one thing; burglaries and muggings are another. A septuagenarian economics professor may balance thoughtfully the benefits of illegal parking against the risk of getting caught, but does a sixteen-year-old with a knife or a gun really weigh up the likely gains from a street robbery against the risk of a spell in jail? Many people intuitively feel not. For example, three authors in the mid-1990s declared in an apparent state of panic that America was now home to ever-growing numbers of violent teenagers who 'do not fear the stigma of arrest, the pains of imprisonment, or the pangs of conscience. They perceive hardly any relationship between doing right (or wrong) now and being rewarded (punished) for it later.'

Who's right – Gary Becker or the panickers? A talk radio host will tell you that prison is the only place for criminals, and harsh punishment is the only language they understand. Push a little further, though, and you may find such opinions are motivated not by belief in deterrence but by straightforward notions of revenge, and by what criminologists call the 'incapacitation effect' – if someone is in prison, he can't rob your house. And despite the best efforts of talk radio hosts, many thoughtful people are doubtful about the idea that prison actually deters criminals.

Even if you believe that harsh sentences do deter potential criminals, how harsh does a sentence have to be? Should we have more prisons and longer sentences, or is the current system already more than strict enough?

These are tough questions. Enter Gary Becker's young colleague at Chicago, Steven Levitt, co-author of *Freakonomics*. Levitt realised that the evidence existed to test Becker's hypothesis of the rational criminal, if only you knew where to look. As with Klick and Stratmann's later work on abortion notification laws, the secret lies in the fact that every American state has a separate system for dealing with young people. Different states use different 'ages of majority' – the age at which a person is deemed too old to be tried in the juvenile courts. The systems also have different severities of punishment in different states. In each state, the juvenile system is more lenient than the adult system but by a differing amount. And throughout the 1980s and early 1990s, the juvenile system became less harsh relative to the adult system across America.

Add up all this and we have enough information to see whether young criminals respond to the threat of prison. In a state where offenders face the adult courts at age seventeen, Levitt compared the difference in behaviour between sixteen- and seventeen-year-olds. In a state where they faced adult courts at nineteen, he looked at the difference in behaviour between eighteen- and nineteen-year-olds. He found that in states where the adult courts were notably more severe than the juvenile courts, the difference in behaviour was very sharp: crime dropped dramatically once kids reached the age of majority. Where the juvenile courts were relatively harsh, the drop didn't happen, because kids were already frightened of contact with the justice system. And across America, as the juvenile justice system became relatively more lenient between 1978 and 1993, violent crime committed by juveniles rose dramatically relative to violent crime committed by adults.

Levitt's method screened out an alternative explanation for the difference in crime rates, which is that harsher sentences cut crime because prisoners can't burgle your house – the incapacitation effect. A ten-year sentence instead of a five-year sentence does have an incapacitation effect, of course, but it won't be noticeable for another five years. Levitt showed that kids on the street responded immediately to the risk of harsher punishment, and that immediate response can only be explained by deterrence.

Levitt's methods were so powerful that he could even estimate how much crime would be deterred by locking up more prisoners. He could calculate the benefits of more prisons, and weigh those benefits against the costs, which range from the suffering and dislocation of prisoners to the expense of running a prison. This is a remarkable application of rational choice theory.

Unfortunately, politicians prefer simple ideological answers. Levitt explained to me that he had been much in demand after his work was published in the late 1990s, because it suggested that many American states should build extra prisons – news that governors liked to hear when justifying tough policies. When he pointed out that several years had passed since he gathered his data, and all the extra prisons had been built and then some more, to the point that America could probably get by with fewer, nobody was terribly interested. Yet the policy recommendations that emerged from Becker's theory and Levitt's data are strikingly clear and precise.

Criminals can be brutal and remorseless, but many of them are far from indifferent to the 'pains of imprisonment'. Prison, whatever its other costs, reduces crime because with a fearsome enough prison system, crime does not pay. Levitt quotes a young man, aged sixteen, who had just passed the age of majority in New York: 'When you are a boy, you can be put into a detention home. But you can go to jail now. Jail ain't no place to go.'

I've repeatedly stated my belief that rational choice theory is useful. It's time to qualify that: useful for what? Think again about Levitt's conclusion that even teenagers respond to the threat of heavier sentences by committing fewer crimes. Does that mean that each juvenile delinquent cuts back a little on the riskier crimes, and commits crimes only when he is fairly sure that he will not be caught? That would be the implication of a rigid interpretation of Gary Becker's rational crime theory. Or does it mean that some teenagers are frightened away from crime entirely, or almost entirely, while others do not respond at all? Since we see crime rates at the aggregate level, there is no way to tell, at least from Levitt's data.

This ambiguity matters in some situations, and not in others. If I'm a politician who wants to know whether tougher prison sentences are likely to reduce levels of crime, I will discover exactly the information I need by consulting Becker and Levitt. If I'm a parent who wants to decide whether the threat of stern punishment will dissuade my daughter from stealing chocolate, I'll be more swayed by my individual knowledge of my daughter's personality than by aggregated evidence from an economics research paper. Rational choice is a powerful theory, but only for some tasks.

Similarly, think of Klick and Stratmann's surprising result that teenagers seem to be worried enough and forward-thinking enough about their parents finding out they are pregnant that they take precautions they might otherwise not have done. We don't know from this statistical analysis if all teenagers respond equally to abortion notification laws by becoming somewhat less risky in their sexual behaviour, or if the effect emerges because some become much more cautious while others remain too drunk, ignorant or turned on to think about Dad's reaction to a pregnancy. The evidence that aggregate behaviour is rational hasn't told us that all teenagers are equally rational, but it has told us something. It doesn't provide a complete psychological explanation of teenage sexuality, but it suggests fruitful lines of research; without rational choice theorists focusing their minds on incentives, it might never otherwise have occurred to anybody to look for a link between abortion notification laws and safe sex.

For many of the world's policy problems, we don't have time to wait for the perfect explanation: we need a way of looking at the world, even if rough and ready, that will work now. To conclude this chapter, let's return to sex and consider the problem of persuading prostitutes to use condoms to prevent the spread of sexually transmitted diseases. It's an urgent question, and if you want an answer now, you could do worse than assume that prostitutes are rational.

Morelia, Michoacán State, Mexico

By day, Jardin de las Rosas is a romantic park in the heart of the sixteenth-century city of Morelia; it is a meditative spot where the weary can seek shelter from the Mexican sun and enjoy cool greenery and the architecture of times past. By night, the garden offers relief of a different kind. It is Morelia's best place to pick up street prostitutes. 'Be there at ten p.m.,' opines one regular. 'The best girls don't last. You'll only find travesties later.'

That sort of charming commentary explains why prostitution is nobody's idea of a dream job. A woman deciding to be a prostitute knows that she will be treated with contempt by both clients and the wider world. There are physical risks, too: interviews with over a thousand Mexican prostitutes, most from the Morelia area, suggested that one in six was suffering from a sexually transmitted infection, while a prostitute can expect to be attacked by a client every couple of months.

On the other hand, the wages are better than these women could otherwise expect. Prostitutes work long hours but they make over half as much again as their peers with more conventional jobs, even before the commissions they get from bar owners by encouraging clients to drink. That's not to say that prostitutes are motivated only by money and don't care about the dangers and humiliations of the job. But they are hardly doing the job because of its prospects for promotion.

After the last shot of tequila has been downed and the client and girl find a quiet place to close the deal, we all have a stake in what they decide about using a condom. If they don't, there is a much higher risk that she will pass HIV or another sexually transmitted disease to him, or he to her. Tomorrow evening, she will be with another client; he will be sleeping with his wife. Whether or not you care much about Mexican prostitutes, the less *they* use condoms, the more *you* have to.

Yet you have little say in the matter. The decision to use a condom springs from negotiations between the client and the prostitute. Often they do indeed use a condom: various studies estimate that in Mexico, prostitutes and their clients use condoms more than half the time, and perhaps as many as nine times out of ten. That is much better than nothing, but since one in six prostitutes complain of a sexually transmitted infection, it is evidently not enough.

It is no surprise, then, to see that health and development organisations are trying frantically to persuade prostitutes to use condoms by providing better information and more access to condoms, while also training the women as negotiators: in all, enabling them to make the right decision and carry it through.

In Morelia, these efforts have been wildly successful in their immediate aims. Prostitutes are well informed, have condoms and negotiate cannily. Nevertheless, these efforts at empowerment have not prevented widespread sexually transmitted infection, and they never will. 'Empowered' prostitutes don't always use condoms. Why not? Because they're a useful bargaining chip.

Men looking to buy sex don't get a bar code on each girl telling them the price. It's something they must haggle over, usually with the woman herself. A pimp, brothel madam, or go-between may agree to a price with the client, but such prices tend to be renegotiated when the door is closed and the lights are off. The price depends on many things. Clients will pay less for 'travesties', and some of the 'girls' are over seventy years old. Clients who look prosperous will be charged more. Extra services attract an extra fee.

The client will also pay more if he sets conditions on the use of condoms. If he insists on using one, he'll pay nearly 10 per cent more. If he insists on 'bareback' sex – no condom – he'll pay a premium of nearly a quarter. The prostitute uses the client's declaration of a preference as a bargaining chip, and she gets more money either way. Obviously the negotiating workshops laid on by local health projects are paying dividends.

This may be hard to believe, but alternative explanations for the unsafe sex do not stand up well. Condoms are cheap and they're easy to find around Morelia: most risky sex takes place with a condom available but unused. Fewer than 2 per cent of sexual transactions are bareback for the prosaic reason that there are no condoms on hand.

It's tempting to argue that the prostitutes do not understand the risks. That's patronising: even without the efforts of the health and development organisations, prostitutes probably know more about the risks of sexually transmitted infections than anyone who thinks of them as simple-minded victims. In fact, the prostitutes know that while the risks are real, they are modest. Only one in eight hundred Mexicans carries HIV, and even among prostitutes it afflicts just one in three hundred. Even if a prostitute is unlucky enough that one of her unprotected jobs is with a man who is HIV positive, the risk that she will catch it is less than 2 per cent if one of them is carrying some other sexual infection, and less than 1 per cent otherwise. None of the prostitutes wants to catch Aids, but the risks of catching it because of one instance of unprotected sex are small, while the pay is substantially higher. Wouldn't you notice a pay increase of 25 per cent?

The risks prostitutes take when they leave the condoms in their purses seem to be strikingly well judged. As far as we can tell, the typical Morelian prostitute is acting as though she values one extra year of healthy life at between eight thousand and twenty-five thousand pounds or up to five years' income. The figure, calculated by economist Paul Gertler, relies on epidemi-ological data on the risk of getting sick, along with a World Health Organisation measure called the 'disability-adjusted life years', designed to estimate the suffering caused by different dis-eases.

Perhaps you're thinking that a rational person would never risk his or her life for mere cash. But most of us know people whose jobs lead them to do exactly that. Consider Staff Sergeant Matthew Kruger. He signed up for a third tour of duty in Iraq and headed to the front lines in December 2005, risking not only his life but his marriage, which had been badly strained by his absences. He's not crazy. But he did risk his life for money: at the age of twenty-nine, with three small children, he simply needed the health insurance the army provided.

Staff Sergeant Kruger sounds like a brave man, but even a

coward like me will risk his life for money. If I saw a twenty-pound note lying on the other side of a busy road, I'd cross over to pick it up. It's not a big risk, but it is a risk none the less.

Far from being rash or stupid, the choices that Mexican prostitutes are making are astonishingly similar to those made by workers in rich countries who accept dangerous jobs in exchange for higher salaries – construction workers, lumberjacks, soldiers. If Morelian prostitutes are being irrational in accepting extra cash in exchange for higher risks, then so are lumberjacks. It's more likely that both the prostitutes and the lumberjacks know what they are doing: a tough, dangerous job that offers some financial compensation for doing it. They both have a degree of negotiating power, sensible preferences, and the same hard-edged view of the world. The difference is that the prostitutes are poorer and so they risk their lives for less.

The most disturbing thing about the decision of prostitutes to have risky sex is just how calculated it seems to be. All the sex-worker education in the world is unlikely to change that decision: unlike US teenagers, the prostitutes already knew about the risks.

Some may find this analysis offensive and absurd. But it's a case study in the use of economics to deal with a social problem. Now that we understand what is motivating the unsafe sex, we have a chance of doing something about it. The sex-worker education programmes have had their uses, but since prostitutes now know about the risks, the people who need to be educated are not the prostitutes, but their clients. That will not be easy.

Prostitutes are smarter about the risks of sexual infection than their clients, and that makes sense, because sexually transmitted infection is a daily occupational hazard for a prostitute but a small risk for a client, who will quite sensibly spend his time worrying about something else. It's just like Professor List's pin traders. The experienced traders (the girls) know what they're doing. The inexperienced traders (some of their clients) do not. Yet again, we see rational behaviour from those who have the strongest incentive to keep themselves informed. The clients remain, to use a piece of economic jargon, 'rationally ignorant': it isn't worth their time to find out more. (We'll meet this concept again in Chapter Eight.) It is very hard to see that changing, but it will certainly not change without efforts directed straight at the men who hire prostitutes.

A trip to the seamy side of Morelia should make it clear that a rational world is not necessarily a wonderful one – something we'll see time and again in this book. Rational individuals make many choices that are bad news for others; risky sex is just a particularly clear example. And when rational individuals face a miserable set of choices, as do the Morelian prostitutes, they cannot do better than pick the best of a bad lot. We will not solve social problems if we pretend that they are caused only – or even mostly – by the mad, the stupid and the morally degenerate. But nor should we shrug our shoulders and declare that all is for the best in the best of all possible worlds. I hope that this book will show that, although people tend to make smart choices, it is possible to offer them better ones.

Let's take stock. Rats are rational because they can spend a budget sensibly. Teenagers are rational because when the risks of sex rise, they switch to safer ways of getting off. Juvenile delinquents are rational because they commit fewer crimes when faced with harsher sentences. I wrote earlier that rational people respond to trade-offs and to incentives, and I hope that the implications of the idea are now clearer. Rational people view the risk of imprisonment as part of the price of committing crime, and the risk of Aids as part of the price of unprotected sex. Rational people, I repeat, respond to incentives, think about consequences, and have intelligible motives.

Certain things should by now be clearer. Although economists often include profit or income as one of our motivations behind our actions, the goals of a rational being don't have to be financial. The rat doesn't care about money – it wants to get enough liquid to survive, and it wants the drink to taste nice. Rational behaviour means acting in such a way as to achieve your objectives, which may be money, but may also be a fast car, status, sex, self-actualisation . . . or root beer.

We've also seen that rationality is not the same as omniscience. The rats did not instantly deduce the changes in pricing or the budget they faced: Kagel, Battalio and Kogut gave them time to work it out. Pin traders made mistakes unless they had some experience. Gay men at risk of contracting HIV/Aids reacted more to an emotional signal than to a real change in the risks of infection. And yet despite these fallibilities, the rats, traders and gay men did, in the end, respond to the incentives in front of them, and often in unexpected ways.

I hope I've begun to persuade you that, while we won't find rational behaviour everywhere we look, we will find that most people in most situations – remember, we spend most of our time within our comfort zone – are rational. We've already discovered that people do remarkable things in response to changing risks, such as exposing themselves to sexually transmitted diseases, or deciding to change their sexual preferences. We've seen that they understand abstract constraints: a budget or a change in the legal system. And the calculations aren't limited to economics professors. Whether we study teenage girls deciding what kind of sex is okay, teenage boys contemplating crime, prostitutes haggling for a better deal or even laboratory rats, we find that they all seem to be economically rational.

But if we're all so smart, why does life seem so crazy? People smoke and gamble. Fools fall in love. Offices are run by morons. City neighbourhoods boom or collapse for no apparent reason. Where is the logic in all this?

It's there, if you look hard enough, and in the next few chapters I'll show you how to find it. Chapter Two describes the most demanding rational choice theory of all, game theory, which was developed by a genius and assumes that other people are geniuses. I'll show that genius is more common than you'd expect, as well as revealing that game theory, unexpectedly, turns out to be invaluable for understanding addictions and other human frailties.

In Chapter Three, I'll argue that rational behaviour can sit comfortably even with our most passionate emotion, that of love. Lovers plan, strategise, negotiate and deal with the harsh realities of supply and demand. Not only does a rational look at love and marriage make sense, it turns out to be the only way to understand one of the great social upheavals of the late twenti-eth century: the sharp growth in the number of professional, educated women, and the rise and fall in divorce rates.

Moving outside the family and into the workplace, in Chapter Four I will look at what happens when rational behaviour meets inevitable ignorance. I'll argue that most offices are full of secrets. Who is smart? Who is hardworking? Who is just lucky? Many of the apparently crazy features of business, from overpaid bosses to office politics, turn out to be rational responses to the ambiguities of office life.

Then I will turn my attention to the often-irrational out-comes of individual rational decisions. Looking at two intertwined issues – race and inner-city deprivation – I'll show that rational behaviour on the part of individuals does not nec-essarily lead to a socially desirable outcome, because the interplay between each person's decision and what happens on a bigger scale is counter-intuitive and often highly destructive.

In the last three chapters, I will use what we have learned on an ever-bigger scale, showing how rational behaviour shapes our great cities, our politics and, finally, the entire history of human civilisation, starting a million years ago. Don't worry, I'll keep it brief.

Two

Las Vegas

The edge of reason

The Rio Hotel, Las Vegas, Nevada

It is hard to say where the check-in queue ends and the casino crowds begin. The bars, restaurants and public spaces of the hotel lobby seem to ooze into the gambling floors. Even in the quiet midmorning hours, as the guests sleep off the night's excesses or enjoy breakfast, the hotel's lobby boasts a bewildering array of flashing lights and garish displays. Elderly gamblers in the Middle American uniform of baseball caps, slack khaki shorts and bulging T-shirts sit and feed quarters into the maw of the nearest slot machines. Sometimes the machines form a cocooning embrace as the seniors ride them like motorised wheelchairs. Occasionally – just often enough – the machines vomit coins into the laps of their riders.

Despite every effort to stimulate the senses, this is a tedious place, but the monotony is interrupted by a strange procession: a long-limbed man, his face concealed by a wall of facial hair, mirror shades and a cowboy hat, strides across the lobby. He is pursued by admirers and stops whenever requested – which is every ten yards or so – to sign an autograph or pose with a fan for a mobile-phone photo. Known to poker lovers as 'Jesus', he is Chris Ferguson, one of the most recognisable and successful players in the world. He's in Las Vegas to try to reclaim his crown as World Poker Champion.

Ferguson, who is reported to have won more than two million pounds in tournament play, is the best of a new generation of players trying to conquer poker with the branch of economics known as 'game theory'. It is a curious struggle, one that has pitted bespectacled geeks against hardened gamblers. It is also an object lesson in the remarkable intuitive rationality of the human mind.

Half a century of struggle by some of the world's smartest economists and mathematicians, backed by computers, has produced an impossibly sophisticated poker strategy. All the while, thugs and hustlers have been bumbling along, playing the game the intuitive way. Don't underestimate the hustlers: we'll discover that fifty years of formal brilliance have yet to provide more than the tiniest advantage over the experienced judgement of 'ordinary' professional gamblers. If you believe that ordinary people aren't rational, first try to outthink them. It may not be as easy as you expected.

Chris Ferguson's poker game aside, Las Vegas isn't the sort of place one links with the word *rational*. Across the lobby from Ferguson, the slot machine addicts mindlessly and joylessly feeding their quarters into machines they can have little chance of beating seem to refute the idea that people can be counted on to behave rationally. But it turns out that the slot machine junkies, too, are more rational than you would suppose.

This chapter traces the limits of rational choice theory as it bumps up against human fallibility. As we saw in the last chapter, economics is the study of how people react to incentives in their environment, such as the chance of going to prison or catching Aids. Sometimes those incentives result not from background factors such as the toughness of the legal system or the presence of the HIV virus, but from the actions of identifiable people: your spouse, your boss or your opponent at the card table.

These other people are not just background; they will try to anticipate one another's desires and strategies, trying to respond to them and perhaps to thwart them. So to understand the complexities of these interactions, we need a special branch of economics, called 'game theory'. In principle, game theory is just a special case of rational choice theory. In practice, game theorists have to be sensitive to small human irrationalities, because they have large effects when people are trying to anticipate and respond to one another's decisions. Game theorists, then, need to understand both rational behaviour and human peculiarities. Far from being fatally undermined by the psychological tics that make us all too human, rational choice theory is offering us insights into our inner battles – thanks to the efforts of a new type of economist, more comfortable with a brain scanner than with the latest inflation statistics.

The Vegas lobby, with poker on one side and slot machines on the other, is a visual metaphor for how game theory has matured – a story that can best be told by contrasting two of the most famous game theorists. Both were Cold War intellectuals, advising the US government at the highest levels and using game theory to try to understand the riskiest of all games, nuclear war. Game theory emerged from the sparkling mind of John Von Neumann, a celebrated mathematical prodigy, when he decided to create a theory of poker. Von Neumann's academic brilliance offered penetrating insights but the cold force of his logic could have led us to Armageddon. It was tempered by the earthier wisdom – usually expressed in witty prose rather than equations – of Thomas Schelling. Tormented by a tobacco addiction he could not kick, Schelling nudged game theory into a direction that now offers us surprising insights into the hapless slot machine addicts.

Late in the 1920s, the most ostentatiously brilliant man in the world decided to work out the correct way to play poker. John

Von Neumann, a mathematician who helped to develop both the computer and the atomic bomb, had been struck by an engaging new conceit. Could his beloved mathematics uncover the secrets of poker, which seemed to be a quintessentially human game of secrets and lies?

Von Neumann believed that if you wanted a theory – he called it 'game theory' – that could explain life, you should start with a theory that could explain poker. His aim was to bring the rigour of mathematics to the social sciences, and that meant turning to economics, because the rational decisions of economics can be modelled using mathematics. Von Neumann thought that he could develop a rational, mathematical explanation for much of life, and his theory would eventually be applied to the breakdown of diplomatic negotiations, the unexpected emergence of cooperation between enemies, the possibilities of nuclear terrorism, even the hidden side of dating, love and marriage – the topic of the next chapter. But as he explained to his colleague Jacob Bronowski, poker was the starting point: 'Real life consists of bluffing, of little tactics of deception, of asking yourself what is the other man going to think I mean to do. And that is what games are about in my theory.'

Bluff, deception and mind-reading are unpromising subjects for a mathematician to study, but if anyone could do it, it was Johnny Von Neumann. His feats of calculation were notorious: at Princeton after the war, he helped to design the fastest computer in the world, before challenging it to a calculation contest and demonstrating that he was faster. Nobody was surprised, either at the result or that the showy Von Neumann had suggested the contest. On another occasion he refused a request to assist with a new supercomputer aimed at solving an important problem, instead furnishing an immediate solution with pencil and paper. Although there were those who delved deeper, nobody was as quick as Johnny. In the popular imagination of the 1940s and 1950s, Von Neumann arguably outshone even his

Princeton contemporary, Albert Einstein, and his colleagues joked that he was a demigod who, having studied humans intensively, was able to imitate them perfectly.

Nevertheless, to understand poker, Von Neumann had to break new ground. Poker was not merely a game of chance, requiring probability, or a game of pure logic with neither random elements nor secrets, like chess. Poker, contrary to appearances, is a far more subtle challenge. In a game of poker, players bet in order to earn the right to compare cards at the showdown. But most of the important information in poker is private. Each player sees only one part of the jigsaw puzzle and must piece together the bigger picture by observing what other players do. The strongest hand takes the 'pot' – all the accumulated bets – so the higher the betting, the more expensive it becomes to lose the showdown. Yet in many hands of poker, especially between skilled players, there is no showdown, because one player bets aggressively enough to scare away the others. In short, there is no straightforward connection between what a player bets and the hand he holds.

Novices wrongly believe that bluffing is merely a way to win pots with bad cards. In the 1972 final of the World Series of Poker, the famous hustler Amarillo Slim took the championship because he had bluffed so often that when he finally put all his chips in the pot with a full house (a very strong hand), his opponent, 'Puggy' Pearson, was convinced that Slim was bluffing again, matched the bet, and lost. A player who never bluffs will never win a big pot, because on the rare occasions that he raises the betting, everyone else will fold before committing much money.

Then there's the reverse bluff: acting weak when you are strong. In what proved to be the final hand of the 1988 World Series of Poker, Johnny Chan (dubbed the 'Orient Express' because he won money so quickly) passed up every opportunity to raise the stakes and meekly called his opponent's bets. By the last round of betting, his opponent, Erik Seidel, became convinced that Chan didn't have a hand and Seidel bet everything he had. Chan matched his bet and turned over a straight, scooping seven hundred thousand dollars and the title of world champion for the second year running.

Trying to deceive your opponent seems like a matter of psychology, not mathematics. Could there really be a rational strategy behind these bluffs and reverse bluffs, one that ignores the idea of reading or psyching out an opponent? Would pure mathematics nevertheless deliver those bluffing moves? Von Neumann thought so. His work on game theory reached its culmination in the 1944 book *Theory of Games and Economic Behavior*, written with the economist Oskar Morgenstern. The book included a stylised model of poker in which two rational players faced each other in a highly simplified setting.

To understand Von Neumann's approach, imagine playing a round of Von Neumann poker. The simple rules dramatically limit your ability to vary your bet or to go back and forth with your opponent, raising the stakes. Still, they capture something of the essence of the game. You and your opponent contribute a small ante to the pot, and then you go first.

You pick up your hand, and think. The simple rules give you two options: you can either check or make a big bet. In this simplified game, when you check, the hands are compared at the showdown and the best hand wins the ante from the worst. (Your opponent doesn't get to make a decision at that point; like real poker, this is unfair, which is why players take turns.) But if you bet, then your opponent faces his own choice: he can fold, quitting the round and conceding the small ante to you, or he can call, matching your bet, which means a showdown for higher stakes. What is the rational move? And what is your opponent's rational response?

Actually, the two answers are related. You shouldn't decide without considering his response, and he should not react to your bet without figuring out what strategy you have. The inter-relatedness of both of your strategies is what makes this a problem requiring Von Neumann's game theory, rather than the probability theory needed to understand roulette.

At first glance even this simple version of poker seems to collapse into an endless chain of reasoning. If you bet even with terrible cards, then your opponent should call the bet with any decent hand. Yet if you bet only with the best possible hands, then he should always fold when you bet. All we have is a thought process that runs, 'If he thinks that I think that he thinks . . .' Can't we say more? Yes we can, if we follow Von Neumann's analysis.

What Von Neumann created was a theory of perfect decision-making; he was looking for the moves that infallible players would make. Game theory finds those moves by looking for opposing strategies that are consistent, in the sense that neither infallible player wants to change once he hears about the other player's strategy. There are plenty of strategies that don't meet this standard. For instance, if your opponent is very cautious and often folds, you should bluff a lot. But if you bluff a lot, your opponent shouldn't be so cautious. The two strategies don't match. They might be played by fools, but not by Von Neumann's perfectly rational players.

Instead, we need to consider both players' strategies in combination. Your opponent's strategy is the simpler. Because the simple game gives you no option to fold it also gives him no chance to bluff, because you can't bluff someone who can't fold. (He, on the other hand, is allowed to fold, which means that you *can* try to bluff.) Since he can't bluff, he should simply call you with his better hands, and fold with his worse hands. The only question is how good a hand has to be before he should call with it. That depends on how often you bluff.

What, then, should you do? With an excellent hand, you should bet: you lose nothing if your opponent folds, while giving yourself a good chance of winning a big pot if he calls. But with a middling hand, you shouldn't bet: if he has a bad hand, he'll fold, and you'll win the ante, which is what you'd have won anyway by checking; but if he has a good hand, he'll call and win. It's heads he wins, tails you lose. You should check instead, and hope your middling hand wins the ante.

What about with a terrible hand? Should you check or bet? The answer is surprising. Checking would be unwise, because the hands will be compared and you will lose. It makes more sense to bet with these bad hands, because the only way you will win anything is if he drops out, and the only way he might drop out is if you make a bet. Perversely, you are better off betting with awful cards than with mediocre ones, the quintessential (and rational) bluff.

There's a second reason for you to bet with terrible cards rather than middling ones: your opponent will have to call you a little more often. Because he knows that your bets are sometimes very weak, he can't afford to fold too easily. That means that when you bet with a good hand, you are more likely to be called, and to win when you are. Because you are bluffing with bad cards, your good hands make more money – just as Amarillo Slim's full house did in the last hand of the 1972 final.

'Of the two possible motives for bluffing,' wrote Von Neumann in *Theory of Games*, 'the first is to give a (false) impression of strength in (real) weakness; the second is the desire to give a (false) impression of weakness in (real) strength.'

What was remarkable about Von Neumann's analysis was the way his tactics emerged rationally from the logic of the game. Von Neumann had met the challenge he had explained to Bronowski and showed that bluffing, far from being some unfathomable human element to the game of poker, was governed by the rules of mathematics. Von Neumann's message was that there is a rational, mathematical foundation even to the apparently psychological game of bluffing at poker. And if he was right that poker was a meaningful analogy for everyday problems, his success implied that maybe, just maybe, there was a rational mathematical foundation to life itself.

*

Von Neumann's book was hugely celebrated, not as a poker manual but as a manifesto for putting economics and the social sciences on a logical, mathematical footing. One contemporary review declared, 'Posterity may regard this book as one of the major scientific achievements of the first half of the 20th century.' But the academics were soon disillusioned: they quickly found that game theory was difficult to apply to the real world. For many years after Von Neumann's death in 1957, academics struggled to bend game theory to problems of economics, biology, and military strategy, but without living up to the expectations raised by *Theory of Games*. The problem was that Von Neumann might have been regarded as a demigod, but for game theory to be useful, it needed to cope with the more limited brainpower of ordinary mortals.

To understand the difficulty, consider how Von Neumann himself saw a 'game'. It was a mathematical description of the link between strategies and possible pay-offs. To work out a rational course of action, simply do the maths. That all seems very abstract, but Von Neumann's game theory *was* abstract. If you're confused, you're beginning to appreciate the difficulties of Von Neumann's creation.

Fundamental to Von Neumann's approach was the assumption that both players were as clever as Von Neumann himself. He wanted to understand what infallible play looked like, and his answer can, in principle, be applied to any two-player 'zero-sum' game, including poker, where one player's loss is the other player's gain. But in practice, there are two problems.

The first is that the game may be so complex that even the fastest computer could not calculate the perfect strategy. The poker model is a perfect illustration of why game theory began to feel like such a disappointment in the real world. While Von Neumann's analysis distilled with great elegance some vital insights of good poker play, it didn't go far as an instruction manual. The Von Neumann model achieves its simplicity by limiting the number of players, their options and the type of hands they draw. Real poker's intricacies quickly become mind-boggling: considering ten possibilities a second, a player would have had to start calculating at the birth of the galaxy to find a game-theoretic solution for just two players of the most popular poker game, Texas Hold'em. And if real poker was too much of a challenge, what about a real economic problem, such as negotiating a pay rise or working out a business strategy?

The second problem is that game theory becomes less useful if your opponent is fallible. If player two is not an expert, player one should play to exploit his mistakes, rather than defending against brilliant strategies that will never be found. The worse the opponent, the less useful the theory is.

This problem is particularly acute for poker. A game-theoretically perfect poker strategy will pass up big opportunities against fallible opposition – that is, against everyone. Over the long run, as chance evens out, the strategy will not lose. But it may win only very slowly against weak opponents. One opponent may be bluffing too much; another may never bluff. Punishing one mistake requires conservative play; punishing the other requires more aggression. Game theory assumes the mistakes will not be made.

A real poker player who wanted to use Von Neumann's theories would somehow need to be able to perform calculations that were beyond even the demigod himself. He would also have to wrestle with the problem of dealing with naïve opponents whose behaviour did not match the perfect play assumed in Von Neumann's solutions.

It's no surprise, then, that Princeton University Press put out a slightly sheepish advertisement in 1949 to celebrate five years of anaemic sales of *Theory of Games and Economic Behavior*. The ad said, 'Great books often take a while to achieve recognition ... their influence far surpasses their readership.' It mentioned 'a few copies bought by professional gamblers' – but there is little evidence that Von Neumann's theories made any immediate impact on poker.

*

It is a safe bet, at least, that young Walter Clyde Pearson was not a customer. 'Puggy' Pearson was born in Kentucky in 1929, making him just a year younger than game theory itself. His family was dirt-poor: the first time Pug saw white bread, then a luxury, he didn't recognise it and assumed it was cake. But while Von Neumann's publishers were defending *Theory of Games*, Pearson was stationed with the navy in Puerto Rico, cleaning up at pool and poker. In his eighteen-month stint he wired home ten thousand dollars – more than eighty thousand in today's money – to his mother. Puggy was to invent the idea of tournament poker, and become world champion in 1973. And he did it all without a mathematical equation in sight.

Like many of the early gambling professionals, Puggy Pearson had a knack for getting himself into trouble. He first fled to Las Vegas in 1962, after cracking the skull of a Nashville bookmaker with a golf club. (The bookmaker swung first, after Pug accused him of cheating.) Puggy was a rough character, but poker was a rough business. He moved to Vegas for good in 1963 after armed burglars tied him and his wife up and ransacked their Nashville home looking for poker winnings. With a gun in his face, Puggy bluffed them out of five thousand dollars by convincing them that all he had was the money in his pockets.

Puggy's close scrapes were hardly unusual. Puggy's rival Amarillo Slim was once robbed of fifty thousand dollars – the stakes on the table – by three armed men who broke into the house where he was playing. On another occasion, in 1976, he was rescued from a pressure negotiation with the Mafia by an army of heavies sent by his friend, poker impresario Benny Binion. 'You've never seen so many big hats and bulges in your life,' Slim recalled.

These characters were a long way from Princeton and *Theory of Games*. Even if a cerebral university professor could have used game theory to clean up from the likes of Puggy and Slim, he might not have fancied his chances of making it home with his wallet intact. But that is not why the professors stayed away from Vegas. It was because they knew that the very best the genius Von Neumann had to offer did not seem to hold out any immediate prospect of beating men like Puggy and Slim, their poker strategies honed not by mathematics but by experience. For all its sophistication, game theory could not offer any improvement on the lessons learned during a life as a road gambler.

It took half a century, and two important developments, for this to change. The first development was social. As the large entertainment corporations moved into Las Vegas, the casinos started to become places where anyone could feel that their physical safety was guaranteed, even if their wealth was not. The second development was technological. The geeks found somewhere to practise, and that place was somewhere that few people had heard of back in 1988: the Internet.

'IRC poker' was the craze among the deep geeks of the time, a simple program that used Internet relay chat, a precursor of today's online chat rooms, to deal cards and moderate a game of poker between players anywhere. This was the pre–World Wide Web Internet of glowing green numbers on black backgrounds, where only experts ventured. None the less, thousands logged in to compete for bragging rights. Although no money was at stake, rising to the top of the IRC rankings meant beating the world's most obsessive geeks.

One of the leading players was a doctoral student at the University of California at Los Angeles named Chris Ferguson. A computer science graduate, Ferguson was studying artificial intelligence and trying to develop a program to play the board game Othello. Chris was exposed to both poker and game theory at an early age. His family were avid games players and his father was a maths professor who taught game theory at UCLA. (Father and son jointly published a paper on Von Neumann's poker model.) On some weekends, Chris drove to Las Vegas and covered his hotel bill by playing conservative poker against the tourists. But IRC poker, with its rapid play and the stream of electronic data it provided, was a much better laboratory for someone who wanted to get inside the game and see what made it tick.

It would be a mistake to think that the secrets of poker simply tumbled out of any computer programmed with the right game-theoretic equations. It was a humbling project. 'If you want to play poker to make money, you're doing it for the wrong reasons,' Ferguson told me a few minutes before sitting down to play at the 2005 World Series of Poker. 'You have to love the game, and you have to like to work hard.'

Just as Von Neumann had had to simplify the game of poker before he could find the perfect strategy, Ferguson started on a simple version of the game: Asian stud, which is played with a deck of only thirty-six cards. But Asian stud, though simpler than the most popular version of poker, Texas Hold'em, is still a real game played in the casinos, and dramatically more complex than anything Von Neumann was able to solve. Ferguson was using exactly the same game theory as Von Neumann, but backed up by technology he was able to work out the strategies required to play first Asian stud and later Texas Hold'em.

Using ever-faster computers to crunch through the numbers, Ferguson began by working out the probabilities of one hand improving enough to beat another. Then came the game theory, which he used to explore which hands to bluff with and how often to bluff, and the trade-offs between raising too little with a promising hand, which ran the risk of being overtaken by a lucky opponent, versus raising too much and scaring people away. He memorised table after table of his results.

Ferguson began to produce some unexpected conclusions. For example, his game theory showed that the old-school poker professionals were raising too much with strong hands. The traditionalists believed that once you were convinced you were ahead, you should raise the stakes to force your opponents out and give them no chance to get lucky and overtake you. But Ferguson discovered that it was worth making smaller raises and encouraging opponents to stay in and try to improve their cards. Sometimes those opponents would indeed get lucky and win, but on balance the strong hand would make more money with smaller raises.

'I showed a lot of my research to well-respected poker players,' recalls Chris. 'They pooh-poohed it, I think because they didn't understand it and disagreed with the results. But I knew that what I was doing was accurate, and that disagreement showed that mathematics could outplay the best players in the world.'

That self-confidence is typical of Ferguson. He knew that game theory would give him an advantage, not because of his winnings at the table but because the theory was right and the best players were wrong. However, while the advantage was real, it was small. Ferguson was uncovering the rational way to play poker, only to discover that there was a huge overlap between the rational approach and the intuitive game played by strong players.

Ferguson guesses that he lost about ten thousand pounds in his first year of professional play. He initially made his name not by his success at the table but by his appearance. By the late 1990s he was one of the most recognisable sights in poker, earning the nickname 'Jesus' as he hid his face behind a long beard and hair that cascaded over his shoulders, buttressed by wrap-around mirror shades and a big cowboy hat. He never spoke during play, trying to remove any sign of human emotion; he didn't pay much attention to other players' nervous tics, either. He drew his information only from the cards, like a computer – or like Von Neumann himself.

The age of rational poker began at the 2000 World Series in Las Vegas. After outlasting five hundred rivals, the last two competitors faced each other under the glare of the television cameras. T. J. Cloutier, a living legend, a sixty-year-old Texan road gambler regarded by many as the best player yet to win the World Series, was playing Jesus. Cloutier was much the more experienced player, but Ferguson had destroyed the field and came to the table with ten times as many chips as his opponent.

Playing brilliantly and riding his luck, Cloutier ate into Ferguson's lead and was only slightly behind when he lured Jesus into serious trouble. With several million dollars at stake, Cloutier's raise of $175,000 seemed timid and it convinced Ferguson that Cloutier was bluffing. Ferguson re-raised to $600,000 and Cloutier pushed roughly $2 million in chips into the pot, going 'all in'.

Ferguson paused for more than five minutes, calculating the odds. Cloutier probably had a stronger hand than he'd expected. However, Cloutier was playing well and if Ferguson backed out of the pot now, his opponent would have a substantial lead. On the other hand, if Ferguson called and won, the World Series was his. He reckoned his chances at about a third – and that that was better than his chances if he folded and conceded all those chips to Cloutier. 'I was getting the right odds from the pot,' he now says. So Chris 'Jesus' Ferguson removed his hat and shades, suddenly shrinking and revealing his human qualities: exhaustion, vulnerability. Then he called, and Cloutier revealed ace–queen to Ferguson's ace–nine.

Since there were no more chips to bet, the five communal cards were revealed at an agonising pace. Ferguson had slightly overestimated his chances. They were one in four: for Ferguson to win, one of the communal cards needed to match his nine, and none of them to match Cloutier's queen. But Johnny Von Neumann's angel must have been watching over Ferguson. When the last card – a nine – hit the table, Ferguson realised what had happened before the hushed crowd did. His arms shot into the air and he leaped up to embrace Cloutier. The great man is famous for receiving his bad luck with equanimity. 'That's poker,' he said. Ferguson, too, took the win in his stride: 'I took all my friends out to a nice dinner, and then two of them drove me home to LA. I slept in the back of the car – that's how the world champion left town.'

Many poker fans remember Ferguson's luck, but he had given himself nine lives by arriving at the final table with more chips than the next five players put together. Since then he's proved that his success was no fluke. Only four men have more finishes in profit at the World Series than Ferguson (Cloutier is one of them) and Ferguson won more World Series events from 2000 to 2004 than any of his rivals had in a decade. He has a particularly strong record 'heads-up', facing just one other strong player. That is not surprising: heads-up poker against another expert is the situation where Von Neumann's game theory works best. All told, Chris Ferguson has a respectable claim to be the most successful tournament player of the twenty-first century.

The fact that it took over half a century for game theory to produce a world champion player might seem like a severe criticism of Von Neumann's approach. The opposite is true. Game theory, remember, assumes rational players. If someone had simply read *Theory of Games* and then cleaned up at Vegas, it would have been proof that poker players were anything but rational. The very fact that Chris Ferguson's achievement was so hard-won and that the level of his play was not notably better than that of someone like T. J. Cloutier is exactly what game theorists need to assume.

Ferguson's struggle was, in fact, another example of what John List's experiments demonstrated in the previous chapter – the way in which experience can produce rational decisions, even if the decision-makers, like Puggy, Slim or Cloutier, are not necessarily conscious of the rational basis for all their actions.

Game theory often throws up such cases of unconscious rationality emerging from experience. Because the situations that game theory analyses tend to be very complex, if you ask ordinary people to play the games in the laboratory, they'll bungle them. Give them a chance to learn the ropes, though, and they will often find their way much closer to the rational strategy, even if they do not know it.

One famous example is the 'winner's curse'. The curse flows from a natural feature of auctions: you only win when every other bidder thinks you're paying too much. I can invoke the curse and produce crazy behaviour whenever I want by holding an auction for a jar of coins. If I ask a large number of people each to estimate the value of coins in a jar, I am likely to get a remarkably accurate answer. Despite that, if I hold an auction for the value of the coins in a jar, offering to write a cheque to the winning bidder for whatever that value is, I am almost guaranteed to make big money, because at least one bidder will be too optimistic. It's the winner's curse in action.

That is not because the auction produces some odd psychological quirk. It's because while the survey of the crowd will produce the average view of the value of coins, the auction will not. Instead, the auction automatically selects the highest bid, the crazier the better. The survey uncovers what *New Yorker* columnist James Surowiecki calls 'the wisdom of crowds'. The auction, by contrast, finds the biggest sucker.

Rational players, knowing this, would dramatically scale back their bids. They would reason like this: 'I think the value of the coins in the jar is twenty pounds. So maybe I should bid eighteen pounds to leave some room for profit. But wait: either I lose the auction, in which case it doesn't matter what my bid was; or I win the auction, in which case a hundred other people in this room thought it was worth less than twenty pounds. What would that tell me? Most likely that I overestimated the value of the jar of coins. Maybe I should bid more like five pounds. That seems very low – but if it happened to be the highest bid in the room, it wouldn't seem nearly so low any more.'

Only game theory experts actually reason this way, for the same reason that few people play good poker the first time they try: it's just too hard to figure out. But just as experienced gamblers work out how to play poker, so do experienced auction bidders work out how not to overbid. For example, managers of construction companies frequently compete for jobs in which the company offering the lowest price wins the contract. When they do, they unknowingly adjust for the winner's curse using rules of thumb that produce rational bidding in the real world. But when economists put the same managers in the laboratory and ask them to bid in an auction, the managers are routinely hit by the curse.

Even professional footballers have been shown to play perfect strategies when taking (or saving) penalty kicks, mixing up the placing of their shots in perfect accordance with the surprisingly complex prescriptions of game theory. It turns out that we don't need to be Von Neumann to master complex strategies, as long as we're in a familiar setting.

That's fine when we have time to practise and familiarise ourselves with a game. But that wasn't true of the most important 'game' to which game theorists applied their thinking in the twentieth century – the game of world dominance, played by the United States and the Soviet Union. The Cold War was a game that had to be played right the first time.

And the creator of game theory was right at the heart of it. By the time *Theory of Games* was published, Von Neumann was a leading mathematician on the Manhattan Project, where his proposal for a way to trigger the explosion of the atomic bomb was credited with dramatically accelerating its development. If it had been up to Von Neumann's purely intellectual reasoning alone, many of the bombs he helped to create would have exploded on the Soviet Union. Thankfully, there was another thinker on hand whose deeper grasp of human foibles added a new dimension to game theory that, among other things, helped save the world from mutually assured destruction. Enter Thomas Schelling.

Camp David, Maryland, September 1961

Some of America's best foreign policy and military strategists were in the room: a young Henry Kissinger; Colonel DeWitt

Armstrong, the Pentagon's top authority on Berlin; McGeorge Bundy, President Kennedy's national security adviser; and John McNaughton, the top arms control aide of Defense Secretary Robert McNamara. They hadn't been sleeping much. The crisis in Berlin had been building for months, since the Soviet leader Nikita Khrushchev had demanded that US troops withdraw from their long-standing bases in West Berlin.

When the phone call arrived from the American base in Berlin, the news was bad. American forces had shot down Soviet planes, killing dozens, and riots were spreading across Eastern Europe. More terse communiqués over the next couple of days made it clear that matters were deteriorating: West German students started rioting, too. Soviet tanks encircled West Berlin and then used the riots as a pretext for entering that sector of the city. As they broke through the barricades, US bombers responded, causing massive casualties. The Soviets had overwhelming local superiority, the Americans nuclear dominance: a nuclear exchange seemed inevitable. Would Kissinger and Bundy decide to press the button?

It wouldn't have mattered if they had, because those men at Camp David were just playing a game. The phone calls weren't coming from Berlin, but from a Harvard professor, the economist Thomas Schelling.

The real Berlin crisis had run out of steam a few weeks earlier without a shot being fired. Khrushchev had indeed asserted Soviet authority over West Berlin and declared that US resistance would be an act of war. The young, inexperienced President Kennedy was being tested. He had turned to Schelling's strategic analysis of the situation ('we should plan for a war of nerve, of demonstration, and of bargaining, not of tactical target destruction') before deciding – correctly – that Khrushchev was bluffing. Instead of invading, the Soviets began building the Berlin Wall in August, sat behind it, and glowered.

Thomas Schelling was just one of many Cold War intellectuals at RAND, the air force's research arm, using Von Neumann's game theory to dissect the possibilities of an event nobody had yet experienced: thermonuclear war. Applying a theory of poker to try to understand the project of mutual annihilation may seem unhinged, but that is exactly what Von Neumann and his disciples did. The theory of zero-sum games wasn't up to the job, as we'll shortly see. But how else to develop nuclear strategy? Practising was not an option, while history, fortunately, could provide no exact parallels.

Von Neumann demanded an aggressive approach. Coincidentally or not, his mathematical analysis backed his instinctive hatred of the Soviet Union, the occupier of his native Hungary. In the late 1940s, he favoured a surprise nuclear assault on the Soviet Union, before it was able to develop the bomb itself. 'If you say why not bomb them tomorrow, I say why not today?' he told *Life* magazine. Von Neumann, who spent the last months of his life in a wheelchair after being struck by bone cancer in his fifties, was an inspiration for the deranged and similarly wheelchair-bound film character Dr Strangelove. (The actor Peter Sellers claimed that the Mitteleuropean accent was based not on Von Neumann but on Kissinger.) He died in 1958, a few years before the Cold War reached its defining crises in Berlin and then Cuba.

In game theory, Von Neumann had crafted a tool that promised to analyse both poker and war. Yet rhetorically pleasing as the analogy is – and delighted as the RAND strategists were with game theory – analytically poker and war had very little in common. Poker is a zero-sum game: one player's loss is another's gain. It is also a game with well defined rules. War is neither well-defined, nor a zero-sum game. (Nor is life. Von Neumann was too quick to draw the parallel between life and poker.) It is much more desirable to avoid war altogether than to fight a destructive war that does not change the balance of power, so while war is certainly a conflict of interests, there is nothing zero-sum about it. Compared to the likely alternative of mutually assured destruction, the Cold War was a win for both sides.

Thomas Schelling's war games were part of his effort to bring about that mutual win.

The war games were, in a way, a prelude to John List's field experiments with Minnie Mouse pins. Schelling realised that however compelling the equations of game theory might be, you could not take the human element out of war. While Von Neumann was the consummate mathematician, Schelling, originally a trade negotiator, was more interested in concepts that eluded mathematical formalisation – credible threats, deterrence and taboos – and his ideas pushed the academic discipline of game theory away from the abstract and intellectual pursuits pioneered by Von Neumann and further into the mainstream of everyday human experience.

Schelling argued that real human strategic interactions were governed not only by Von Neumann's mathematics but by 'focal points' that were invisible under a mathematical formulation of the problem. Schelling did not believe that game theory was useless, merely that most human interactions were so shot through with ambiguity that these focal points could be the ultimate guide to what might or should happen. For example, a trade union leader might try to gain leverage in a negotiation over pay by publicly stating that his members won't accept less than a 10 per cent rise. Ten per cent is a figure of no mathematical significance. Von Neumann would have seen no basis for it. Yet Schelling knew that once the declaration is made, it becomes significant. (And it will be a round number such as 10 per cent, not 10.32 per cent or 9.65 per cent.)

Schelling's most famous example of a focal point was inspired by a time he'd lost a friend in a strange town and tried to work out where to meet him. Schelling used to pose the problem as follows. You have arranged to meet a friend in New York tomorrow, but because of a breakdown in communications, neither of you knows where or when you should meet. What do you do? When Schelling asked his students, they suggested going to the clock at Grand Central Terminal, at noon. (Those students would have travelled to New York by train. Tourists might have a different focal point – perhaps the top of the Empire State Building.)

All this was still game theory, in that each player was acting rationally and trying to anticipate and respond to the strategy of the other player. But it was game theory of a simpler, more common-sense sort than Von Neumann had conceived. And for Schelling common sense was exactly the point, because the players of such games needed to understand one another.

With his emphasis on communication, it is not surprising that Schelling was the man who came up with the idea of the hotline to Moscow. He realised that a nuclear war could easily start as the result of some accident: a misunderstanding or a mistake by a radar operator. If a crisis started, the leaders of the United States and Soviet Union could be looking at the wrong focal point, one in which there was a nuclear exchange. They would only be able to fix the situation before it escalated out of control if they could reach each other quickly, and talk. Yet no hotline existed, so Schelling proposed one to both sides in 1958. The famous 'red telephone' was in fact a teletype machine with multiple back-ups. Even in the darkest hours of the Cold War, the American and Soviet operators tested it every day by sending one another greetings. In retrospect the idea was obvious – especially after the superpowers had lurched through the Berlin and Cuban crises before the system had been established – but it took Schelling to realise how important quick, reliable communication might become.

Schelling also applied his focal point idea to trying to strengthen the taboo against using nuclear weapons. In the 1950s, while Von Neumann still lived, the US government was desperate to avoid the sense that such weapons were beyond the pale. Dwight Eisenhower's secretary of state, John Foster Dulles, argued that inhibitions in the use of nuclear weapons were based on a 'false distinction' between nuclear and conventional weapons that needed breaking down. 'Somehow or other we must manage to remove the taboo from the use of these weapons,' he stated in 1953. President Eisenhower appeared to agree, approving a doctrine that nuclear weapons should be 'as available for use as other munitions'.

Schelling did not agree. His argument was that 'bright lines, slippery slopes and well-defined boundaries' were everything in this debate. In the quest to avoid a full-blown nuclear exchange only one focal point should be emphasised: that nuclear weapons could never be used. There was no such thing as a 'minor' use of nuclear weapons any more than one could become slightly pregnant. The taboo was purely psychological, invisible to a mathematician like Von Neumann, but real and very useful. He put forward this view, as part of a broad theory of deterrence and arms control, in a series of seminars that he organised at Harvard University and the Massachusetts Institute of Technology in 1960. Later that year, John F. Kennedy was elected President. Schelling later reflected,

> The timing was perfect. Kennedy appointed as his national security adviser a Harvard dean who had participated in the autumn discussions of arms control, and as his White House science adviser an MIT professor who had been one of the group; another member became Deputy Assistant Secretary of Defense for Arms Control, another General Counsel of the State Department.

Schelling became the intellectual godfather of the Kennedy and Johnson administrations, introducing Robert Kennedy to his war games, advising his former pupils as they held the reins of power, and providing the leading intellectual justification for the taboo against nuclear weapons. By the time he broke off his connections with the government in 1970, that taboo was as strong as it has ever been. When he accepted his Nobel Prize in 2005 – economics, not peace – Schelling began by saying, 'The most spectacular event of the past half century is one that did not occur. We have enjoyed sixty years without nuclear weapons exploded in anger.'

Schelling compared the 'minor' use of nuclear weapons to 'one little drink' for an alcoholic: it is a slippery slope. The analogy was close to home: Schelling was fighting his own personal battle with cigarette addiction. In his 1980 essay 'The Intimate Contest for Self Command', he tried to understand the person 'whom all of us know and who some of us are, who in self disgust grinds his cigarettes down the disposal swearing that this time he means never again to risk orphaning his children with lung cancer and is on the street three hours later looking for a store that's still open to buy cigarettes ... who spoils the trip to Disneyland by losing his temper when his children do what he knew they were going to do when he resolved not to lose his temper when they did it.'

Despite our obvious fallibilities, Schelling believed that addiction could be analysed using the rational choice perspective offered by game theory. But he came to realise that his views were unorthodox when he was asked in the 1970s to join the National Academy of Sciences committee on substance abuse and addictive behaviour. All the other members of the committee – psychologists, sociologists, lawyers – believed that addicts were irrational and helpless. The reasoning was common sense: since smoking or taking heroin is addictive and can have horrible effects, people who choose to take up the habits must be irrational. Schelling wasn't quite so sure.

The extreme opposite view was most explicitly set out, not by Schelling, but by the economists Kevin M. Murphy and Gary Becker. We've met Becker, the rational criminal from the Chicago car park. Murphy, his young co-author, was inspiring the same sort of 'demigod' anecdotes that had once surrounded Von Neumann. One colleague recalled telephoning Murphy for advice on a mathematical problem that had been troubling him for weeks. 'I imagine him sitting at his kitchen table, pencil in hand, scribbling equations on a napkin. He's dropped everything to help me with my problem, and in ten minutes he's explaining aspects of it to me that I would never have seen. Then I hear a splash, and a squeal, then another splash, and it dawns on me: There's no pencil, no paper. Kevin's holding the phone to his left ear with his shoulder while he's giving his kid a bath.'

Perhaps it will not be surprising to hear that Becker and Murphy produced, in 1988, a conclusion worthy of Von Neumann. Addiction, they said, was entirely rational. People who consume addictive products – cigarettes, alcohol, slot machines – calculate that the pleasure of the habit will outweigh the pain. For Becker and Murphy, a stroll through the lobby of the Rio Las Vegas hotel would have proved no challenge to the rational choice view of the world. Yes, the slot machine players were losing money. Some of them might even be addicted. But they had made a rational decision to start playing the machines, knowing there was a chance they'd end up miserable and hooked, and now they were making a rational decision to continue playing rather than endure the greater misery that would be involved in kicking the habit.

A rational decision not to kick an addiction, and even to start one? It sounds less outlandish if you consider a more commonplace addiction. I like to start my day by grinding freshly roasted coffee beans and brewing them into a rich, aromatic cup of coffee. Every now and then I am careless and run out of beans. My head aches, I'm grumpy, I can't concentrate. I'm an addict in withdrawal. Of course I know that if I wait a few days the withdrawal symptoms will have gone and I will be free of my addiction. Instead, I buy more beans: the coffee is worth it. Am I really so irrational? According to Becker and Murphy, the slot machine addiction, even a heroin addiction, is different only in degree.

It can also be rational to get hooked in the first place. Imagine a young man who is thinking of trying a new drug. He knows that everybody who tries it loves it, at least at first. Then some users find their lives degenerate into an increasingly desperate and futile attempt to recapture that initial buzz, leading to the pain of cold turkey or the anguish of eternal, unfulfilling addiction. Others seem able to enjoy the highs and remain quite content for the rest of their lives. He has no way of knowing into which category he will fall. Is it rational for him to ingest the drug?

If you say 'no', read the paragraph above again but replace 'trying a new drug' with 'getting married' and 'cold turkey' with 'divorce'. Getting married is not so different from getting hooked. It might not work out, it will restrict your future freedom of choice, and quitting if things turn sour is going to be extremely difficult and painful. But it will probably be a lot of fun, too. The first-time drug user (or the newlywed) might be making a mistake, but he or she thinks that on balance the decision will pay off. That, according to Becker and Murphy, is what addicts do.

Becker and Murphy were not merely expressing their faith in rationality, but making some clear predictions. Rational addicts know that drinking or smoking today reinforces drinking or smoking tomorrow and is reinforced by drinking or smoking yesterday. So an alcoholic who knows that an incoming government is promising to raise taxes on booze may decide that this is an opportune time to work on kicking the habit, even if vodka is cheap right now. Rational addicts respond to predictable price changes before they even happen. So if Becker and Murphy are right, this is how real addicts should behave.

It sounds implausible, but it's true. Becker and Murphy found that reductions in cigarette consumption occur when a price increase is expected, but before the price actually rises. Another researcher discovered that gambling also looks like a rational addiction: an increase in the share of gambling revenues taken by racecourses reduces the amount that is bet not only in the current year, but in the next year and even in the previous year. Gamblers anticipate that betting will become more expensive and work on kicking the habit in advance.

This behaviour is easier to understand through an imperfect but revealing analogy: dealing with a forthcoming increase in your rent. It is difficult and costly to switch flats, just as it's difficult to kick an addiction. So if your landlord gave you three months' warning of a rent increase, you might rationally start looking for a new place right away. If it were a local restaurant that was announcing its prices would rise in three months' time, on the other hand, you wouldn't feel any need to start trying out alternative restaurants immediately – you'd simply enjoy eating there while it was still cheap. It's pushing it to say you are 'addicted' to your flat (and not to the restaurant), but certainly you have a tie to the flat that is difficult to break, and that has effects just as an addiction does.

Becker and Murphy also predict that because addiction is self-reinforcing, with each fix creating a greater desire for the next fix, cold turkey is the rational way to quit. The surprising implication is that addictive goods can be *more* sensitive to price changes than non-addictive goods, and addicts may pay more attention to price than light users do. The light users can cut back if prices rise, while the heavy users might prefer to stop entirely. It sounds ridiculous, but turns out to be true: when liquor taxes are raised, the consumption of alcohol falls but the death rate from liver cirrhosis falls more sharply. In other words, when the price of booze increases, alcoholics are the ones who cut down most on their drinking.

Economists have also found that advertising for nicotine patches and gum seems to encourage non-smoking teenagers to smoke. That's easy to explain if teenagers are rational: the advertisements tell them that there are new ways to help them quit, so rationally it is less risky to start the habit. Kevin Murphy told me he thought the discovery was 'obvious' and completely unsurprising, 'although it's always nice to see the evidence support the theory'.

So is addiction really rational, as Becker and Murphy argue, and their data tend to suggest? Or is it irrational, as Schelling's fellow committee members were claiming? Schelling thought that neither was true. It was possible to reconcile both the intuitive sense that it was crazy to risk addiction with the logic and evidence that said it was rational. For Schelling, addiction was neither purely irrational nor purely rational. It was a war, a battle for self-control. Schelling didn't mean this as a casual, poetic analogy. He meant that it was a battle that an addict could win, if only he had the right tactics.

Schelling sometimes told a story about a man whose wife was trying to quit smoking. Imagine, he said, that she had quit, but was having a tough time of it. Then a friend came to visit and accidentally left a packet of cigarettes lying around. The husband should pick up those cigarettes and flush them down the toilet before his wife's short-term cravings forced her to do something she didn't want. It was a simple contest in which the husband, able to appreciate the bigger picture, outwitted his addicted wife and her overwhelming impulses.

But then Schelling would recast the story. The man was single. He was the one who was trying to quit smoking and struggling. When his friend left the cigarettes behind, the man tucked them into his pocket so that he could return them later. But after a glass of whisky, the man started to find the cigarettes dangerously tempting. Before his impatient, addicted side gave in, the man's more strong-willed self realised what was likely to happen. He dumped the cigarettes in the toilet and pulled the chain. This is the same simple contest between two decision-makers, one patient and the other eager for a quick hit – but both decision-makers were in the same body.

Schelling had to rely on introspection to develop what he called 'egonomics', the view of addiction as a kind of mental civil war. Now a bold new group of researchers armed with both brain scanners and rational choice theory, calling themselves 'neuroeconomists', are starting to develop a view of the brain that provides some startling evidence for Schelling's split-personality model of decision-making. Rather than reflecting and speculating, they can use high-tech scanners to see the 'impatient' part of the brain.

This impatient part of the brain is called the dopamine system. You can give a snack to a monkey in a brain scanner and watch his dopamine system light up like a Christmas tree. The system seems to be designed to make instant forecasts of pleasure ('the snack will be delicious') as a way to make quick decisions about what to do ('eat it!'). But addictive chemicals can cause the dopamine system to misfire, and some researchers even think that non-chemical addictions such as playing slot machines can do the same thing.

The other side in the mental civil war is the cognitive system. Better able to guide longer-term choices in uncertain environments, it can be slow to operate. The dopamine system is fast and usually reliable, but produces mistaken forecasts in some circumstances. Humans combine information from both, apparently a compromise produced by the forces of natural selection. *Voilà*: Thomas Schelling's 'egonomics', reborn as 'neuro-economics'.

Lower-tech experiments can easily reveal the tension. In one, the experimenters offered some subjects a snack: fruit or chocolate. Seven out of ten subjects asked for chocolate. But when the experimenters offered other subjects a different choice, the answer was different, too: 'I'll bring you a snack next week. What would you like then, fruit or chocolate?' Three-quarters of subjects chose fruit.

When subjects were offered the choice of watching a lowbrow movie or a sophisticated critical success, well over half opted to watch something like *Mrs Doubtfire*. Asked what they wanted to watch in a week's time, suddenly *Three Colours: Blue* or *Schindler's List* seemed like the better choice for almost two-thirds of the subjects. When asked to make choices in advance, students seemed to value the fact that watching *Three Colours: Blue* would make them a wiser, more cultured person for the rest of their lives. Offered the choice right now, having a relaxed couple of hours watching jokes about fake breasts outweighed those longer-term benefits.

One of the researchers, economist Daniel Read, told me that when he subscribed to an Internet movie rental service, he kept changing his ranking of requested films so that the highbrow films never quite made it to the top of his waiting list. Clearly, if you want to watch more cultured films, order them well in advance and then stay away from the rental website.

Schelling was not the first person to point out these tensions or to describe addiction as a battle for control of the self. But he was the first to think explicitly of the problem as a strategic one. He made a woeful strategic error in his own battle. He quit smoking in 1955, but in 1958, sitting in a restaurant in London, he bought a cigar from 'one of those ladies who used to go from restaurant to restaurant selling them'. He thought he was immune, but spent many years 'tormented', trying to quit.

Schelling's days as a strategist gave him a book of tricks and tactics to try to recover from that initial stumble. Not all of them were successful. He realised he didn't have the strength of will simply to quit smoking, but he also knew that a vague promise to himself to cut down would be easily dodged by his impatient, cigarette-craving side. So he decided to create a 'bright line', just as he had argued for a taboo against the use of nuclear weapons. He told himself that he would not smoke until after the evening meal. He obeyed that rule for years, but unfortunately Schelling's weaker half was also an expert strategist, and the hapless professor found himself hunting for sandwiches at around 5.30 p.m. so that he could have a smoke without having violated the letter of his self-imposed law.

Schelling's strategy was right from the negotiator's textbook: make a specific and (apparently) unambiguous commitment. That was what President Kennedy had done when facing Khrushchev over Berlin. Rather than saying something vague such as 'we will take the steps necessary to defend our interests', he made an unambiguous statement. Four days after reading Schelling's analysis of the problem, he announced on television, 'We have given our word that an attack upon that city will be regarded as an attack upon us all.' That public commitment made it hard for Kennedy to ignore any attack, and thus dissuaded Khrushchev from making one.

But as a good negotiator knows – and as Kennedy showed later in the Cuba crisis – when the line causes irreconcilable differences, you work out a way to compromise without erasing the line. You can see the same tactics at play when a trade union leader publicly declares that members will not accept less than a 10 per cent pay increase. The whole idea of that sort of announcement is to add credibility to the threat to walk away from the talks. And you can also see, from pay negotiations, why the tactics don't work as well as the negotiators might hope. The clever response is to find weaselly ways to undo the commitment: what about 10 per cent staggered over the next three years? Or what about a 10 per cent rise this year, provided certain onerous productivity targets are met?

Or what about a sandwich at 5.30 in the 'evening', and a cigarette at 5.33?

No economist has yet come up with a convincing explanation for why these taboos and focal points work. But work they do, albeit imperfectly. Why else do people try to quit smoking on 1 January rather than on 24 February?

An addict, like a negotiator, may be able to gain an advantage by making binding decisions in advance. An everyday example is the dieter who shops for food over the Internet, and only after a good meal, so that he is not tempted by the sight of cakes and chips. A more sophisticated example, designed by economists Richard Thaler and Shlomo Benartzi, is a financial scheme called 'Save More Tomorrow', in which corporate employees boost their pensions by earmarking a proportion of future pay rises to go into their pension funds. The idea has nearly quadrupled retirement savings.

In both cases, the forward-thinking person outwits the impatient or weak-willed person who inhabits the same body. Schelling wryly observed that it is not always easy to tell whose side you should be on. People can save too much, exercise too much, diet too much, and commit themselves to 'improving' activities – subscriptions to the *Times Literary Supplement* or membership of the Royal Opera House – that they do not really want.

In real negotiations, too, a negotiator can strengthen his position by tying his hands. This is what any shop assistant does when they tell you they're not authorised to offer you a discount. But such tactics can backfire, just as they do for the person who never uses her gym subscription. In the film *Dr Strangelove*, the Russians build a doomsday device, a computer that will launch every Soviet warhead if it detects any signs of an American attack. Such a device is obviously risky, but by making retaliation certain it should make the surprise attack far less likely. This is reasoning that Dr Strangelove, the fictional Von Neumann, explains. Needless to say, predictable human error intervenes and things do not go quite according to plan. (Who did the director Stanley Kubrick consult while scripting the movie? None other than Thomas Schelling.)

Suddenly it is not so hard to see how an alcoholic's rational side can successfully decide to quit after reading about an increase in liquor taxes in the newspaper – but that the very same person could kill herself drinking if she got hold of another bottle. While addicts can make the wrong choices, contradict themselves and be tormented by their frailties, as Schelling was, they can also weigh costs and benefits, anticipate temptations, and take steps to put those temptations out of reach.

Schelling himself won his personal civil war after a fifteen-year struggle. When I met him in 2005, he had gone three decades without smoking. At the age of eighty-four, he was the picture of health.

*

Thinking back to Las Vegas, it is clear that Ferguson's triumph at the 2000 World Series of Poker was a landmark in the history of game theory. But in many ways, it was atypical. Ferguson's approach was directly descended from Von Neumann's pure mathematical brilliance, but while modern economics still drips with mathematics, much of the most successful game theory is of the Schelling variety: simpler in theory, and more aware of the messy details of real situations.

Just three weeks before Ferguson's victory, for example, the British government had scored a little win of its own, raising twenty-two billion pounds in an auction for mobile phone licences that was designed by game theorists – arguably the most high-profile success of game theory in recent years. Paul Klemperer, one of the lead designers of the UK mobile phone auctions, later explained that successful auction design did not require fancy mathematical game theory, but basic economic ideas that any undergraduate could explain: encouraging bidders to come to the auction, closing loopholes and preventing cheating. Success or failure depended on getting the fundamentals correct in an ambiguous world. Like Ferguson, the auction's designers used banks of computers to explore all the possibilities, but unlike him they were looking for simple strategies, clear focal points and glaring errors.

And while Ferguson's grasp of advanced game theory continues to make him one of the most feared faces at the poker table, more humble Schelling-style battles for self-control are being fought out at the doors of the Rio. Some gambling addicts cannot reach the slot machines, because the casino manager and his security guards will intercept them and politely guide them to the exit. These men and women have been barred from the Rio, and all the other casinos owned by the world's largest operator, Harrah's. Who barred them? Not the police or the management of Harrah's, but their better halves. Anyone who suffers from a gambling addiction – a misfiring of the dopamine system when the slot machines are in sight – can call Harrah's or log on to the web-site and volunteer to be banned. The rational decision-maker outwits the short-sighted addict with the help of Harrah's, their image recognition software and a couple of friendly bouncers. If you can't win the battle with yourself, you can recruit allies.

Game theory shows us the hidden logic behind poker, war and even addiction. It is inevitably a way to view the world through the lens of rationality, but it is most effective when it uncovers simple, common-sense rationality in unexpected circumstances – such as the slot machines in Vegas. Von Neumann, the self-confident 'demigod', would fully have expected his beloved game theory to be achieving triumphs at Las Vegas. He might have been more surprised to learn that modern game theory has as much to do with the internal dilemmas of the slot machine junkies as with the brilliance of Chris 'Jesus' Ferguson on the other side of the lobby.

Three

Is divorce underrated?

There are 1.3 million single men in New York, 1.8 million single women, and of these more than three million people, about twelve think they're having enough sex.

– Carrie Bradshaw (Sarah Jessica Parker), *Sex and the City*

Tiger Tiger Bar, Haymarket, London, 2006

Tiger Tiger is a large bar in the heart of the theatre district, its air thick with smoke, loud music and pheromones. If you like that sort of thing, it's a good place to meet friends and have cocktails or a glass of Chardonnay. Not a bad place, either, to find love. When I went there, to one of the smaller, quieter lounges towards the back, I was interested in meeting people who had signed up for a little extra romantic help.

The occasion was a speed date. Twenty or so hopeful boys and girls had gathered together for an evening whose format is growing increasingly familiar. Everyone got a name badge, a pen, a list of check boxes and a large drink. The women took their seats at small tables dotted around the room. The host – a rep from the speed dating company that organised the event – rang a little bell, prompting all the men to hurry to their assigned 'dates', which lasted all of three minutes. When the time was up, the bell rang again, the daters shook hands (or, if brave, gave each other a peck on the cheek), and the men hopped to the next table and the next woman. Half an hour later, everybody had met everybody else and ticked 'date' or 'no date' for each name on his or her list. That information wouldn't be revealed until the next day, over the Internet, but they all could chat in blissful ignorance at the bar or, *au choix*, slink off home.

I was there in a professional capacity, using economics to 'help' ordinary folk for a television show I was filming. The victim in this case was a volunteer called Andy, who bravely agreed that he would use some harebrained piece of game theory I'd cooked up to persuade his favourite girl to go on a real date with him. He crashed and burned on national television while I berated him for getting the game theory tangled up. It was not a high point for Andy, nor for my project of using economics as a tool for self-improvement.

You might think that was the first and last time any economist has dared to show his face at a speed date, but not at all. We can't get enough of them. Economists at Columbia University even went to the trouble of organising one. Ever since John Von Neumann's game theory promised to help us understand love and marriage, economists have been interested in how people choose their partners and how relationships work. And if you want to understand the way people choose their partners, a speed date is a great place to start. At a speed date you can get information about how each person responded to dozens of potential partners, something that would be impossible to collect in more traditional dating situations without binoculars, snooping devices and a good private investigator.

There is, obviously, a lot more to love, dating and marriage than rational choice theory, but rational choices are an important part of the story. A biologist or a poet might explain why we fall in love, and a historian can trace the way the institution of marriage has changed over the centuries. But economists can tell you something about the hidden logic that underlies love.

This chapter looks at competition, supply and demand in the marriage market. Hold on – does competition really apply to love? If you think not, you're lucky: evidently the object of your affections never ran off with your best friend. Or perhaps you think those staples of the economist's analytical tool kit, supply and demand, don't belong in a discussion of romance. Tell that to the (mostly male) engineering students and the (mostly female) nursing students who, in universities across the world, organise 'nurses and engineers' parties.

Specifically, we will see how rational people respond in places where there are imbalances between the numbers of men and women available. Carrie Bradshaw, the character from *Sex and the City* whose quote opened this chapter, told us plenty of stories about the difficulties facing single women when they outnumber single men in New York. We shall see that even a small discrepancy between the sexes can have surprisingly far-reaching effects.

We'll then go on to look at the rational – if often implicit – bargaining that takes place within a marriage or other long-term relationship: who goes to work, who looks after the kids, who spends the money, and who files for divorce. Husbands and wives love each other (we hope) and enjoy each other's company; they are a romantic couple. But they are also an economic unit, dividing labour and sharing the costs of bringing up children or putting a roof over everyone's head. Economic changes – which is to say, rational responses to changing incentives – were behind the rapid rise of divorce in the 1970s; they are also behind the dramatic but as yet unfinished strides women are taking towards equality in the workforce. We'll see how rational reactions have turned divorce, the contraceptive pill and women's achievements in the workplace into a reinforcing loop: these questions are all connected closely to the negotiations between men and women in long-term relationships.

First of all, though, it's time to dispose of an age-old question. Do people spend their lives looking for 'the one', the one person – or, less ambitiously, a particular type of person – who is the perfect match for them temperamentally, socially, professionally, financially and sexually? Or do people adjust their standards depending on what they can get? In other words, are the romantics right, or the cynics?

I'll admit that I can't answer that question definitively – not even the most ingenious of today's new generation of economists have devised an experiment that will prove whether people lower their sights in response to market conditions when it comes to marriage. But there is some suggestive evidence from the study of speed dating, courtesy of the economists Michèle Belot and Marco Francesconi.

Speed daters are able to propose to anyone and everyone they meet, and do so electronically after the event, so the embarrassment of rejection is minimised. That should mean that, for most people, a proposal of a date is a simple, uncomplicated expression of approval, and that nobody would propose a date they didn't want accepted or hold back a proposal even though they wanted a date. Belot and Francesconi persuaded one of Britain's largest dating agencies to release information about the activities of 1,800 men and 1,800 women who, over the course of nearly two years, attended eighty-four speed dating events. The researchers were able to see who went to which event, and who proposed to whom.

It won't surprise many people to hear that while women proposed a match to about one in ten of the men they met, men were a bit less choosy and proposed a match to twice as many women, with about half the success rate. Nor will it shock anyone to hear that tall men, slim women, non-smokers and professionals received more offers. But what might raise the odd eyebrow is that it became clear from about two thousand separate speed dates (that's one hundred hours of stilted conversation) that people seemed systematically – and rationally – to change their standards depending on who showed up for the speed date. They didn't seem to be looking for 'the one' at all.

For example, men prefer women who are not overweight. You might think, then, that if on a particular evening twice as many overweight women as usual show up, it will be a night where fewer men propose. Not at all. The men propose just as frequently, so that when twice as many overweight women turn up, twice as many overweight women receive offers of a date.

Similarly, more women prefer tall men than short men, but on evenings where nobody is over six feet, the short guys have a lot more luck. Most people prefer an educated partner, but they will propose to school dropouts if the Ph.D.s stay away. If people really are looking for a partner of a particular type, we would expect them to respond to the absence of such people by getting the bus home with a disappointed shrug, resigning themselves to spending Saturday night in front of the televison, and hoping for a better turnout at the next speed date. But that simply isn't what happens. Instead, people respond to slim pickings by lowering their standards.

Note that this experiment doesn't suggest that people aren't fussy: even the men turn down 80 per cent of the women, and the women are choosier still. What it does show is that we are more fussy when we can afford to be and less fussy when we can't: crudely speaking, when it comes to the dating market, we settle for what we can get. Francesconi told me that, according to his estimates, our offers to date a smoker or a non-smoker are 98 per cent a response to – there's no nice way to put this – 'market conditions' and just 2 per cent governed by immutable desires. Proposals to tall, short, fat, thin, professional, clerical, educated or uneducated people are all more than nine-tenths governed by what's on offer that night. Only when there is an age mismatch do people even seem to consider waiting for another evening and hoping for a more suitable range of potential mates. Even then, the importance of preferences is still less than the importance of the market opportunity. In the battle between the cynics and the romantics, the cynics win hands down.

'Who you propose a date to is largely a function of who happens to be sitting in front of you,' Francesconi explained to me.

(He is a charming Italian who I imagine would do rather well if forced to participate in a speed date.) 'In this case, that is largely random.'

Now, of course, the fact that people seem happy to settle for what they can get when contemplating asking someone out for a date next Saturday doesn't prove that their standards are equally malleable when it comes to contemplating marriage. But we choose our first dates from among the people we meet, and we choose our marriage partner from among the people we've been on dates with. Moreover, if you turn down everybody on the marriage market, you're going to die alone; if you turn down everybody on the speed dating market on a particular evening, you get to try again in a few days, and the organisers will even pay for it. (People who make no proposals get a courtesy invitation to another speed date.) If our standards for marriage are as inflexible as a romantic might like to believe, why do they become so stretchy on a speed date, given that the cost of maintaining those standards is so low? My suspicion is that since we adjust to conditions when dating, we also adjust to conditions in longer-term relationships.

That may be enough to put you off the economists' analysis of dating and marriage already, but I hope not. Yes, economists think of dating and marriage as taking place in a 'marriage market', but that does not mean a market where husbands and wives are bought and sold. It simply means that there's a supply, there's a demand – boy, is there a demand – and, inevitably, there is competition. Carrie Bradshaw, with her little statistic about 1.3 million men and 1.8 million women, understood that very well. So does anyone who ever complains to friends that 'all the good men are taken' or that everyone is suddenly pairing off. None of this is to deny that true love exists. But while love is blind, lovers are not: they are well aware of what opportunities lie ahead of them and they rationally take those opportunities into account when they are dating. They also make big, rational decisions to improve their prospects or to cope when prospects look grim. I'll show that supply and demand in the dating market motivates people to work, to study and even to move in search of better prospects. We'll see that in places where men are scarce, women respond by staying in school longer. In cities where men are particularly rich, women are particularly plentiful. (Did Carrie Bradshaw ever stop to think that there's a reason why so many women live in Manhattan?) Love is not rational, but lovers are.

The rationality of lovers has surprisingly far-reaching effects when one sex outnumbers the other, even by a small margin. To see why, we need to visit a place that exists only in the curious imagination of economists: the Marriage Supermarket.

The marriage supermarket, somewhere in economic space

It takes two to tango, and it also takes two to get married. Marriage therefore requires that you go out and find someone you want to marry, and persuade them to marry you. It's a matching problem, and it is not unique to marriage. Getting a job is emotionally a different proposition to finding a wife or husband, but in some ways it's similar: you need to consider a range of jobs, work out which ones you prefer, and persuade the employer that he likes the match as much as you do. And just as in the job market, who matches up with whom, and on what terms, will depend on what the competition is offering.

Imagine twenty single guys and twenty single girls in a room. This is the Marriage Supermarket, so called because shopping is simple, there's nothing exciting about any of the products, and everything's under one roof. Getting 'married' at the Marriage Supermarket is easy: any man and woman who present themselves at the checkout can collect a hundred pounds (a simple way to represent the psychological or financial gains from getting married) and leave. Naturally, nobody agonises about whether to get married in the Marriage Supermarket. It's a no-brainer, because any partner is equally good, and you get cash with no strings attached.

The Marriage Supermarket is a very simple model of marriage. Like all economic models, it leaves out many complicating details in an attempt to tease out something interesting about the core issues that remain. And they are? That most people would rather be married than remain single, and that your gains from getting married depend on the supply of marriage partners. Of course, we know that in reality there are contented lifelong singletons and married people who curse the day they walked down the aisle. But to the extent that we accept these two premises as embodying a recognisable kernel of truth about the real world, the Marriage Supermarket can tell us something useful.

The gains from marriage in reality are not measured in pounds – or, at least, not in pounds alone. But for the purposes of this model, we do not need to know whether women (or men) in reality are looking for men (or women) who will give them money, orgasms, sparkling conversations or a warm glow of security. All we need to know is that they would rather be married than single.

Since any couple can collect a hundred pounds to split between them, the only question is how to divide the spoils. With equal numbers of men and women, we can expect a fifty–fifty split. Yet it doesn't take much to change that conclusion utterly.

Imagine an unusual evening in the Supermarket, when twenty single women show up but only nineteen single men. What happened to the other guy? He's gay. Or dead. Or in prison. Or has moved to Scotland. Or is studying economics. For whatever reason, he is not available – like the half-million single guys Carrie thinks have gone missing in Manhattan. You might think that the slight scarcity of men would cause the women some modest inconvenience, but in fact even this tiny imbalance ends up being very bad news for the women and very good news for the remaining men. Scarcity is power, and more power than you might have thought.

Here's why. One woman is going to go home with neither a spouse nor a cheque from the cashier. That's bad news for her. What is less immediately obvious is that the women who *do* get a spouse are also going to be worse off – and their loss is the men's gain. Remember that a couple get to split a hundred pounds when they show up at the checkout; assume that the nineteen couples have provisionally agreed on a fifty–fifty split.

The odd woman out, contemplating going home empty-handed, will make the obviously rational decision to muscle in on an existing pairing. The unwanted woman could certainly offer a better deal than a fifty–fifty split, perhaps agreeing to accept only forty pounds. Her rival, being a similarly rational soul, won't want to lose out entirely, so she'll counter-bid – maybe offering to accept just thirty pounds. The bids will fall until the woman who faces leaving alone is offering to walk through the checkout with some lucky guy and accept just one penny as the price of doing so. He'll get £99.99, but her one penny profit is better than nothing.

The trouble doesn't end there. Economists talk about 'the law of one price', which says that identical products on offer at the same time, in the same place, with the prices clearly visible, will go for the same price. This is the Marriage Supermarket, so that's exactly the situation the women find themselves in. No matter what deals are agreed, there will always be one girl left over, offering to pair up for just one penny. The law of one price says one penny is what all of them will get: anyone on the verge of getting a better offer will be undercut. The nineteen men will each get £99.99. Nineteen women will get a penny each, and the last woman will get nothing.

That's remarkable: a shortage of just one man gives all the other men massive scarcity power. The intuition is straightforward, though. Just one 'leftover' woman can provide an outside option for every single man, and spoil the bargaining position of every other woman.

That's how it would work in the Marriage Supermarket. You may have noticed some minor differences in reality. The conditions for the law of one price are never perfectly met. The bargaining process is not quite as calculating, although it is probably just as brutal. Most importantly, because the Marriage Supermarket measures the benefits of marriage in pounds, those benefits are easily transferred from one party to another. In reality, it's not as easy for suitors to bid against one another as marriage prospects ('I'll match Brian's guarantee of three orgasms per week, and add in at least one candlelit dinner') – although the marriage of twenty-six-year-old former *Playboy* centrefold Anna Nicole Smith to billionaire eighty-nine-year-old J. Howard Marshall II (both now sadly deceased) suggested there are some circumstances in which one potential marriage partner can compensate the other, at least to some extent, for whatever shortcomings he or she might have.

Although the Supermarket produces overly stark conclusions, even in a more realistic setting the same underlying forces would be at play. A seemingly modest shortage of men leads to a surprisingly big disadvantage for women. The dramatic increase in bargaining power of men doesn't harm merely the women who don't get to marry, but also those who do. Their potential partners just have too many options to allow a fair bargain. Later in the chapter we'll see a striking example by looking at what happens to women when many of the young men they might have married go to prison instead.

There is another big simplification involved in this thought experiment, which, when we shine the spotlight on it, tells us what strategies the real-world equivalents of women in the Marriage Supermarket can rationally pursue, given that offering cash to get a husband doesn't work so well. Outside the Supermarket, you can go to college, set up a business, get plastic surgery or work out at the gym. In short, there are all sorts of ways you can make yourself a more attractive catch than the other guys and girls. This is indeed how rational women tend to respond to a shortage of men, as we shall see.

To take us there, though, let's take a step backwards and ask why Carrie Bradshaw and the girls were facing such a shortage of eligible men in New York. There's a rational explanation for this, too.

The ancestral environment, the African savannah, a long time ago

Men and women have different approaches to sex and marriage. This is because it takes a woman nine months to make a baby, while it takes a man about two minutes. This simple biological fact, allied to the inexorable force of natural selection, lies behind the folk wisdom that all males (not just human males) are always available for sex. Men typically do not need much persuading to invest a short amount of time in having sex, with the chance of spreading their genes as a result, because they are the sons of men who did not need much persuading. For all females (not just human females) sex tends to lead to pregnancy, and pregnancy is a serious commitment of time and resources. It is best only to risk pregnancy when the time and the partner are right, so women have higher standards and take more persuading. Women are cautious because they are the daughters of women who were cautious.

Since I am now talking about the evolved biological preferences of men and women, rather than their considered opinions, you might think I'm straying a long way from rational choices. Not at all: these preferences emerge from the economic logic of risks, costs and benefits. Robert Trivers, the evolutionary biologist who first explained why males and females have such different attitudes to sex, titled his analysis 'Parental Investment and Sexual Selection'. His reasoning was explicitly economic, and the preferences of men for indiscriminate sex and women for more cautious behaviour are rational not because of conscious choice but because of evolution.

Of course, evolution has also generously bequeathed us big brains with the capacity to understand, reflect upon and choose to reject our evolved biological preferences. But we have already seen evidence, in this chapter, that we do not appear to have been entirely successful in doing so. In the speed date, remember, women were half as likely as men to suggest a follow-up date. In another experiment that is now famous, three-quarters of men approached by a random woman agreed to have sex with her. Admittedly, they were students on campus, so might have been unusually free-spirited. Yet no female student agreed to have sex when approached by a random man. Such things happen only in a certain exuberant genre of movies, or so I am told.

So much for sex – what about marriage? In the ancestral environment, it is fair to assume, a baby with two parents looking after it stood a much better chance of reaching adulthood than a baby whose single parent had to do the rearing as well as the hunting and gathering. Hence the evolution of the pair-bond. But what characteristics would men and women have been looking for? Since a woman needed the physical strength to bear and rear the baby, youth and health – for which beauty is a reliable indicator – would top the list of male desires. We can imagine that a father's role in raising children, primarily, was to provide and protect: perhaps the most able hunters would have been in most demand as long-term partners, or the strongest fighters, or the canniest at making political alliances. All these attributes would have translated into high status. And in modern times, we have a very reliable indicator of high status: wealth.

On the African savannah, then, our rational male forebears wanted young and beautiful partners while our rational ancestors down the maternal line would have preferred high-status males. Have these preferences, like attitudes to sex, survived to the present day? Folk wisdom would certainly say so. In the song 'Summertime' from Gershwin's opera *Porgy and Bess*, there's a reason why Bess soothes the baby with the line 'Your daddy's rich and your momma's good looking' rather than the other way round. And how often do you hear of a twenty-six-year-old Chippendale marrying an eighty-nine-year-old heiress?

As ever, economists aren't satisfied with folk wisdom. And fortunately, there's a data source to settle all (well, almost all) controversy on the matter: Internet dating success rates. Economists have been studying Internet dating just as assiduously as they study speed dating, and have found that men attract a lot of replies if their Internet dating ads claim a high income. The situation is reversed for women: if a woman claims a high income in an Internet dating ad, she will receive *fewer* replies than if she had claimed a modest income. It is official: rich men are a turn-on and rich women are a turn-off.

Perhaps you don't think Internet dating responses are really a window on to the soul. You may be right, but there are other sources of evidence. If, as George Gershwin, evolutionary biologists and Internet daters suggest, women are particularly interested in netting themselves a rich man, then presumably we should find lots of women in places where there are lots of rich men: that is, in the cities. Since men aren't as interested in marrying someone with high earning power, the good marriage prospects in the cities are less of an attraction to men than women. As rents rise, it will be the unskilled men who give up and move to the country before the unskilled women do – or who never bother to move to the cities in the first place.

The economist behind this idea is Lena Edlund of Columbia University. She explained the implications to me. First, men would always be in shorter supply in cities than in the countryside. In forty-four out of forty-seven countries studied by Edlund, they are. (In the three exceptions, the sex ratios are equal in the cities and the countryside.) Within the United States, you find the same pattern in the big cities. In Washington, DC, women outnumber men nine to eight. In New York, there are 860,000 men between ages twenty and thirty-four, but there are 910,000 women. (Carrie Bradshaw's numbers were different, but she was including octogenarians!) There are more men, though, in rural states: Alaska, Utah and Colorado.

Another implication of Edlund's theory is that since unskilled men are most likely to stay away from cities, unskilled urban jobs that could easily be done by either sex would tend to be done by women. (Waitressing? Secretarial work? There is nothing inherently, or historically, female about these jobs.) And we would also expect to find that the higher male incomes go, the greater would be the supply of – how to put this? – spare women. That is exactly what Edlund finds in a detailed study of Sweden: areas with high male salaries are areas where a lot of women live, especially young women. Consciously or not, plenty of women seem to have decided they would rather compete for scarce, wealthy males than move where the males are poorer but more plentiful. Manhattan's women may constantly grumble about the lack of marriageable men in the city, but it is their rational choice not to relocate to Alaska.

It's not only by geography that marriage markets in the United States are fragmented: whom you marry does tend to depend on where you live, but also on how old you are and what race you are. Most people marry people of the same race, of a similar age and from the same area. Ninety-six per cent of married black women have black husbands, and over 96 per cent of married white women have white husbands.

What might cause an imbalance in some of these local marriage markets? We've seen that imbalances in cities might be caused by unskilled young men rationally deciding to give up and move to the country, or stay there in the first place. But another major reason for men being absent from local marriage markets is prison. There are two million men in US prisons and just a hundred thousand women; and the men in prison are spread unevenly across age, race and geography. Huge numbers of young black men are in prison, and that is bound to pose a problem for the young black women they might otherwise have married. (It might also pose a problem for women of other races and in other states – but only if some women were inclined and able to hop from a marriage market where men are scarce to one where they are plentiful. That does not seem to happen often enough to cancel out the effect of the shortage of marriageable young black men.)

In New Mexico, for example, 30 per cent of young black men, ages twenty to thirty-five, are in prison (or, less commonly, in a secure mental institution). That is an extreme case, but there are thirty-two states with more than one in ten young black men in prison, and ten states where one in six young black men are behind bars. That is a serious business for young black women. In the Marriage Supermarket, even one missing man puts every woman in a weak bargaining position. Does it translate to real life?

Yes it does, according to economists Kerwin Kofi Charles and Ming Ching Luoh. Where a large number of a particular racial group is in prison, women of the same age and race in that state do not enjoy the gains from marriage or a stable relationship that women in a more equitable situation do.

In the Marriage Supermarket, a weak bargaining position means that women have to bribe men to marry them. In life, another option is open: women can try to increase their attractiveness as marriage prospects. Charles and Luoh show that young black women facing a shortage of men do exactly that. The more men are in prison, the more likely women are to get themselves a job, and the more likely they are to go to college. College-educated people are much more likely to marry other college-educated people, so an education doesn't just make you smart, it wins you a smart husband or wife.

Improving their bargaining position in the marriage market is, of course, not the only likely reason for these decisions. Since the high incarceration rates of young black men mean young black women are less likely to marry, a college degree and a job look like a rational investment for a single girl who can't rely on a partner as a source of income. What's more, the likelihood of young black women not marrying is greatly exacerbated by a trend that the simple Marriage Supermarket couldn't model, but that wouldn't surprise an evolutionary biologist: it appears that young black men who are not in prison typically take advantage of their strong bargaining position by not bothering to marry at all.

Charles and Luoh are able to examine this statistically because they have data across all fifty states and from the 1980, 1990 and 2000 censuses. So they are able to compare the situation of women in different times and places, taking into account background trends as they vary across the country and from decade to decade. They estimate, for instance, that a one-percentage-point rise in the proportion of young black men in prison reduces the proportion of young black women who have ever been married by three percentage points. In states where 20 or 25 per cent of the available men are in prison, young black women become very unlikely to marry. The effect is even more dramatic for uneducated women, since women tend to pair up with men of a similar education level, and uneducated men are particularly likely to end up in jail.

There are a lot of African-American single mothers around, and some commentators are inclined to blame this fact on 'black culture' – whatever that phrase might mean. But 'black culture' doesn't explain why the single mothers are disproportionately in the states where lots of young black men are in prison. Economics does: women's bargaining power is badly dented by the imprisonment of potential husbands. The better-educated guys stay out of jail, and they are smart enough to realise that with the competition locked up, they don't have to get married to enjoy themselves. 'Culture' is a poor explanation; that women respond rationally to a tough situation is a much better one.

If these seem like very large effects, think back to the Marriage Supermarket: even a small shortage of marriageable men puts every woman at a disadvantage, because each single woman is capable of providing competition for many women who eventually marry. The shortage of men does not have to be large to present a large problem for women.

Even though it is mostly uneducated men who end up in prison, Charles and Luoh show that the negotiating position of women is so weakened that they end up more likely, not less, to 'marry down' – that is, to marry men who are less educated than they are. So there's another reason for young black women to put more effort into getting a degree and a job: even if they could find a husband, we could understand them being concerned that he wouldn't be a high-quality husband. Maybe they couldn't rely on him to stay around and be a reliable father or a provider for the household. As the song goes, sisters are doing it for themselves – but not, in this case, for very encouraging reasons.

It's a commonplace observation that the contraceptive pill wrought major changes in society. But when most people hear that, they probably think that the effects were mostly to do with college parties becoming a lot more fun. In fact, rational responses to the pill have had effects remarkably similar to those that come from imprisoning a significant chunk of the male population.

What's the similarity? Both heat up competition among women in the marriage market. Young black men who stay out of prison in a place like New Mexico rarely marry, and this is probably because they realise they do not need to marry to get sex. The contraceptive pill also makes it easier for men to get sex outside of marriage. The logic of evolutionary psychology says that women should be choosy about whom they have sex with, because pregnancy in the wrong circumstances is extremely costly – but the logic of a woman who has control of reliable contraception is quite different. The preferences that evolution has shaped still exert powerful influence on our instincts, and many women remain extremely choosy and refuse to have sex outside marriage. But others, once armed with the pill, decide they can afford to have more fun.

The choosy ones are unlucky: the existence of other women who are a little freer with their favours weakens the bargaining power of the Madonnas, and means that men have less incentive to marry. Some men will not bother at all, feeling that they can get all they want from a playboy lifestyle. Others may delay marriage until middle age, cutting down on the pool of marriageable men and increasing male bargaining power.

As we have seen, the rational response is for women to go to college, bringing them better prospects in both the job and the marriage markets. Meanwhile, the more capable women become of looking after children by themselves, the less men need to bother. It's a textbook case of free-riding: with highly educated women in excess supply, men have realised that they can get sex, and even successful offspring, without ever moving too far from the armchair and the TV. Statistics seem to bear this out. Nowadays, four US women graduate from a university for every three men, and this is not a particularly American phenomenon: in fifteen out of seventeen rich countries for which the data are available, more women are graduating than men. The most educated generation of men in the United States was born just after the Second World War and graduated in the mid-1960s – male graduation rates dipped after that, and have not yet returned to that peak. The rational choice perspective suggests it is probably not coincidental that this decline set in roughly when women got hold of the contraceptive pill.

Women's rational responses to the pill wrought other, socially far-reaching changes. The ability to delay, and to some extent control, the timings of their pregnancies also allowed women to plan their careers in a new way: rather than hurrying back to work after having children, they could decide to postpone their departure. That made it rational to invest in training for a career with a long prequalification period, such as law, medicine or dentistry. Female enrolment in law and medical colleges soared as the pill became available, because women knew they could qualify and establish themselves in a career without becoming a nun.

Delaying motherhood means big income gains for educated women, because of the economies of scale in education and work that reward those who spend a long time in college and then work long hours early in their careers. For every year by which a woman delays having her first child, her lifetime earnings rise by 10 per cent. Of course, someone who delays having children might earn more simply because her career is her priority, but you can get around that statistical minefield by looking at women who, because of miscarriages or accidental pregnancies, do not have children at the time they would have chosen. These random misfortunes, which lead to women having babies later or earlier than they would have done, all point in the same direction: a year's delay adds about one-tenth to lifetime earnings.

The pill also meant women felt more able to postpone marriage – why hurry? They could enjoy sex and a career without rushing to get married. And as more intelligent women delayed getting hitched, that meant that more intelligent men would be floating around, unattached. The dating scene became a more interesting place to dip in and out of for a decade or so, and the risk of being 'left on the shelf ' plummeted. The fewer people sprinted up the aisle, the less need for others to hurry. It looked like a cultural shift, but it had rational roots.

Another side-effect was on the expectations of potential mentors and employers. They had more confidence that women would not give up on their training or careers because of an accidental pregnancy; that increased confidence meant that more women got a fair chance in the workplace. This, too, was not merely the blinkers of discrimination being lifted from employers' eyes: it was a rational response to a world that had changed.

As we are about to see, the pill also contributes towards a rational explanation of one last, much-discussed social phenomenon of the last fifty years or so: skyrocketing rates of divorce. To set the scene for that discussion, though, we need to move on from thinking rationally about competition for partners and start to think rationally about what happens next. Once you have found yourself a partner – or decided that you would rather stay single – how do you manage the household? What, to an economist, is a family? To answer that question we need to take a short detour to an eighteenth-century pin factory.

Kirkcaldy, Scotland, 1776

Adam Smith, the father of modern economics, travelled around Europe as tutor to the Duke of Buccleuch. (His employer was the Duke's stepfather, the Chancellor of the Exchequer Charles Townshend, a man who set a political time bomb by imposing tea duties on America and appointing a customs commissioner to Boston.) But despite his travels, Adam Smith never visited a pin factory. While sitting at home in Kirkcaldy and penning the most famous passage in economics, he was inspired by an entry in an encyclopedia. The passage is no less important for that.

Smith argued that a general handyman who turned his hand to the business of making pins

> could scarce, perhaps, with his utmost industry, make one pin in a day, and certainly could not make twenty. But in the way in which this business is now carried on, not only the whole work is a peculiar trade, but it is divided into a number of branches, of which the greater part are likewise peculiar

trades. One man draws out the wire, another straights it, a third cuts it, a fourth points it, a fifth grinds it at the top for receiving the head.

Smith reckoned that ten specialised pin-makers, using equipment designed and built by specialists, could produce forty-eight thousand pins a day. Ten general handymen could produce perhaps one pin each. In the 'trifling' business of making pins, quite rudimentary division of labour multiplied the output per person almost five thousand times. From a rational choice point of view, dividing labour is a no-brainer.

The division of labour is utterly fundamental to the wealth we enjoy in modern economies. Complicated products, such as the computer on which I am typing this paragraph, are unimaginable without the combined cumulative efforts of the countless specialists who worked out how to manufacture integrated circuits or how to control a word-processing program using a mouse and a pointer on the screen. Most of those specialists couldn't boil an egg, let alone survive alone on a desert island. They are dependent on other people's expertise, if only the expertise of the cooks at the local Chinese takeaway, and computer users the world over are dependent on theirs.

Even simple products like the cappuccino I have beside me would be impossible without the division of labour. Is there anyone in the world who has mastered ceramics, dairy farming *and* the art of the perfect espresso roast? I'd be bowled over by someone who had even two out of the three.

That is all very well, but what does it have to do with marriage? There is not much reason to think that Adam Smith gave the matter much thought. A bachelor, he lived with his mother. Yet marriage used to be one of the fundamental ways to gain from division of labour. Before there were well-developed markets for anything much, and long before you could order a cappuccino, men and women were able to enjoy some of the gains from the division of labour by getting married, specialising and sharing. Back on the savannah, one might hunt and the other might gather. In the more recent past, one might be good at guiding a plough and sewing while another would specialise in cooking and household repairs. Nothing about Adam Smith's story suggests division of labour according to traditional sexual roles, but make no mistake: the family has rational roots. It is the oldest pin factory of all.

By the 1950s, those traditional sexual roles were fundamental in the division of labour within marriage. The ideal husband specialised in breadwinning, getting an education, a good job, working whatever hours were necessary to win promotion, and earning ever more to supply the family with a car, a fridge, a nice house in the suburbs and frequent holidays. His adoring wife specialised in homemaking, cooking, cleaning, entertaining, bringing up the children to be smart and wholesome, and taking care of her husband's emotional and sexual needs.

That was the idea, at least, and in 1965 the average married woman worked fewer than fifteen hours a week in paid employment. For the typical woman, a stay-at-home mum, that would be zero hours. The average was pulled up by empty-nesters and the very poor. Meanwhile, the average married man worked over fifty hours a week. The roles were neatly reversed for household work: married women did almost forty hours a week of non-market work, men fewer than ten. This was division of labour all right, and it was division of labour along sexually lopsided lines.

It was Gary Becker – committed evader of parking fees and champion of the rational slot machine addict – who showed the implications of Adam Smith's pin factory for marriage in the modern age. How had the division of labour become so sexually lopsided? The answer was the interaction of three economic forces: the division of labour, economies of scale and comparative advantage.

As Becker knew, division of labour works because it unleashes economies of scale. In plain English, one full-time worker earns more than two half-time workers. That is often true for the most basic jobs, but much more so for the most demanding positions. How many top lawyers do half a law degree and then work twenty-hour weeks? How many successful business executives work only Mondays, Tuesdays, and Wednesday mornings? And the top earners, at the peak of a long, full-time career, earn much, much more than those halfway through their careers. It is a harsh truth about the world of work that for many professionals, the more work you have done in the past, the more productive each additional working hour becomes: a perfect example of economies of scale.

This means that a household in which both parents work part time on their careers and part time looking after children and the home does not make rational economic sense. Two halves are much less than a whole. Economies of scale dictate that, logically, one partner should apply himself or herself full time to paid work. The other should work at homemaking, and work for money only if there is some spare time available after the household chores.

So far this is classic Adam Smith. Where did the traditional gender roles of the 1950s come from? Becker pointed out the implications of the third economic force, the principle of comparative advantage. Comparative advantage says that division of labour is governed not by who is most productive in some absolute sense, but in a relative sense. In Adam Smith's pin factory, if worker Elizabeth can sharpen two pins a minute and mount four pins a minute on paper, while worker James can sharpen one pin a minute and mount one pin a minute on paper, the logic of comparative advantage says that James should be sharpening pins, even though Elizabeth does the job faster. The relevant comparison is not whether Elizabeth sharpens pins faster than James but whether, relative to him, she sharpens pins faster than she mounts them on paper.

Imagine that James and Elizabeth are married; now, replace mounting pins on paper with looking after babies. Elizabeth is a more productive worker than James but also a more effective parent. James is a bad worker but a worse dad, so Elizabeth takes the rational decision to stay at home baking and looking after the kids, while James tries to scrape together a living as an estate agent. The logic of comparative advantage highlighted something that most men – except economists – have found it hard to get their heads around: there is no reason to believe that men were breadwinners because they were any good at it. They might simply have been breadwinners because getting them to help around the house would have been even worse.

Gary Becker's contribution was not to suggest that women make good parents, but to realise that because of economies of scale even a very small difference in innate capabilities could lead to titanic differences in how people spent their time. A small difference in relative expertise between men and women would be enough to cause a sharp division of labour across traditional sexual roles. That difference might be because of biological differences, because of socialisation or because of discrimination against women in the workplace, quite likely all three. Rather than arguing for any particular explanation, Becker showed that the difference didn't have to be big to have big effects.

In the late 1970s, Gary Becker was a widower and a single parent, pouring all his intellectual energy into *A Treatise on the Family*, published in 1981. (A happy footnote: he remarried shortly before the Treatise was published.) One of his aims was to understand what was happening to the institution of marriage. Divorce rates had more than doubled in the past two decades, in the United States and in many European countries. It was clear that the world of marriage had changed dramatically.

Some commentators have blamed changes in divorce laws for the trend: Ronald Reagan, when Governor of California, signed a bill introducing 'no-fault' divorce in 1969, meaning that either partner could simply walk away from the marriage by demanding a divorce. Other states followed. But Becker knew that couldn't be the answer: if the husband wanted a divorce to run off with his mistress, no-fault divorce didn't make it easier for him to do that, just cheaper. Before no-fault divorce, he had to get his wife's agreement, which might mean higher alimony payments. This reasoning suggests that no-fault divorce rules wouldn't change divorce rates at all. The only thing that would change was who paid whom to get the divorce. And sure enough, although there was a brief spike in divorce rates as no-fault divorce allowed a backlog of divorces to be processed more quickly, the legislation appears to have produced no more than a blip in a strong, steady upward trend.

Instead, the divorce revolution was driven by a more funda-mental economic force: the breakdown of the traditional division of labour identified by Adam Smith. At the beginning of the twentieth century, housework took many hours, and only the poorest and most desperate married women had jobs. As the decades rolled past, technological change made housework less time-consuming. It became easy – and quite common – for older women to enter the workforce after their children were grown and housework was more manageable.

Once divorce rates began to climb, it was no surprise that they increased dramatically. There was a rationally self-reinforcing loop at work: the more people divorced, the more divorcées – that is, potential marriage partners – you could meet. That meant that it was easier to get divorced yourself and find a new spouse.

Furthermore, once divorce started to become conceivable, women knew they could no longer think of themselves as one part of an economic unit. Rationality, you will recall, is about thinking ahead and responding to incentives. Realising that the economic unit might break up, at which point a woman who simply specialised in having children was in serious trouble, it became rational for a woman to maintain career options as divorce insurance. In the division-of-labour world of the 1950s, unhappily married women would rationally stick it out: they had few alternatives. But as more older women were finding jobs, managing their housework more quickly with the aid of washing machines and electric irons, women started to realise that there was an alternative to an unhappy marriage. Divorce was still financially tough but it was no longer economic suicide. And then the contraceptive pill came along, making women – as we have seen – more highly educated, career-minded and employer-friendly.

Did women really need career options before they could get divorced? In all but the most desperately unhappy marriages, they did. Contrary to the popular bar-room grumbles of divorced men, alimony alone doesn't take women very far financially. In the US, fewer than half of single divorced mothers get any child support at all, and for those who do, it is just a few thousand dollars a year, typically about one-fifth of the mother's total income. If a woman, especially a mother, was determined to get a divorce, she almost always needed to find a job. More and more women realised that they had the ability to do exactly that.

That started a second reinforcing loop (some people regard it as a vicious circle). Because divorce was conceivable, women preserved career options. But because women had career options, divorce became conceivable. It became less and less likely that a woman would become trapped in a miserable marriage out of pure economic necessity.

A close look at the statistics backs up this story. Even today, when so many women work for fun or the enjoyment of spending the cash they earn, women tend to work more when they face a higher risk of divorce. There are several ways to guess at that higher risk: you can look with hindsight at who did get divorced and assume that the woman involved might have seen it coming beforehand; you can look at variables such as age, religion and whether parents went through a divorce; or you can ask women how happy they are with their marriages. Whichever way you slice it, women at risk of divorce are more likely to head off to work. The increase in divorce is not because of a change in the psychology of love: it is a rational response to changed incentives.

The changing incentives also altered the way couples behaved within the relationship. In US states that introduced 'no-fault' divorce, while divorce rates did not show a lasting increase, women knew that their husbands could walk away from the marriage without having to buy their agreement with a generous side deal. That made it riskier to make an expensive commitment to the relationship: riskier to have children, riskier to support a husband financially through school, and riskier to become a homemaker while hubby focused on his career. The economist Betsey Stevenson explored this question using a research approach that should now be familiar: looking at the timing of the new law, state by state. And she found that when states introduced no-fault divorce and thus gave the husband an easy escape from the marriage, wives were less likely to work while their husbands went through college, but more likely to work full time and less likely to have children. All these effects were quite large: for each of these decisions, between 5 per cent and 10 per cent of women changed their behaviour as the law changed.

A young woman in the early 1970s faced a different world from the one her mother lived in two decades earlier. She could see that career opportunities for women had opened up, and there were jobs available if she wanted them. She could see, too, that divorce rates were on the rise and she should not, if she was wise, simply rely on a husband to provide her with an income, because extreme division of labour was too insecure for an age of divorce. Other women her age were marrying later, meaning that there were more men to date and marriage could be postponed. To cap it all off, she had access to a safe, reliable way of postponing children until she was ready to have them, meaning she could plan for a long education and several years to establish herself in a serious, high-powered career.

This analysis links divorce, the pill and women's increasing power and achievement in the workplace in a reinforcing loop. But it would be wrong to 'blame' an increase in divorce rates on an increase in women's professional achievements. There is, after all, no evidence that people are more unhappy with their marriages than in 1950. The opposite is likely to be true, because when they are unhappy with their marriages they can do something about it. One influential study by economists Andrew Oswald and Jonathan Gardner finds that divorcées, unlike widows and widowers, are happier one year after the marriage ends than they were while still married.

Perhaps a more positive way to express the trend is that women's entry into high-powered careers has given them the option to get divorced if the marriage isn't working out, and the recognition that that option is important is one of the factors encouraging women's entry into high-powered careers.

That may sound a little abstract, but Betsey Stevenson and Justin Wolfers discovered a chilling example of the way that the increased availability of divorce empowered women. As states passed no-fault divorce laws, women acquired a credible threat to walk out of the marriage. (The statistics suggest that many of them did not actually do this. But the threat is enough.) Stevenson and Wolfers show that the new laws had an unexpected – but rational – effect: by giving women an exit option, they gave men stronger incentives to behave well inside a marriage. The result? Domestic violence fell by almost a third, and the number of women murdered by their partners fell by 10 per cent. Female suicide also fell. It is a reminder that the binding commitment of marriage has costs as well as benefits.

Perhaps we should celebrate divorce just a little bit more. First, we should recognise that divorce is no longer increasing. That is rational. The peak in divorce in the 1970s was not, fundamentally, caused by legal changes but by changes in the underlying economics of family life, changes that reduced the incentives to be married.

In the long run, the rational response is not for couples to marry early and marry often; it is to divorce less and marry less, too. Now that the stock of marriages has been decimated by divorce, romantic couples are moving from the boom and bust of marriage and divorce to a more stable arrangement where marriages are delayed until couples are more sure of themselves. And they are perhaps delayed indefinitely – two of the leading economic researchers in the field, Stevenson and Wolfers, have been a romantic couple for ten years, and remain unmarried.

While the divorce rate has been falling for three decades, it would be a shame if it fell too far. Justin Wolfers comments, 'We know there exists something called an optimal divorce rate, and we're 100 per cent sure it isn't zero.'

Only an economist could put it like that, but he has a point. Marriage is an uncertain step and sometimes couples find that they made the wrong choice. Earlier in the chapter I compared finding a partner to finding a job. Returning to that analogy, we know that a job market where nobody could quit or be fired would not work very well: too many people would find themselves trapped in jobs they were incompetent to do or unhappy to do. A marriage market is not so terribly different.

Some people long for a return to the stable, traditional marriages of the 1950s, even if that means a firmer division of labour between the sexes again. They might do well to remember what Adam Smith wrote about the excessive division of labour: 'The man whose whole life is spent in performing a few simple operations ... has no occasion to exert his understanding or to exercise his invention in finding out expedients for removing difficulties which never occur. He ... generally becomes as stupid and ignorant as it is possible for a human creature to become.'

Smith's argument applies just as well to ironing and baking cakes, his use of the male pronoun notwithstanding. Division of labour creates wealth but can sap our lives of variety. The serious entry of married women into the workforce has meant that they spend a little less time baking, and perhaps also that their husbands spend a little more time with the children. It has empowered women to leave marriages that are not working, making them happier and safer from abuse. It has truly been a revolution, and the price of that revolution is more divorce and less marriage. That price is very real – but it is almost certainly a price worth paying.

Four

Why your boss is overpaid

Dilbert: 'My problem is that other people keep trying to drag me down, Bob. My theory is that people denigrate me because it makes them feel superior in comparison.'

Bob: 'Sounds like a stupid theory to me.'

– Scott Adams, *Dilbert*

Not many people lie on their deathbeds wishing that they had spent more time in the office. Ah, the office: the mournful gloaming under the fluorescent strips, the monotonous swish of the photocopier, the 'ping' as e-mails arrive from bullying bosses, work-shy colleagues and backstabbing rivals. Much of it is little better than spam. In fact, spam is a blessed release: a missive from another world, sent by a transparent crook and wasting no more than a second or two. Real e-mail also comes from time-wasting criminals, but it takes a lot more effort to deal with.

But why is office life so frustrating? Why do your colleagues stab you in the back while your idiot boss is paid a fortune for lounging around behind a mahogany altar? And why do your undoubted talents go unrewarded? The office is now routinely satirised as the world's most illogical place: could there possibly be a rational explanation for it all? And would a rational explanation make you feel any better or, more likely, just angrier?

All the problems of office life stem from the same root. To run a company perfectly you would need to have information about who is talented, who is honest and who is hardworking, and pay them accordingly. But much of this vital information is inherently hard to uncover or act upon. So it is hard to pay people as much or as little as they truly deserve. Many of the absurdities of office life follow logically from attempts to get around that problem: sensible pay schemes have unwelcome side-effects that range from encouraging treachery to overpaying the boss. Unfortunately, that doesn't mean they can be improved. A rational world isn't necessarily a perfect world, and nowhere is that more true than in the office.

Perhaps the easiest way to appreciate this is to start by looking at a couple of counter-examples. These are situations where working life is simple and civilised, and the reason is that the workers in question are turning in a performance that is clearly measurable: first, authors of books about economics; and second, windscreen installers. For such people, the problems of office life simply evaporate.

South Water Kitchen, Chicago, April 2005

I met Professor Steven D. Levitt just a couple of weeks before his book, *Freakonomics*, was published. I was interviewing him for the *Financial Times*. We met in an unpretentious restaurant-bar in Chicago, ate burgers and drank Coke, and chatted about his work and the book. There was a lot of pre-release hype about *Freakonomics*, but nobody expected the publishing phenomenon that was to follow. He laughed at the press release I had received from his publisher claiming that the first printing of the book would be 150,000 copies: like so much of the behaviour he studied (by cheating sumo wrestlers, estate agents, schoolteachers) it was just a self-serving piece of public relations. He reckoned that thirty thousand copies was a more realistic estimate.

Levitt had also had a disagreement about money with his coauthor, Stephen Dubner. Levitt was the academic powerhouse behind the book but it was obvious that Dubner, an accomplished author and journalist, was the one who was going to do much of the writing. What, then, was a fair division of the advance and the royalties? Levitt said he wouldn't settle for less than a sixty–forty split. Dubner dug his heels in: he wouldn't accept less than sixty–forty, either. When it transpired that both of them had assumed the *other one* would get the 60 per cent, they agreed to do the book together.

Levitt's account suggests that he would have done the book for far less money than he eventually received. I don't know what advance he was offered, but if he really thought the book would sell thirty thousand copies and he was willing to write it for 40 per cent of the royalties, that would be about twenty-five thousand pounds. What he actually received, having sold well over a million books, would have been more than a million pounds. But would anyone seriously go to the barricades with a Kalashnikov to demand that he should be denied this extra income? Levitt was paid by the book, sold a lot of books, and so made a lot of money. Because his performance was so easy to measure (at least in the terms that mattered for the bottom line), he has been spared any need to justify his earnings to colleagues, friends, or underlings; his work may be controversial, but his royalty statement is not. For most of us, justifying our salary is a rather more fraught experience – especially for anyone, such as the CEOs we consider later in this chapter, lucky enough to have incomes that dwarf even Levitt's.

There's a second point of interest in the way Professor Levitt was paid. It's possible that a rival publisher could have lured him away on the cheap by exploiting his scepticism about the book's likely success, and offering a big advance but no royalties. That would have insulated Levitt from the success of the book – flop or blockbuster, he would have been paid just the same. As long as Levitt was unduly pessimistic about the success of his book, that would have been possible.

But it wouldn't have been rational for the publisher.

Publishers *want* to offer contracts that pay authors more money when they sell more books, partly because it encourages authors to write good books and energetically promote them. Who wants to commission a book from an author who has no financial interest in whether the book succeeds? Performance pay encourages performance. That is what publishers think, at least. And experience from the windscreen replacement business appears to prove them right.

Colombus, Ohio, 1994

The new bosses of the Safelite Glass Corporation, Garen Staglin and John Barlow, were not happy. Safelite's workers fitted replacement windscreens – slowly. Staglin and Barlow wanted to speed things up.

Safelite workers were paid an hourly wage. Whether they worked diligently or whiled away the hours flicking through *Playboy*, their contracts specified the same salary. Perhaps this was in deference to the wisdom of psychologists who argued that attempting to pay for performance simply dampened 'intrinsic motivation' – that is, the love of a job well done. Similarly, workers were supposed to be kept in line by peer pressure; if they installed a faulty windscreen then another worker from the same repair shop – one who knew very well who had done the bad piece of work – would have to fix his colleague's mistake. This was thought to be more effective than a more direct financial incentive to get things right the first time.

Staglin and Barlow ignored all this and decided that workers were rational. If you paid them more to install more windscreens, they would install more windscreens. And if you made them work without pay to fix their own shoddy workmanship, they would take care not to make mistakes. It was a reductive view of human motivation.

It was also entirely correct. Productivity at Safelite soared under the new piece-rate system, with work per worker increasing by nearly half. Half of this effect was because workers tried harder. The other half was because the fastest, most skilled workers made much more money and stayed with the firm, while slow, clumsy workers, who weren't making much money, tended to drift away. The quality of work also increased, and the number of botched jobs fell.

The Safelite case is unusual: only one in thirty occupations typically uses piece rates. So why aren't we all on straightforward performance contracts? It's not that Safelite's workers were unusually rational, but that their jobs were unusually easy to measure. With the help of a then-sophisticated computer system it was very easy to see who was performing, tracking not only quantity of work but quality. When I wrote 'performance pay encourages performance', I was right, but with a crucial hidden premise – that performance can be measured, and thus rewarded. That was true for Safelite, and for Steve Levitt. But sadly, for most jobs, it is not so easy.

An accountant or an auditor, for example, is hard to keep tabs on. To know whether an auditor did a good job, you need to get a second auditor to audit the first auditor – not cheap, and what about the third auditor to audit the second auditor? You can't check whether a FedEx courier is smiling at the customers, although you can track the packages. It's not easy to do even that with lower-value letters sent by regular mail. So who's to say whether the postman is stealing the mail, or even getting drunk on the first Thursday night of each month and dumping much of Friday's mail in the bin? Customer complaints might find him out eventually, but if the lost mail is sporadic enough, who's to know? And if you could bunk off without being caught, wouldn't that be the rational thing to do?

Even when performance can be sort-of-measured and targets set, it is often all too easy to manipulate those targets. Say, for example, that your job is to process customers' complaints, and you're given a target that no customer should wait more than ten days for a reply. That means anybody who has been waiting seven or eight days becomes a priority, while you have nothing to gain by processing customers whose complaints have just arrived. If you aim at the target, your average response time might easily slow down. So then a new target arrives: keep the average response time to a minimum. Responding to the incentive the new target gives you, you ignore any complaint that is difficult to resolve and send back quick letters when a response is easy. The average response improves but the customers with the most serious complaints never get a reply. Now a third target arrives: hit *both* of the previous targets. You can do that, sure, and present a handsome claim for overtime. So the fourth target restricts overtime. Now you send out a simple form letter: 'Dear sir/madam, Thank you for your letter/email/fax/telephone call. I am afraid there is nothing we can do. Yours, etc.'

These problems have plagued all kinds of bureaucracies, from Soviet dictatorships to local councils to the ordinary businesses in which many of us work. It's simply too difficult for managers to work out the details of what should be done, and to judge whether what *should* be done *is* being done. The frustrations of working life are a direct result of that struggle. Sometimes the problem is that there is just no way to tell the difference between a brilliant worker and a lazy charlatan, and at that point there is nothing to do but throw your hands in the air and hope for the best.

But it's far more common to have a pretty good idea of who's performing, but to be unable to reward them directly for their efforts. To find out why that might happen, we need to take a trip to the local shopping mall.

A supermarket, somewhere in the western United States

For all the manufactured cheer, few places are less welcoming than the checkout in a busy supermarket. Queues of irritable shoppers stretch back to the cheese counter while overworked staff point their scanners at shrink-wrapped junk food just as fast as they can. We don't all find it easy to spare a smile for these underappreciated citizens, but there is now one more reason to give checkout staff all our sympathy: they are guinea pigs in an economic experiment.

The economists in question, Alexandre Mas and Enrico Moretti, figured out that by sweet-talking the bosses of a supermarket chain, they could get access to every detail about the productivity of the chain's cashiers. Using the computerised records from the stores' scanners, they could track every 'bleep', every transaction, for 370 cashiers in six stores, for two years. They could measure each cashier's productivity by the second, and note how it changed depending on who else was working at the same time.

Mas and Moretti wanted to find out whether people work harder if surrounded by productive colleagues. The answer is yes: when a quick worker sits next to you, you immediately start scanning your items more quickly. And you do so because you don't want to be accused of slacking, rather than because you are inspired by their speed. Mas and Moretti know this because they observed the way that supermarket checkout aisles are arranged: each worker is looking at a co-worker's back, with his or her own back being watched by a different co-worker. Mas and Moretti found that checkout staff do not speed up when they are looking at fast colleagues – that would not be rational. They only speed up when fast colleagues are looking at them.

That's an interesting piece of work in itself, but equally interesting is the supermarket's response to the study. The managers acknowledged that the scanning records made it perfectly clear who was pulling their weight and who was not. They could have used Mas and Moretti's study to arrange a schedule in which quicker workers were keeping an eye on slower ones. Mas and Moretti calculated that this would have reduced the need to pay for 125,000 hours of labour per year across all the branches of the supermarket chain, or about $2.5 million of wages, health-care and other labour costs.

But the supermarket managers did not use their information in modifying anything explicit about the workers' contracts. They didn't rearrange staff hours, and neither did they pay piece rates. They simply paid workers by the hour and allowed them to work out their own shifts. This was partly because the labour union resisted piece rates and the workers placed a high value on being able to fix their own hours. But it was also because paying by the beep, or even arranging the register assignments to put pressure on slower workers, might well have encouraged some unwelcome results at the sharp end of the business: yes, shorter queues, but also more bruised or improperly scanned produce and staff who rationally refused to spend time dealing with cus-tomer queries or complaints.

The supermarket chain, then, had detailed information it could trust but did not wish to write directly into a contract. This is a common situation: the boss knows that Phil is lazy, Suzanne always puts in whatever hours are needed to get the job done, Felicia is smiley but slow, and Bob is a lecherous pervert. Managers will certainly want to take this sort of thing into account when it comes to the annual salary review, but good luck writing it into a piece-rate pay agreement. And the supermarket managers might well have used the data from the scanners when deciding whom to promote and whom to let go; they just would not have been explicit about it.

So it makes sense not to rely too much on objective perform-ance measures. They worked at Safelite, and they work for authors, but those are rare cases. Such measures are often easy to manipulate. It is hard to think of a more objectively measurable task than the pole vault: the higher the bar when you clear it, the better the performance. Yet an attempt to pay for performance was outwitted by the great pole vaulter Sergei Bubka. He was paid a cash bonus every time he broke the world record, and so he was motivated to beat his previous marks by the smallest increment possible, rather than aim for his best jump. Bubka often broke the record by a single centimetre. The bar steadily crept upward until the mid-1990s, when Bubka was past his best and was unable to beat his most recent height. Only Bubka and his coaches know what he had been able to achieve in private practice sessions. The incentive pay produced plenty of world records but it probably discouraged Bubka from producing his greatest vaults in public.

Not all objective performance measures are so easily fooled – or, frankly, so badly designed – but smart managers know these risks often lurk below the surface. Even if some aspects of performance can be measured, there is a risk that relying on them will lead to skewed staff effort – as the supermarket feared, if you pay only for speed, rational staff won't give you quality. For Safelite, objective performance worked because only two things mattered: speed and whether the windscreen later broke or not. Safelite could devise a way to reward both speed and reliablity. But in most jobs, there are more than two variables at play and some are very hard to pin down. For those jobs, managers need a more holistic, all-encompassing measure of performance.

So bosses will rationally search for more informal ways of rewarding their best staff. Rather than writing down a specific, objective measure of performance, they give themselves discretion to reward 'good work' without being too precise about what 'good work' is. The thinking is, quite sensibly, that while they can't define good work, they can recognise it when they see it. And with this discretion over pay rises, promotions and bonuses, they have plenty of flexibility to dish out rewards and punishments in line with what everybody knows but nobody could prove in court.

There the story would end, but for one important problem: managers are lying weasels. If performance bonuses are purely discretionary, the boss can weasel out of paying them, and so the workers won't be motivated by them. Why would anybody believe a manager who promises pay rises and promotions but can't be specific about what they will be and what his staff would have to do to earn them?

It turns out that there is a way around this problem. Unfortunately, it gives your boss a perfectly rational reason to pay himself a perfectly crazy bonus. The solution is to turn office life into a tournament. The economists who spotted the idea now call it 'tournament theory', and it explains the misery of the office with remarkable accuracy.

In a tournament, you pay people for relative performance – how they do in comparison to other people doing the same thing. In most tennis tournaments, the winner of each match is guaranteed to make about twice what the loser does, and with a chance at further progress, too.

Paying by relative performance has some merits in a world where objective yardsticks are hard to find. It's easy to find out if Steve Levitt sold more books than Milton Friedman, but impossible to say whether Roger Federer is a better tennis player than John McEnroe was. That is why Steve Levitt is paid by the book – an absolute measure of performance – but Roger Federer is paid for beating Rafael Nadal at Wimbledon, a relative measure of performance. Federer isn't paid to try hard, nor to produce brilliant tennis. He is merely rewarded for beating his rivals in a tournament. That is enough to get the best out of him.

You might think that Federer's performance is easy to measure objectively, but in fact the measures that determine the size of his pay cheque are relative ones. All the statistics – aces served, return winners, even unforced errors – are artefacts of who Federer is playing. (If Federer played *me* I am quite sure he could win with no unforced errors.) 'Federer is better than McEnroe was' is a subjective judgement. 'Federer served thirty-five aces' is an objective statement, but without knowing who the opponent is, an empty one.

That's a tennis tournament. What about a workplace tournament? It works as follows. The boss promises to give a thousand-pound bonus to the best worker in the department. He gets the degree of flexibility he needs because he doesn't have to specify what he means by an excellent performance. At the same time, his staff get the degree of credibility they need because there's little scope for him to weasel out of the promise to pay the thousand-pound bonus.

Admittedly, it is easier to identify the winner of a tennis tournament than that of a workplace tournament. Nevertheless, think of all the information that managers have at their disposal (in the case of supermarkets, in frightening detail) but that they cannot put into a written contract. Even if it is not always easy to spot the best performance, it will often be easier to assess how workers perform in comparison to one another than according to any objective criteria.

Some workplace tournaments are explicitly that: a bonus for the best worker, and perhaps for second and third place, too. More commonly the workplace tournament has a bit less structure. Instead, it emerges from the fact that there is a limited fund for bonuses: the better you look relative to your colleagues, the less they will get and the more you will get. Or the tournament prize is a promotion to the next management tier. However the tournament is structured, its merit is that it allows a weaselly manager to keep options open while making a believable promise to reward good work.

Tournaments also protect workers against risks they cannot control. Companies can be affected by recessions, unexpected competition and hurricanes. As long as every worker is equally affected, the incentives to try hard remain the same. Paying workers in other ways – for example, by giving them stock options or a profit share – often exposes them to misfortunes beyond their control, or rewards them just because the company is going through a lucky patch.

It is all so rational, but workplace tournaments are also a reason – perhaps *the* reason – why work can be such a miserable experience. The first problem is not difficult to see. Once you start handing out large quantities of cash to people for outperforming their peers, they will work out that there are two ways to win this game: either do a great job or make sure your colleagues do a bad one. Roger Federer hasn't yet resorted to tying his opponents' shoelaces together or replacing their racket strings with spaghetti, but there are plenty of examples of sportspeople trying to rattle their opponents. It is often regarded as being part of the game.

Tournament-style incentives make it perfectly rational for workers to stab one another in the back. It turns out that they respond rationally to the incentive just as surely as the Safelite workers responded to being paid for quick, accurate windscreen installations. One study compared twenty-three firms from Australia and found that those giving big pay rises to their best workers encouraged all workers to put more effort into the job, for instance by taking fewer days off work. That's as we would expect. But the study also found that workers in those firms refused to lend equipment and tools to their colleagues, which is also a rational response to the incentives the tournament gives them.

Some personnel experts have argued that tournaments fail to motivate workers, because they are perceived as being unfair, but that's a misdiagnosis. Tournaments motivate workers very well indeed; unfortunately, they motivate backstabbing as well as dedication. If you want to introduce a tournament-style system of promotion and performance pay for your subordinates, all you need to do is work out whether each worker's efforts to improve his performance will outweigh his efforts to drag down everyone else's. Even the most cut-throat tennis tournament has not offered players incentives to undermine their own doubles partners; if you're a manager, you may want to bear this in mind.

Overcompetitive colleagues are not the only depressing workplace phenomenon we can blame on tournament theory. Another surprising outcome is the way in which many workers appear to be rewarded simply for being lucky. That doesn't seem to make rational sense, but, surprisingly, it is perfectly logical. The more luck is involved in work, the larger the pay gaps need to be between the winners and the losers if the tournament is to motivate anyone. If your promotion is 95 per cent luck and 5 per cent effort, it is rational to slack off in the face of most incentive schemes. After all, who works hard to win the lottery? It's 100 per cent luck and so requires zero effort, which may explain why so many deadbeats love to play. But if working extra hard gave you a 5 per cent chance of winning the lottery, you'd put everything you had into the attempt because the prize would be so huge.

So, too, with office life: if hard work is everything – as with, say, filing, photocopying and manning the phones – then workers know that working harder than their colleagues will guarantee a pay rise, and the pay rise can be kept modest. But if luck is a big factor in deciding who succeeds – say, for those working in management consultancy – then encouraging any effort at all is going to require a large disparity between what the winners get and what the losers get. (There are limits: if hard work really is unimportant, there is no point in paying to encourage it.)

So, workplace tournaments encourage workers to sabotage one another and to demand higher bonuses if success is largely a matter of luck. Evidence is mounting that tournament theory is the most convincing explanation of why work sucks, but it doesn't stop there. Tournaments also require increasingly absurd pay packages as workers get higher up the corporate hierarchy. At the lowest level, a promotion may not need to carry much of a pay increase, because it opens up the possibility of future, lucrative promotions. Nearer the end of your career, you don't work hard just because it opens doors for the future. Only a fat cheque is likely to spur you on.

Tournament theory has stood the test of time and has been supported by many subsequent pieces of empirical research. It also makes a perverse kind of sense: the more grotesque your boss's pay, and the less he has to do to earn it, the bigger the motivation for you to work with the aim of being promoted to have what he has.

One of the creators of tournament theory, the economist Ed Lazear, has commented: 'The salary of the vice president acts not so much as motivation for the vice president as it does as motivation for the assistant vice presidents.' So there you have it. Economists don't even pretend that your boss deserves his salary. Suddenly, everything is clear.

As the CEO of Walt Disney Corporation, Michael Eisner pocketed £400 million over thirteen years. That puts into perspective the trifling few million that Steve Levitt earned by writing *Freakonomics*. We saw that there can be minimal controversy over Levitt's pay: even after he cashed his royalty cheque, there was plenty left over for his publishers, and the prospect of a bigger royalty cheque probably motivated him to contribute more to the book than if he had been on a modest flat fee. Is the pay of Michael Eisner quite so easy to justify?

Not really. Applying the same logic, the £400 million of Disney shareholders' money that Eisner took home would have been money well spent if it motivated him to do his job in a way that made more than £400 million for those shareholders. Or, more to the point, if it motivated him to do his job in a way that made more than £360 million *more* for Disney's shareholders than he would have done if he'd been paid a mere £40 million over thirteen years – a level of pay that still, you would think, might have been sufficient to get him out of bed in the mornings and encourage him to stay awake in board meetings. Since investors in Disney would have done better investing their money in government bonds over the thirteen years in question, it's a big 'if'.

As we've seen, though, tournament theory shows that the £400 million pay package didn't need to motivate Eisner him-self to do such a good job that he personally added all of that

£400 million to Disney shareholders' wealth. It would still have been value for money if it motivated Eisner's would-be replacements to work so hard that they created the remaining portion of wealth between them. In fact, when you think about it, if Eisner's pay motivated his underlings throughout the company to add more than £400 million of value, then it would still have been rational for Disney's shareholders to pay Eisner £400 million to spend all day with his feet up on his desk watching *Tom and Jerry*.

This is one of tournament theory's more entertaining implications, one that's not necessary to the theory, but is fully consistent with it – the idea that a CEO's pay could be entirely unconnected with any decisions the CEO might make. In this view, CEOs have been removed from the productive flow. They are mere figureheads, more like the Queen or the recipient of a lifetime achievement award than people who do anything important.

Tournament theory has given us one satisfying explanation for why the overall level of CEO pay might be so stratospheric – though, as we will see at the end of the chapter, it is not the only factor at play. But we need to leave it behind in the quest to understand *how* that pay is structured. While much of Eisner's pay may have been an attempt to motivate his ambitious lieutenants, to be fully effective the pay package should also have encouraged him to be honest, diligent and smart. Did it?

The really huge CEO payments that one reads about in the papers, such as Eisner's, or Larry Ellison's $706 million payout from Oracle in 2001, are almost always the result of stock options. Stock options, put simply, are contracts that allow their owner to buy shares at a specified price. If the actual price of the share rises above the price specified in the option contract, then the option can be cashed in for money. So, if Oracle stock is trading at $100 and I have a million options to buy at $50, I can immediately make $50 million by using my options to buy shares at $50, and then selling them on the stock market at $100. Stock options seem like a sensible way of paying CEOs because the higher the company's share price rises, the more valuable the options are. Stock options should encourage the CEO to put all his efforts into boosting the share price – and the share price is, after all, the market's best guess at whether the company will make money in the future.

The stock option revolution that culminated with Larry Ellison's mega-payout arguably began with a dry academic paper published in 1990 by two economists, Michael Jensen and Kevin J. Murphy. The best way to understand the paper is to think about dining out at a restaurant with a big crowd of people and then splitting the bill equally. As we all know, this can be a vexing experience. Most of what you pay goes towards other people's meals and most of your meal is paid for by other people. Under those circumstances, the rational strategy has occurred to everyone: order oysters, lobster and plenty of champagne. Sticking to soup and bread with iced water on the side will save money for everyone else, but your taste buds alone will be the ones suffering. Your merest whim will persuade you to order the most fulsome luxuries, because you will pay such a small fraction of their cost. Splitting the bill may have its merits, but encouraging honest choices from the diners isn't one of them.

Jensen and Murphy pointed out that at the time they were researching, the mid-1980s, America's CEOs were being paid in a particularly bizarre variant of 'split the bill'. For every extra million dollars of shareholder wealth, a CEO received just twenty dollars in this year's bonus or next year's pay rise. Because the CEO received such a small slice of any profits, he would happily use company money for his own convenience instead. It would cost the CEO just twenty dollars in lost pay to put a million-dollar painting on the wall of his office using the shareholders' cash; for a mere two hundred bucks, he could splurge on a ten-million-dollar corporate jet. This is like splitting the bill with fifty thousand other people. More champagne, please!

That slightly exaggerates the problem. Jensen and Murphy reckoned that there were other incentives at work besides simple performance pay. For one thing, the CEO might be fired for doing a terrible job. They estimated that this risk was probably worth a rather chunkier $750 per million dollars of shareholder wealth. The chance of being fired wasn't high, but it was there. The typical CEO and his immediate family also held one-quarter of 1 per cent of company stock, which meant that spending a million dollars on a Picasso sketch would cost another $2,500 in personal wealth. All in all, the manager would spend $3,270 in putting the Picasso on the wall, while the company's other share-holders would pay for the remaining $996,730.

Any way you look at it, Jensen and Murphy found that your boss's performance pay was so small that he would only make decisions designed to boost his employer's prospects if doing so didn't look too much like hard work. Empire-building, gold-plated executive lavatories and Picassos on every wall should rationally be the order of the day. For every extra hundred dol-lars the shareholders would get, the CEO took home a measly 32½ cents; rather than being paid too much, perhaps bosses were being paid too little.

The obvious solution to the split-the-bill problem would be for the CEO to own all the stock in the company. If she owned all the stock, and used company funds to buy a million-dollar Picasso to hang on her office wall, nobody could complain. We could stop worrying about embezzlement because the CEO would only be picking her own pocket: it wouldn't even *be* embezzlement.

Obviously, there's no point in maximising the value of the company if you have to give it away to do so. But there is a way for CEOs to hold all the stock without getting anything for free; shareholders would simply sell their shares for the right price. Rather than getting high average pay, the CEO would get pay-outs that were highly sensitive to corporate results, which is not the same thing. This is not as crazy as you might think. In fact, it already happens and it's called a leveraged management buy-out. A company's managers borrow money and buy the firm. If they do well then they make a lot of money, but if they do badly they go bankrupt. Incentives are strong, but pay packages bulge only if the results are good.

That all sounds so satisfactory that we might want to broaden the scheme. The CEO can't be the only person in the company who affects how much money the company makes. Any old cubicle slave can make the company ten pounds poorer by stealing ten pounds' worth of paper clips and selling them on eBay. The obvious answer is to sharpen the incentives. If every worker in every company owned 100 per cent of the company stock, then nobody would ever steal paper clips again. Now, there's not enough stock to go around to make this idea work, so each worker could instead sign a contract that linked his salary to the share price: if the company lost a billion pounds, so would each worker. If the company made a billion pounds, so would each worker. Even in a less extreme implementation of the plan, workers could borrow hundreds of thousands of pounds to buy corporate stock, thus giving them an incentive to improve company profits.

This is an insane idea, but it's worth thinking about why it's insane: it's not because the worker couldn't borrow the money required to buy a lot of stock. (He couldn't, but do you see anybody even trying? How many workers are required to borrow £100,000 or even £10,000 to invest in company stock?) Rather, it's insane because the contract would be impossibly risky for the worker long before it provided any sort of incentive: owning 0.1 per cent of a ten-billion-pound company would expose a worker to ten million pounds of risk, but wouldn't dissuade him from stealing paper clips for a second, because 99.9 per cent of the costs of the paper clips would be paid for by other shareholders. And subjecting ordinary workers to too much risk isn't an abstract worry: just ask the workers at Enron who were strongly encouraged to invest their pensions in Enron stock. That simply meant that many of them lost almost everything when the company collapsed; it didn't persuade them to work any harder, because few of them would have felt personally responsible for the stock price.

For the CEO and other senior executives, things are a little different. CEOs are paid so much money, and could conceivably have so much personal influence over the share price, that it might indeed be rational to ask them to bear the high risks that come with sharp incentives. A rational, self-confident CEO would be happy to accept the risk in exchange for a chance of higher pay, while shareholders would be happy to provide that chance if it motivated the CEO to do a good job.

What's more, if the CEO gets drunk one Friday lunchtime and reorganises his company's entire corporate structure, he might do so much damage to shareholder wealth that his personal wealth – even with a small percentage ownership of the company – would take a noticeable hit; but if the cubicle serf gets drunk on duty, all he will reorganise is the Post-it notes around his computer monitor. Even if the CEO owned only 0.1 per cent of the company, that would still mean he lost ten thousand pounds of personal wealth if he made a ten-million-pound mistake by dozing off in a meeting. But if the office cleaner somehow acquired a massive 0.1 per cent of the company, that wouldn't motivate any action because 0.1 per cent of his contribution (good or bad) to the firm's profits is not going to be a big deal.

There's a third important difference between the CEO and the cubicle serfs: it is usually easier to find other ways of controlling performance of those lower down the corporate hierarchy. If the cleaner doesn't clean the office, that's plain to see and he can be fired. If the regional sales manager doesn't make any sales, she can be fired, too. As we discussed earlier in the chapter, these problems are hard to solve, but with the help of tournament pay they are not impossible. Yet with the CEO, it's harder still: not only has he already won the tournament, but his performance is particularly hard to measure. If it was so easy to see what decisions needed to be made, who would need the CEO to make them?

So, because the CEO can handle quite a bit of risk, and because modest incentives might make a difference to CEO behaviour, and because it's hard to give the CEO the right incentives otherwise, it makes sense to link the CEO's pay closely to the share price – or, in other words, to give him a lot of stock options. But not so fast. On closer inspection, there's a twist in the tale.

Jensen and Murphy grumbled in the *Harvard Business Review* in 1990 that 'on average, corporate America pays its most important leaders like bureaucrats' – and in the 1970s and early 1980s, that was certainly the case. A CEO who captained a firm to profit growth of 20 per cent a year would earn just 1 per cent more than one who managed only 10 per cent growth a year. Under the circumstances, it would not be surprising if CEOs neglected the key job of making the company more successful and retreated into covering their backs and ticking the right boxes.

That was then. Times have changed, and CEOs are no longer paid like bureaucrats but rather like plutocrats – or, arguably, like kleptocrats. In 2005, incentive-based pay schemes – variable bonuses, perks and long-term incentives – were the chief sources of CEO pay in the United States and almost every other rich country. Starting in the 1980s, CEO pay started to become much more responsive to how well the company actually did. For instance, by the mid-1990s in America, a CEO at the helm of a company in the bottom third of share price performance relative to other companies would make about one million dollars a year; a CEO running a top-third company would make five times more than that. This is a big difference between modest success and relative failure, and at the root of the pay disparity is a huge increase in the use of stock options.

This all seems to make good economic sense: CEOs are given a lot of stock options to stop them from ripping off the shareholders. But there's another possibility that will not have escaped the sceptical reader: perhaps CEOs *have* ripped off the shareholders, and the stock options are their ill-gotten gains.

Big pay packages are not, in themselves, a guarantee that the shareholders are being ripped off. Sure, CEOs were paid six times more in 2003 than in 1980. But the value of large US companies also rose sixfold over the same period. If a smart decision at the head of a $60-billion company is worth six times more than a smart decision at the head of a $10-billion company, perhaps that is all there is to the rise in CEO wages.

Yet some of the design features of these stock-option-based compensation plans are a little suspicious. Options are often reset when share prices fall: what was once an option to buy shares at a hundred dollars apiece becomes an option to buy shares at fifty dollars apiece, as long as the company is doing badly enough. Where are the sharp incentives here? Instead, the offer to CEOs seems to be: 'If the company share price does well, your options will make you a killing. If the company share price falls, don't worry: we'll make sure you make a killing anyway.' How rational is that incentive?

There are other suspicious aspects of CEO pay. I shall spare you the technical complexities – these schemes seem to be designed to be impenetrable to the casual observer – but one favourite is the 'reloadable' option, which rewards CEOs if the share price bounces around a lot, because they can lock in the most fleeting gains. Another is the 'backdated' option, where companies hand out particularly generous options but disguise their generosity by fibbing about when the option was actually awarded. Economists spotted the backdating trick by noticing how often options were being handed out just before the share price rose, making the option very valuable. Either the timing was impossibly lucky, or the official dates were phony, and the options had been backdated to maximum advantage. Backdating can be fraudulent if not properly disclosed, and when the practice was discovered, it claimed the jobs of six CEOs in just one week in October 2006. (One of the most remarkable examples of backdating was at Apple, the makers of iPods and Macs. They granted backdated stock options to their CEO, Steve Jobs, some of which were supposed to have been approved at a 'board meeting' that Apple later admitted didn't actually take place.)

Let's be clear: the problem with these various fishy-looking options isn't that they're too generous. There are lots of ways for firms to overpay their CEOs. But the odd options produce odd incentives (which is bad for shareholders) and are also harder to spot (which is also bad for shareholders, but good for greedy CEOs).

It doesn't seem to make any rational sense. Why would shareholders sit by and let their cash be spent on lavish executive pay that was unconnected – or shakily connected – with performance? It's the shareholders' money. They can vote to dismiss the board. Why don't they? It turns out that there is a perfectly rational explanation.

A pretentious restaurant, London, 2006

It was surely the most miserable evening I've spent at any restaurant. It was the sort of overblown place that attracts a lot of one-time visits from customers eager to admire the famous toilets and the like. The food was overpriced, but that's not uncommon for London. What was remarkable was the variety of barely legitimate techniques used to suck cash from our pockets. My wife asked for a salad: the waiter brought four. Bottles of wine were uncorked and placed in front of people who weren't drinking.

What was going on? It was another game of split the bill. There were a dozen of us there, largely unable to communicate with one another because of the noise. It was supposed to be a fancy night out, so nobody wanted to spoil the occasion. You'd see the four salads and figure that they were only going to cost you, personally, a pound or so. You might assume somebody else had ordered them. The same with the open but untouched bottle of wine. It was relentless, but at no point was it worth my while – or anyone else's – to stand up and tell the waiters that we refused to put up with it any more. In the end I left before the desserts had arrived, and left a gigantic wad of cash to cover my share of the bill. I am still not sure that it ended up being enough.

As with the restaurant, so with a big company. The shareholders can feel the drip, drip of cash out of their pockets and into those of the managers, but what can they do? Successful shareholder protests are difficult at the best of times. If I held a total of ten thousand pounds' worth of stock in FTSE 100 companies, I'd say I had a real interest in how the stock market was doing. But I wouldn't care about any particular CEO pay deal: with about a hundred pounds' worth of stock in each of one hundred companies, a CEO who helped himself to a titanic 1 per cent of corporate wealth would only be costing me a pound – and with the right camouflage I might never find out that it had even happened. Collectively, the CEOs are taking a hundred pounds from me, but I can't pursue them collectively, I can only try to beat them up one at a time. And I'm only one shareholder – how much effort am I really going to put into contacting my fellow shareholders and trying to persuade them to vote down the board?

Actually, the situation is worse than that: it's a game of split the bill inside a second game of split the bill, because even if I and my fellow activist shareholders do manage to get together and rein in an overly generous board, the immediate result is likely to be a damaging succession crisis at the company. Shareholders of *other* companies will benefit because other boards will look over their shoulders at our little shareholder revolution and tighten their belts just a little. But we brave revolutionaries are likely to be out of pocket for our pains.

That means that directors simply need to avoid provoking their shareholders too severely. Had a waiter tried to take my wallet I'm pretty sure I would have stood up for myself. But another bottle of wine that nobody was drinking? If I even noticed it arrive at the other end of the table, what would I do about it?

The easiest way to avoid shareholder outrage is to keep them in the dark: the panoply of odd stock option awards are a great way to pay executives a lot while making the smallest possible ripples in the company accounts. There are other tricks, too, involving soft loans or 'consultancy' pay for retired executives. This sort of camouflage makes it harder for shareholders to spot fishy compensation packages and do something to complain about them.

Not all CEOs get away with this. While most CEOs are 'paid for luck', skimming hefty bonuses for profits that are due not to their own efforts but to external factors such as commodity prices, this happens much less at companies where there is at least one substantial shareholder. That makes rational sense. A large shareholder goes a long way to solving the split-the-bill problem, for the same reason that you do not order champagne if your wife's father is paying for everyone and watching you like a hawk. Unfortunately, it's in the nature of public companies that shareholders tend to be widely dispersed.

Some problems cannot be easily solved. After all, I never promised that *rational* meant 'wonderful'. Rational choices lock us into a situation in which your boss will always be overpaid, and the CEO of your company even more so. They also doom you to paying too much when you eat out with twenty other people. But at least you now understand the logic behind it all. And I am afraid there's worse to come over the next two chapters.

Five

In the neighbourhood

The economics of not being stabbed in the street

World Bank, Washington, DC, 2003

I had plenty on my mind: a new job, a new city, a new country and a baby on the way. But since the World Bank recruits from all corners of the globe, most new employees are unsettled. The Bank provides a small office to help new staff understand the healthcare system, the way the local bureaucracies operate, and of course where to live in Washington. It was in that office that I first truly felt what I had previously only registered intellectually: the nation's capital is a city divided.

After some chit-chat about the different options for housing, I explained that I wanted to live downtown, near the Bank itself. It was then that the Bank's housing officer got down to business. She unfolded a large map of the downtown area. She gestured at the northwest quadrant of the District of Columbia. 'This is all safe,' she said, waving her hand over Georgetown and Cleveland Park. Then she took out a blue ballpoint pen and slowly, carefully, drew a line along Sixteenth Street. The line began at the White House and ran north. The pen dug into the paper, gouging an inked-in trench that I saw every time I unfolded the map in my travels around my new home city.

I looked at the line as she continued: 'A realtor isn't legally allowed to say this, but I am. Stay on the west side of that line.' I folded up the map, slipped it into my bag, and walked down the stairs and out of the door, dazed and blinking in the bright October sunshine.

The precise location of 'that line' is a matter of controversy in DC, but its existence does not seem to be. What you experience in DC depends overwhelmingly on where you live. In the area carved in two by Sixteenth Street and the ballpoint pen, the police department's third district, there were twenty-four homicides in 2005. Elsewhere the situation is much worse: across the river in Anacostia, the seventh district, where we were repeatedly advised never to venture, there were sixty-two homicides in 2005. In leafy Georgetown and Cleveland Park, the police department's second district, there were none at all.

That isn't the only way in which Georgetown and Cleveland Park are nicer places than Anacostia. Fewer than one child in thirty lives in poverty, fifteen times less than in Anacostia. The overall poverty rate is 7.5 per cent, five times lower. There were just two violent crimes per one thousand people, ten times fewer. And who gets to enjoy the difference in conditions? Suffice it to say that Georgetown and Cleveland Park are 80 per cent white and Anacostia is 93 per cent black.

There does not seem to be any rational reason why a city like Washington, DC, incorporates such deep pockets of deprivation, nor why racial segregation remains so stark. And indeed, the geography of the inner cities is not rational – it is pathological. Even though each person makes rational choices, the result can be something that none of them wanted; you might say that rational behaviour by individuals can produce irrational results for society.

This and the next chapter are closely linked. In this chapter, I will focus on the way city neighbourhoods work, and the way mild preferences and smart decisions from individuals can produce desperate, extreme outcomes for neighbourhoods. I discover why neighbourhoods can get locked into deprivation, and why the rational responses of ordinary people perversely make their neighbourhoods extremely difficult to rescue. Throughout the United States, as in Washington, DC, there is a connection between city geography and race: the most deprived areas are often ghettos, packed with immigrants or with African Americans and shunned by whites. But there is more to city neighbourhoods than race, and more to race than geography, so in the next chapter I focus specifically on the question of racism and racial inequality. There again we will see that rational decisions from individuals can produce tragic outcomes for society as a whole.

First, though, we'll look at a juncture of race and geography: the extreme racial segregation in some American cities. That segregation seems to suggest deep racism, but that might be a misleading impression. Segregation – by race, by class, by income level – can be a stark symptom of surprisingly mild prejudices. Given some simple props, you can prove that to yourself in the comfort of your own home.

Please put down this book for a moment, and find yourself a chessboard and a bunch of black and white draughts pieces. Place the pieces on alternate squares of the chessboard, black-white-black-white-black-white. Leave the four corner squares blank.

Now, pretend that these little black and white pieces are two different types of person: black and white is the obvious possibility, but it could be native and immigrant, or rich and poor. Each one has up to eight neighbours, or as few as four for those near the corners. Each is motivated by a single concern, which is to avoid being dramatically outnumbered in her own immediate neighbourhood. Everyone is perfectly happy to live in a mixed

Thomas Schelling's chessboard: a perfectly integrated utopia

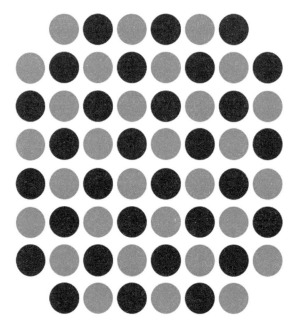

The chessboard after removing twenty pieces and adding five at random

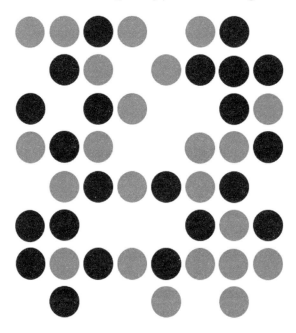

The final, segregated position, after pieces have been moved to
their preferred places

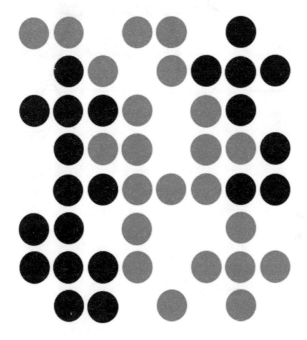

neighbourhood, even to be slightly outnumbered, but if anyone
finds that more than two-thirds of her neighbours is of the other
colour, she will become unhappy and move.

What will happen? You will see at a glance that this perfectly
alternating arrangement of neighbours makes everybody happy.
White pieces near the centre of the board have four black neighbours, vertically and horizontally adjacent, and four white
neighbours, diagonally adjacent. Black pieces are in a similar situation. A white counter at the edge of the board has three black
neighbours and two white neighbours, but that is also well
within the bounds of her tolerance.

We might look upon this chessboard as a model of an integrated society. Blacks and whites live – literally – side by side. It
is not a racially harmonious utopia, because every member of
this society has racial preferences that are nothing to be proud

of. At the same time, the preferences are relatively mild and the society is completely integrated. Things could be far worse.

Unfortunately, if this is a model of an integrated society it suggests that such a society is horribly fragile. To see why, let's make a small change to the set-up. Remove some of the pieces at random – say, twenty of them. Then add a few at random, perhaps just five.

The board now looks messier but it is still highly integrated, as you would expect with forty out of forty-five pieces in their original, alternating positions. The blank spaces are dotted here and there and a very small number of new arrivals have slotted into what is still a mixture of black and white.

Yet the small difference turns out to be critical. Scanning the board you will find an unhappy black piece with more than twice as many white neighbours as black. Move it to the nearest blank space where it is not so badly outnumbered. Find white pieces in the comparable situation and move them, too. You will find a chain reaction: as a black piece moves away from too many white neighbours, another black piece becomes more isolated and will follow, and another, and another.

Keep moving the unhappy black and white pieces and you will find the whole melting pot separating out like a fancy sauce gone wrong. No matter how thoroughly you mix the pieces together, they seep apart, congealing in their own ghettos. It is an uncanny process: a mixed group of people, all happy to live in a mixed neighbourhood, end up segregated into homogeneous lumps of black and white by the steady unravelling of diversity.

This striking demonstration of a simple process was discovered by Thomas Schelling, the pragmatic game theorist whom we've met before. He started doodling on a long flight, drawing a grid filled haphazardly with pluses and zeros to try to figure out what happened when one person moved to avoid being racially isolated. 'It was hard to do with pencil and paper,' he told me. 'You had to do a lot of erasing.'

When he got home he sat down with his twelve-year-old son,

a chessboard and the boy's coin collection, and played around with some simple rules about what the pennies 'preferred'. He discovered something rather profound: 'A very small preference not to have too many people unlike you in the neighbourhood, or even merely a preference for some people like you in the neighbourhood . . . could lead to such very drastic equilibrium results that looked very much like extreme separation.' In other words, mild causes could lead to extreme results.

Schelling's chessboard model is justly famous, and became even more so after he was awarded the Nobel Prize for economics in 2005. But exactly what you think it demonstrates rather depends on your character. Consider the observation that Anacostia is 93 per cent black, while rich, safe Georgetown and Cleveland Park are 80 per cent white. If you are in a glass-half-full mood, you might consider Schelling's model to indicate that even these extremes of segregation do not count as evidence for racial hatred. As Schelling's model showed, all it takes is a mild preference not to be heavily outnumbered. Pessimists, however, would point out that Schelling's model suggests that extreme segregation is almost inevitable. It is all very well to say that racial prejudices might be mild, but what does that matter if the consequences remain severe – if, indeed, the consequences really are severe?

Schelling himself offered a somewhat hopeful observation based on the cafeterias at Dodgertown, a baseball training camp, in the late 1960s. The Minor League players were served cafeteria-style and then took their tray to the first vacant seat. 'If a white boy doesn't want to eat with a colored boy, he can go out and buy his own food,' declared the manager of the day. The tables, naturally, were mixed as a result of this system. The Major League players chose their own seats, however, and seg-regated tables were more common than mixed tables.

At first glance that suggests nothing more than that whites and blacks will sit and eat together if they are forced to. The truth is more hopeful. As the manager observed, committed bigots could always buy a meal off campus. Even easier, they could simply meet with others of their own colour and enter the cafeteria queue together. There was no rule against that, but nobody bothered to think ahead for the thirty seconds necessary to practise apartheid. The racial preferences that led to so many segregated tables in the Major League dining room turned out to be mild, at least in the context of choosing a neighbour for lunch. Perhaps, after all, there is hope.

In the next chapter, we shall look more carefully at racism and racial inequality. But for now, I would like to focus instead on the oil-and-vinegar transition of Schelling's chessboard. Such sharp separations are not only seen in racial segregation; in various guises, they are an everyday feature of urban life. They happen so often, in fact, that most of us have stopped noticing them, as we shall discover on a trip to my local park in London.

Hackney Downs, London

The children's playground at the heart of the Downs changes as sharply as Thomas Schelling's chessboard, and with as little provocation. The weather is typically to blame, or the time of day. I visited at four o'clock on Saturday afternoon, an unseasonably warm and sunny late September day, and counted fifty people packed in and around the modest little place: children tearing around as children will; a Jamaican man with a beret, black tracksuit and bookish spectacles dribbling a football around his toddler daughter; Polish mothers leaning on strollers and talking while their children tugged at their handbags; an Indian father doting on his little girl as he softly pushed her on the baby swing. The crowd thinned a little as the shadows lengthened, but the mix of people did not change.

Come six-thirty, twenty people, mothers and fathers and toddlers in little family groups, were still enjoying the playground in the twilight. But the playground's little social system was about to tip into a different state. Parents admonished their children:

'five more minutes', 'last go on the slide, then we leave'. Very suddenly, the playground emptied of families. Two gangs of young teenagers took up position at opposite sides of the playground, one on the swings and the other lined up along a seesaw: they seemed harmless enough, grouped together more for their own reassurance and conviviality than to prepare for trouble. But the park had, within a brief interval, changed dramatically.

A similarly stark difference can be observed if the weather changes. When I visit the park with my daughter on a grey day, cold enough to wear a pullover or a light jacket, perhaps with a sniff of rain or some dew on the playground benches, I know that we are likely to be the only people there.

So what? Parks vary with the weather and the time of day. People like to go when it's sunny; they do not sit around at night unless they are teenagers bent on some sort of mischief. That much is obvious, or so it seems. But hang on. We are quite happy to sit in our gardens or in a pavement café on a balmy evening; why not in the park? A grey day makes a park less fun, but it's hardly a blizzard or a hurricane. Why is there such an extreme difference in a park environment, so that the change of a few degrees or a few minutes can be the difference between fifty people going to the playground, and nobody at all?

The difference is interaction. Any urban space is full of humans interacting, but parks particularly so. When my daughter and I go to the playground on a grey day, we do not stay for very long. It's not because the weather is intolerable but rather because the park is dull. With nobody there, there's nothing to see. As the weather improves and a few people come out to enjoy it, suddenly the playground bursts into life. Everybody is able to watch everybody else. People are there because the playground is lively, but the playground is lively because people are there.

What an economist sees behind the crowds of jostling children has the deceptive name of a 'positive externality'. When I show up at the playground with my daughter, I am bestowing a positive externality on the playground: other people enjoy the fact that we are there, but we do not get to enjoy their enjoyment. It is the opposite of pollution or congestion, where the culprits hurt others without feeling their pain. And as such, positive externalities sound rather wonderful.

They are not. If I enjoy the park only when you're there, and you enjoy the park only when I'm there, it's quite likely that neither of us will go – or if I go, I'll stay only briefly before giving up, leaving too early to see you arrive. A positive externality, all too often, is a purely hypothetical benefit, enjoyed at a destination that is never reached via a road not taken. If people in the park are an unpaid attraction for other people in the park, do not be too surprised if, quite rationally, they find the zero wage is not enough to persuade them to show up as often as we might like.

The behaviour of Hackney Downs park is also unpredictable because of what economists would call – more jargon – 'multiple equilibria'. A single equilibrium is a predictable, stable state, like a swing hanging still. Even if you give the girl on the swing a push, the swing will eventually settle back down to that same equilibrium. But the park has more than one equilibrium. If you go to the park, I'd like to be there and we'll both be glad we went. If I don't go, you wouldn't want to go either, and we'd both be glad we stayed at home. Either situation is an equilibrium, although one of them makes much better use of the park than the other does.

Conventional economics doesn't say much more than that, but Thomas Schelling does. You might remember, from Chapter Two, Schelling's idea of a 'focal point'. Focal points are the little things that make a big difference – the difference between reaching one equilibrium and reaching another. If a local football team comes to practise near the playground every Saturday morning, or a group of stay-at-home parents arrange a regular trip at three o'clock on a Wednesday afternoon, that can create a focal point around which others coordinate. With the team at practice, the park will feel safe from muggers and there will be something to look at, so families will come along to use the park. Other families will come because the first families will be there; after the football season is over and the team no longer comes to practise, Saturday mornings can still be lively at the playground simply because everybody expects that they will be. A lively park playground can therefore be created by a football practice session that doesn't even take place any longer: that is an indication of how whimsically unpredictable these multiple equilibria can be. Yet while the outcome is whimsical, the causes are rational.

While parks are the clearest example, this story applies much more widely, to the intimate structures of city neighbourhoods themselves, why one location is for millionaires only and another, perhaps very near, is dangerous, boring and impoverished. The fine details of city design, coupled with individuals acting rationally, determine which neighbourhoods thrive, which wither – and even who lives and who dies.

Had they ever met, Margaret Muller and Sarah Stefanek (not the latter's real name) would have had plenty to talk about. Both were the daughters of European immigrants; both originally lived in Washington, DC. Both of them were talented young women – Margaret, an artist; Sarah, an economist – whose ambitions drew them to move to England. But what they really had in common was horrifying: both Margaret and Sarah were attacked in broad daylight, in rush hour, in the heart of a busy city. Both were attacked by men they did not know. But they will not meet, because while Sarah survived the attack on her, Margaret did not.

Margaret was jogging in Victoria Park, London, at eight-thirty on a sunny February morning. Victoria Park is a beautiful space but a quiet one, even at the height of rush hour. Where is there to rush to, after all? The park is over a mile long and several hundred yards across, and there are few reasons to cross it. The east side is bordered by an impassable road in a deep concrete cutting, the busy A102. On the south side runs Regents

Canal, an occasionally charming but always quiet waterway with few bridges. On the north side of the park are rows of council housing blocked off behind high brick walls and a tall iron railing. With so many boundaries blocked, few people walk through the park.

Even on a sunny morning, anyone with anywhere to go had no business being near the park's secluded rose garden, hundreds of yards from anywhere busy, where Margaret was attacked. Less than five feet tall, she was defenceless and alone. She was stabbed almost fifty times, and although the park contained passers-by near enough to hear the screams and summon help, nobody arrived in time even to see her murderer.

Sarah might easily have suffered the same fate. It was a similar attack, but instead of a quiet park, Reginald Jones chose Washington, DC's Fifteenth Street as the venue for his assault. On a sticky July evening, the locals were out in force. Some were walking to or from the bars, restaurants and ice-cream shop on Seventeenth Street; others were heading to the Whole Foods supermarket just around the corner. Many were simply sitting out on their front steps, watching people go by.

When Sarah – tall, slim and beautiful, wearing white trousers and a crop top – passed Jones in the street, he evidently saw something he did not like. 'White pants – white bitch,' he declared, and began to chase her down the street. Immediately, passers-by tried to intervene. One man pulled over and tried to get Sarah into his car. Jones punched her and she hit the pavement hard, screaming for help. Jones began stabbing her, puncturing her belly and back, hitting her in the face, and reducing her arm to tatters as she tried to ward off the blows. It was a few seconds before one man had sprinted from his doorstep and barrelled into Jones, sending the knife skittering across the street. Others were quick to follow the neighbour's lead. Jones was slick with Sarah's blood, strong and quite determined to kill her. He failed. He was pulled off her several times and half a dozen dazed onlookers sat on him until the police came. When they did, the officers were overwhelmed by witnesses offering statements.

Such was the ferocity of the attack that Sarah would have had no chance without the ordinary folk of Fifteenth Street who rushed to her aid. She owes her life to the neighbourhood in which she was attacked, and to the protection it gave her.

Most city dwellers are not so unlucky as to attract the attention of maniacs, but we still rely on the city streets for protection. Usually we do not need passers-by to pull muggers off us or apprehend pickpockets, because rational muggers and pickpockets do not act when there are passers-by.

Jane Jacobs – an unconventional observer of economies, especially city economies – famously argued that successful neighbourhoods provide 'eyes on the street' to protect us from crime, just as they protected Sarah but could not protect Margaret. It is yet another example of a positive externality: when I go to the park, I not only make it more interesting for other people but make it feel safer. That may attract more of them and they will make me feel safer. Empty streets are dull and feel dangerous, so they stay empty. Bustling streets are interesting and safe. Is it any wonder that they are bustling?

Jacobs emphasised the importance of the fine details of streets and building design. She would not, I think, have been much surprised by the quiet spots in Victoria Park, given how hemmed in it is by other parks, the canal and a busy road. Nor would she have found the oscillations around Hackney Downs playground unexpected. The playground and park are the only green space for a mile or more around in a relentlessly urban setting. If they felt safe and interesting they would be well used, but they get little support from their environs, bordered on one side by a railway line, another side by a high-fenced school, and a third side by faceless high-rise council housing. These neighbouring uses do not encourage people to stroll across the park, except at the beginning and end of the school day. So the playground has to be completely self-sustaining – which on good days, it can be.

Architecture, too, mattered a lot to Jacobs. There was more than aesthetics at play when a high rise was built. These tall buildings tended to lift eyes away from the street and make the streets more dangerous: you cannot leap up from your vantage point on the front step and dash across the street to rescue the victim of a stabbing if you live on the fourteenth floor.

Jacobs was a brilliant student of urban life, and her theories have hypnotised many readers. But while plausible, those theories have not always been easy to put to the test. Two economists, Ed Glaeser and Bruce Sacerdote, have now managed to put together data to test whether these big buildings really do cause crime.

Some of the subtleties of architecture are simply impenetrable to a number-crunching approach, but Glaeser and Sacerdote studied nearly fourteen thousand city dwellers and were able to examine Jacobs's thesis with surprising precision. Comparing high-rise public housing with high-rise private housing, low-rise public with low-rise private, and using statistical tools to adjust for other factors such as race and poverty, they found that Jacobs seems to be right. They discovered that residents of big high-rise blocks were more likely to be victims of crime and were more likely to fear becoming victims. And it wasn't because large blocks are often public housing: the size of the building itself was the problem.

You might think the reason for this is not rational but psychological: perhaps big tower blocks squeeze people into small spaces and make them angry and more likely to commit crime. Or perhaps the problem is purely physical, as it would be if high-rise flats were more vulnerable to burglary.

Glaeser and Sacerdote don't think so. They found that buildings do not create an environment that encourages crime in general. They don't, for example, facilitate petty larceny (say, lifting a purse from your bag) or even burglary. Big buildings encourage only street crime, such as car thefts or robberies with violence. That suggests that the big buildings are exerting a sphere of malign influence over the streets around them – or, perhaps more accurately, they are failing to exert an aura of safety, which smaller homes naturally do.

The architectural effects on crime were all about eyes on the street. Glaeser and Sacerdote found, for example, that it was tall buildings (rather than simply large ones) that really failed to keep the streets around them safe. Each additional floor in your building increases your risk of being robbed in the street or having your car stolen by two and a half percentage points – if your building has twelve storeys rather than two, your chance of being mugged rises by a quarter. The higher the building, the more people are lifted away from the front step and the street. Since Glaeser and Sacerdote adjusted for poverty, public housing and many other factors, that is a big effect coming from mere steel and concrete. Jane Jacobs was right: the architecture of city neighbourhoods isn't just about what looks nice. It's about whether the neighbourhoods themselves live or die. And the pernicious effect of the tower blocks falls unevenly. In the United Kingdom, for example, whose population is 92 per cent white, racial segregation is vertical: whites are in the minority of those who live above the fifth floor of a tower block. The British ghettos are up in the sky.

The 'eyes on the street' model, like the chessboard model of segregation, tends to push towards extremes. Either the neighbourhood is interesting, lively and safe, in which case it will bustle with activity and stay interesting, lively and safe, or it is dull and dangerous, in which case it will be shunned and will stay dull and dangerous. But the encouraging thing about eyes on the street is that, unlike Schelling's chessboard model of segregation, there is nothing fundamental pulling cities towards the bad equilibrium. The good equilibrium, where diversity and liveliness are self-sustaining, is always there under the surface, waiting to get out if given half a chance by urban planners.

Fifteenth Street itself, where Sarah was stabbed, went through just such a transition. All the elements were in place, with decent housing stock and proximity to Washington's downtown and to the lively Dupont Circle. First, Dupont Circle spilled east to Seventeenth Street, as bars and restaurants sought out cheaper rents not too far from the action.

Many of the eager consumers of the bar culture that would transform the neighbourhood were gay, and this again reflects a kind of hidden rationality. We all have to weigh up costs and benefits. For many people, cheap housing and convenient access to nightlife are benefits, while the fear of crime, dangerous streets, and bad schools are costs. But for gay men, the nightlife was a particular benefit, and the bad schools and dangerous streets were lower costs. It wasn't that they didn't care about or fear the crime that blighted deprived areas – it was just that there was a bargain to be had, and they worried less than couples with kids.

That sparked a positive spiral. The busy, fun, safe streets the gay men helped to populate are attractive to everyone, and soon all kinds of people were moving into what had previously been an impoverished enclave. The clincher was when the organic supermarket Fresh Fields (now Whole Foods) opened a large store even further east, on P Street between Fourteenth and Fifteenth. It quickly became a focal point for further developments: apartment blocks, restaurants, coffee shops and even art galleries. By 2005, when Sarah was attacked, Fifteenth Street had become a very bad place to try to murder someone: day or night, it was one of the busiest and most diverse areas in the city.

Schelling's chessboard model suggests that transformations such as Fifteenth Street's should be impossible: things always fall apart, people always give in to their prejudices, and small anxieties lead to big divisions. But Schelling's model is not a forecast, just an illustration of the kind of unexpected transitions that can emerge from individual interactions. Its successors, sophisticated simulations using modern computers with hundreds of thousands of simulated decision-makers rather than a chessboard with forty pieces, often find the same sort of sudden transitions, but not necessarily to the worst possible outcomes.

One model was developed by a political economist who was then at the Brookings Institution, just a few blocks away from Whole Foods and the Fifteenth Street attack. Ross A. Hammond developed his model in 2000, at a time when the Washington, DC, community around him was becoming safer at a dramatic rate. Perhaps it was this startling transition that inspired him to develop models of artificial societies that move from a corrupt, crime-ridden state of nature to being the most genteel, law-abiding communities.

Hammond's computer creates a simple world populated by artificial people. Watching it work is a little like watching speeded-up footage of a Schelling chessboard. Little patterned tiles cascade down the screen, each representing a person and with a colour that shows how each person is acting. And how do they act? The computer randomly pairs up people each 'day' (actually, many times a second). The computer gives them a simple choice: act honestly or act corruptly. If both sides of the pair act corruptly, both enjoy a kickback; if only one side acts corruptly and the other honestly, the crook will go to jail.

The magic of the computer model is in seeing how quickly the artificial world can change. At first, it is populated by self-interested crooks, with a few honest citizens sprinkled among them. The few honest citizens don't respond to incentives; irrationally, if heartwarmingly, they will always act honestly. The crooks do respond to incentives, being corrupt or honest depending on whether they believe the other side will recipro-cate. The chances of honesty being the best policy are quite small at first, and many days go by with corruption thick in the air and the honest folk unable to stem the tide.

But when Hammond's crooks fear that even other crooks will decide to act honestly, they will do the same. That fear of an out-break of honesty can spring up suddenly as the result of a few random events, a few honest citizens clustered together creating the impression of a legal crackdown. After a long period of pure corruption, Hammond's model displays a change even more dramatic than Schelling's: suddenly, very quickly, everybody in the world decides to be honest. The moment the process starts it is impossible to stop: offering a corrupt deal becomes irrational and suddenly the world is full of crooks who have decided that honesty is the best policy. It is a self-fulfilling decision. The cascade of tiles on the computer screen changes colour abruptly as honesty breaks out everywhere.

Hammond's model is still a vast simplification, of course. But it does provide a hint at why some societies do seem to move from awful corruption to relative lawfulness very suddenly. The model confirms that the transitions can be dramatic; they can have tiny causes, or even no cause at all, just being the product of random events. Each rational individual decision changes the decisions of others, just as small stones rolling down a hill can build into a landslide. In life, as in the model, the collective outcome of such rational interactions may not resemble the typical individual's desires, even if it is a change for the better.

Unfortunately, it is uncommon for neighbourhoods to break out of the vicious circle of poverty. While estate agents love to describe particular areas as 'up-and-coming', relative to one another, neighbourhoods do not tend to 'up-and-come' at all. Anyone who doubts this should look at Charles Booth's famous map of London's rich and poor areas at the end of the nineteenth century. Booth graded the inhabitants of each block from G ('upper class and upper middle class, wealthy'), through F, E, D ('small regular earnings'), C, B, and finally A ('lowest class, vicious and criminal'). Overlaying Booth's map with today's poorest areas is a sobering experience: with few exceptions, yesterday's poor areas are also today's poor areas. This is despite the fact that London is much richer than it was, and each individual neighbourhood has improved over time. This persistence of relative poverty over the decades is a shock to most people (and anathema to estate agents). But it should not be surprising, given what we have learned about the tendency of cities to self-segregate, and the way in which safe, lively neighbourhoods become safer and livelier while dangerous, dull neighbourhoods become more dangerous or more dull. It makes perfect, rational sense.

But perhaps it does not matter if a given neighbourhood is always poorer than others. After all, there will always be a poorest place and a richest place, a place with the least crime and a place with the most crime. That does not matter very much in a society where people can move around freely. Much more worrying would be if the people who populate a poor area today are the descendants of the people who populated the same poor area a couple of generations before: that would suggest that geography and history are simply destiny, a trap from which it is impossible to escape.

That is all too plausible. In Chapter Three, we briefly discussed the possibility that discrimination was holding back women. In the next chapter, we will try to uncover the truth about racial discrimination. But there is an important difference between sexual and racial inequality: blacks have black parents, are more likely to be brought up in a largely black area and are more likely to have grown up in a poor family. Women, on the other hand, have no tendency to grow up in female families or female areas. That may mean that young blacks today inherit disadvantages – poverty, geography – from their parents in a way that young women simply do not.

Take a young black man living in a largely black community. We know, statistically, that things are not likely to work out well for him. The trouble is, it is very difficult to say why. There are too many explanations. Perhaps the existence of crime in the neighbourhood is somehow contagious. Perhaps underachievement itself is contagious, and his friends tease him if he works hard at school. Perhaps he won't enjoy the social connections that lead to a good job unless he can get out of the ghetto and meet a more diverse group of people. And perhaps he is simply the victim of discrimination by employers who won't give him a chance. After all, the oldest, most obvious explanation need not be the wrong one.

It is important to try to untangle these explanations – and we shall, over the remainder of this chapter and the next one. If the problem is basically geographical – young black men are not doing well today because they are brought up in deprived areas – then the solution would have to be geographical, too, looking for some way to renew or regenerate those areas. But if the problem lies somewhere else, attempts at regeneration will either fail, or succeed only by displacing and dispersing the poor without helping them.

Economists, frustrated by years of trying to understand a complicated world with very limited information, have started to get very good at tricking the numbers into telling the truth. Some of those tricks are purely statistical, but many involve uncovering or even creating new types of information that reveal new stories. The results tell us much of what we need to know to understand what is really going on for the residents of the ghetto.

Boston, Massachusetts, 1994

Economists occasionally grumble that, unlike physicists, they cannot carry out experiments to test their theories. But that is not quite true. Admittedly, a physicist in his laboratory can vary one factor of interest – the temperature of a liquid, perhaps – while keeping everything else the same. Economists can't do that, because they are interested in the behaviour of people and everyone is different.

But this is a problem that has been solved already, by medical researchers. They, too, want to test treatments on people, and each person is unique. Give a drug to a sick man and he may get better – or worse – regardless of whether the drug works. So medical researchers use the next-best thing to a perfectly controlled experiment: a randomised trial. They give a real drug to a thousand sick people and a placebo, a fake, to another thousand sufferers, and if the typical recipient of the drug is doing better than the typical recipient of the placebo, then the drug is almost certainly working. Some of the placebo crowd will get better, and some of the patients receiving the genuine treatment will get worse, but with two thousand people in the experiment, all the little chance elements will cancel each other out. The only thing that can explain a systematic difference is the drug.

In fact, you may not even need two thousand people if the drug is powerful. I don't need a coin to come up heads two thousand times in a row to tell me that something is wrong with the coin: twenty heads in a row is already a million-to-one long shot.

Yet if clinical researchers can do this, why not economists? Why not test the effectiveness of a new policy designed to help people – textbooks for schools, more police on the streets, housing vouchers – by giving some schools or councils or households access to the help, while others – chosen at random – get nothing?

In 1994, selected residents of public housing projects in very poor areas of Boston, along with those in similar situations in Baltimore, Chicago, Los Angeles, and New York, became lab rats in an ambitious economic experiment. Many were offered, however, something more substantial than the root beer doled out by Ray Battalio and John Kagel in Chapter One. One-third, chosen at random, were offered nothing additional, although they continued to qualify for residence in public housing, built by the government and with rents fixed at 30 per cent of household income. One-third were offered so-called 'Section 8' vouchers, which enabled them, if they wished to move, to live in private housing under similar conditions: they paid 30 per cent of their household income, the voucher covered the rest. The final third, also chosen at random, were enrolled in the 'Moving to Opportunity' scheme.

Moving to Opportunity aimed to find out what happened when households moved away from the ghettos and to areas with low levels of poverty. Participants in the scheme were offered special relocation counselling to help them find a home in a new area of town and were given housing vouchers that covered all rent above 30 per cent of their income. But there was a catch in all of this: the vouchers were valid only if the family managed to find a place to live in a neighbourhood with a poverty rate below 10 per cent. This was an ambitious target: remember that even Georgetown and Cleveland Park, super-safe and with an average family income of two hundred thousand dollars a year, have a poverty rate of 7.5 per cent. Participants in the programme were moving out of neighbourhoods with a poverty rate of at least 40 per cent.

Moving to Opportunity held out the promise of a new life away from the isolation, poverty and crime in the ghettos. To economists Lawrence Katz, Jeffrey Kling and Jeffrey Liebman, it offered something else as well: a real chance to work out how much neighbourhoods really mattered. Were these residents of public housing pulled down by their surroundings and their peers? Or were they held back by something unrelated to the neighbourhood, such as family poverty or racist employers? Because there was no systematic difference between those who stayed and those offered a chance to move, any difference in what happened to the families had to be put down to the effects of the move.

What Katz, Kling and Liebman discovered defies easy categorisation. The experiment proved that neighbourhoods matter very much indeed for some facets of life, and not at all for others. Adults and children who moved to richer neighbourhoods were much safer and much happier. Children were four times less likely to be seriously injured; behavioural problems fell by a quarter for girls and by 40 per cent for boys; severe asthma attacks fell by two-thirds. Children were five times less likely to be attacked, robbed or threatened. Adults were about a third less likely to suffer major depression, to say they rarely felt happy or rarely felt peaceful. Their overall health improved. One mother who moved with her family recalled the time she tried to take her four-year-old daughter to visit the old neighbourhood. 'Even now, we can't drive up the street. My baby, she so scared that she start cryin' "No no no." She don't even want to go near there. It's amazing how little kids remember that stuff.'

At the same time, the experiment showed that adults who moved to the new, low-poverty neighbourhood were no more likely to find a job. Children in the new neighbourhood did not improve academically after they moved. As for crime rates, it turns out that, contrary to popular belief, crime is not contagious: of the families who moved to richer neighbourhoods, it did not matter whether the new neighbourhood had high crime or low crime – the kids who moved were as likely to get into trouble with the law after the move as beforehand.

What does all this show? It shows that your neighbourhood makes a big difference to your health and happiness, but that it will not drag down your test scores, lead you into crime, or prevent you from finding a job. Your neighbourhood matters, but it is not your destiny.

The young people who 'moved to opportunity' moved away from the worst of the gangs and crime and drugs, and consequently became happier, less fearful, even saner. But their employment prospects did not improve and nor did their exam results – at least, not in the early years after the move. (Over time, perhaps those who have moved will be more likely to find jobs. There is some evidence, for instance, that living in a poor neighbourhood in Paris is a serious obstacle to getting a job.) The fact that ghettos do not seem to ruin job prospects might seem surprising, especially since we are used to people moving out of the ghettos as a prelude to doing well. But we need to remember that the people who move are self-selected, not randomly selected. If Jennifer moves away from the poor neighbourhood and starts a new life, is that because of the new neighbourhood or because of Jennifer?

The real message of the 'Moving to Opportunity' experiment, though, is that neighbourhoods are not the only things in life that can hold people back. That's a story we'll explore next.

Six

The dangers of rational racism

University of Virginia, 2003

Some students at the University of Virginia have signed up to earn a bit of easy money by taking part in a classroom experiment devised by economists Roland Fryer, Jacob Goeree and Charles Holt. The experiment seems like a funny little game, but the result is anything but funny, as the group of idealistic university students begins to behave in ways that frustrate and outrage one another.

The experiment divided students into roles – 'employers' and 'workers'. The workers were randomly assigned one of two colours, green or purple. Hunched over their computers and logged into a simple Web interface, the unsuspecting students were put through three experimental stages. First, the 'workers' were asked to decide whether to spend a specified sum to get an 'education', which would improve their chances on a 'test'. Then came the test itself, actually a random throw of the dice, but with the odds loaded in favour of those who'd paid to be educated. Finally, there was the hiring decision. Each employer was presented with two pieces of information about each worker: the result of their test – which hinted at whether they had paid to get an education, but didn't confirm it – and, fatefully, whether the applicant had been randomly designated as 'green' or 'purple'. Using that information alone, the employers had to decide whether to offer each worker a job.

These three steps were repeated twenty times, and as the experiment went on, the Web interface was revealing the average test scores and hiring rates for green and purple workers in the previous rounds. That was potentially useful information, because the students playing the role of employers had been told that they would be rewarded with extra dollars every time they hired a worker who turned out to be educated, but fined every time they hired one who turned out to be uneducated. Students playing the role of workers knew they would be paid every time they got a job, but at the start of each round they had to weigh that potential pay-off against the cost of paying for an education. Both sets of students, then – employers and workers – were in a position where they had to assess the odds and take a gamble to earn more of the experimenters' cash.

So what happened? In the first round, employers looked only at test results when deciding whether to hire. Their hiring decision was colour-blind. How could it not have been? The game started with a blank slate. 'Green' or 'purple' conveys no information at all in the first round of the game.

But from the second round on, employers had a history to work with. As it happened, more green than purple workers had gambled on getting an education in the first round, so the green test scores tended to be better. The colours had initially been assigned at random, so this was pure chance. This didn't stop employers figuring that greens appeared to be more disposed than purples to invest in an education. They became more willing to take a chance on green workers with a low test score, and less willing to hire purple workers even with a high score.

With the Web interface also revealing the average hiring rates for greens and purples in previous rounds, the workers quickly responded: green workers kept investing in an education, and purple workers did not. Why bother to pay for an education if employers are less likely to hire you because you're purple? And so a vicious circle took hold.

At the end of the experiment, it was time for a class discussion – and the frustration came pouring out. 'I was amazed,' Fryer told me. 'The kids were really angry. The purple workers would say, "I'm not investing because you won't hire me," and the employers would respond, "I didn't hire you because you weren't investing." The initial asymmetries came about because of chance, but people would hang on to them and wouldn't let them go.'

It sounds bizarre enough that young and idealistic students were so quick to create their own colour stereotype of lazy purples and hardworking greens, despite having no prior information whatsoever on which to base their discrimination. Even more bizarre is that the way they ended up behaving was rational. Although the initial disparity was purely a matter of chance, and although there was no fundamental difference between the greens and the purples, the students playing the role of employers were absolutely correct in their view that green workers were more likely to be educated. (If we were to split hairs about their rationality, they jumped to the conclusion too quickly: John Von Neumann or Chris Ferguson would have realised that what looked like an early sign of a pattern might easily have been random.)

The employers' view became self-fulfilling as purple workers rationally abandoned hope of getting hired and stopped paying for education. And once the downward spiral set in, a determinedly colour-blind employer would actually have lost money compared with one who took note of the colour of the applicants. Fryer and his colleagues had witnessed the emergence of 'racial' inequality, of stereotyping, of treating people as members of a group rather than as individuals in their own right, and of the systematic abandonment of hope by the purple workers. All this happened in a game where everyone started off from an equal position. How much worse should we expect things to be in the real world, where our starts in life are far from equal?

This chapter is about the dangers of rational racism. Let me make it clear that when I say that some forms of racism can be rational, that is not an attempt to justify them. I talked in Chapter One about the rational criminal, who only commits crime when crime pays. Similarly, the rational racist is only racist when racism pays. The fact that both profit from their actions is no justification at all.

Indeed, the reason why I think it's important to face up to 'rational racism' – even though the phrase is unpleasant – is the same as why we have to face up to rational crime: because we want to stamp it out. We hire police and build prisons in an effort to change the incentives and make sure that crime doesn't pay. We need to figure out when and how it is possible to change the incentives for racists, too.

In this chapter I'll focus particularly on the predicament of African Americans, because it has been closely studied by economists. African Americans are not doing well, whether you look at life expectancy or infant mortality, employment or earnings, years in education or exam results. But why? It seems utterly crazy that the colour of a person's skin could be the marker for such disparities. And some of it will, indeed, be crazy – there are still bigoted employers around who just don't want a black man on the staff. But the classroom experiment suggests that some of it, disturbingly, might be all too rational – if it saves time and trouble for employers to treat job applicants as part of a group that's known to be educationally struggling, rather than taking a closer look at their individual qualities.

We'll look at both types of discrimination, the crazy and the rational, and see how the vicious circle that took hold in the experiment – purple workers giving up on education because they thought that employers were paying more attention to their colour than to their test scores – plays out in reality. We'll also see that there is even a harsh logic to the controversial idea that studious black kids are systematically bullied by their peers. This is, I'm afraid, for the most part a depressing story. But there is some cause for cheer, as we'll see at the end of the chapter.

First, though, we need to establish that the highly simplified experiment at the University of Virginia is, in fact, mirroring reality. Are real-life employers really as quick to jump to conclusions about African-American job applicants as the students in the experiment were about 'purple' ones? Isn't it possible that real employers are colour-blind, and the only reason why fewer African Americans get good jobs is that fewer African-American applicants are well qualified? Despite the woeful litany of statistics about the gap between whites and blacks, it was until recently possible to make a plausible-sounding case for this hypothesis. Then a pair of economists came along with a devastatingly simple experiment that utterly destroyed it.

Marianne Bertrand and Sendhil Mullainathan are immigrants who have made good in America. Bertrand came from Belgium and studied for her doctorate at Harvard. Mullainathan spent his early childhood in a remote village in India before arriving in Los Angeles at the age of seven. A photograph of him, at age five, shows him proudly wearing a tiny three-piece suit with the waistcoat on top of the jacket; his uncle and grandfather had been his inexperienced sartorial advisers. But Sendhil did not let isolated beginnings get in his way. He is now a tenured professor at Harvard; before he was thirty he had received a half-million-dollar 'genius' grant from the MacArthur Foundation, and around the same time he was one of three young founders of the Poverty Action Lab at MIT, devoted to understanding the causes and cures of poverty in the developing world. It is something of a wonder that he also had time to study racial discrimination, but then there was something absurdly simple about the way he and Marianne Bertrand did it.

Their researchers generated five thousand realistic-seeming CVs, based on real documents posted on job-hunting websites, and modifying contact details, addresses and some other information. Some of the CVs were graded as being high quality, and the researchers reinforced this by adding some icing to the cake, such as summer work experience, extra computing skills or some military experience. Others were lower quality, and the researchers left these untouched. Only then did the research team have a computer assign names, at random, to the CVs. Some of the CVs received distinctively black names, such as Tyrone Jones or Latoya Washington. Others got lily-white names, like Alison Walsh or Brendan Baker. (Who says these are black or white names? Perceptions were important here, so the researchers went out with clipboards to ask people in the street what they thought. Names such as Maurice, which despite being common among African-American men is not perceived as being a black name, were set aside.)

Any difference in call-back rates could therefore be attributed to only one thing: the name of the applicant. This was a fully randomised trial, along the lines of those used to test the effectiveness of new medicines – only instead of isolating the effect of taking a new headache remedy, Mullainathan and Bertrand were isolating the effect of having a black-sounding name such as Jamal or Ebony.

The researchers responded to over a thousand advertisements in the *Boston Globe* and the *Chicago Tribune*, sending out to each employer two 'black' CVs, one good, one mediocre, and two 'white' CVs, again one good and one not-so-good. They set up voice-mail boxes to collect the responses, and waited. The results were depressing. White names received 50 per cent more invitations to interview. With such a large sample size, the odds of this happening by chance in a colour-blind world are less than one in ten thousand. Exactly as 'employers' in the classroom experiment dismissed applicants when they saw the word *purple*, real-world employers were dismissing applicants when they saw a black-sounding name. This simple experiment demolished any idea that racial discrimination is a thing of the past in America.

Mullainathan and Bertrand discovered something else in the course of their experiment, something that is arguably even more disturbing. Remember that the CVs were divided not just into 'white' and 'black' but into 'good' and 'mediocre', with white and black names assigned to each grade of CV in equal proportions. High-quality applicants were more likely to be invited for an interview, but only if they were white. Employers didn't seem to notice whether black applicants had extra skills or experience. It certainly didn't make any difference to the response rate. It was as though there were three categories: 'gifted and white', 'ordinary and white' and simply 'black'.

That categorisation is far more corrosive than the raw racism of a lower interview rate for all blacks, because it sets up the same vicious spiral that Roland Fryer and his colleagues discovered in the classroom at the University of Virginia. Why bother to get a degree or work experience if you are young, gifted and black? Employers won't even notice. Don't bother. And that rational response makes things even worse. Even enlightened employers will start to realise that many black applicants aren't educated or experienced. After a while, in a hurry as all recruiters are, they will stop looking. All they will need to see will be the name 'Tyrone'.

Economists distinguish between two kinds of discrimination. One is known as 'taste-based' discrimination, although I tend to prefer the less euphemistic term 'bigotry'. This happens when racist employers refuse to give blacks a job because they don't like blacks. The other is 'statistical' discrimination, or what I am more starkly calling 'rational racism'. Statistical discrimination happens when employers use the average performance of the applicant's racial group as a piece of information to help them decide whether to hire that applicant.

What happened in the experiment at the University of Virginia was, clearly, pure statistical discrimination – unless you seriously believe that students acquired a visceral dislike of clicking a button to 'employ' a 'purple' worker. It's less obvious what was going on in the minds of the real-world employers in Bertrand and Mullainathan's experiment. Some recruiters could be disregarding a CV on seeing a black name because they don't want black people in their company. Others could be doing so because they have a hundred applications to get through before lunch and experience has taught them that their time will pay better dividends if they spend more of it considering Brendans than Jamals.

Does the distinction matter? In some ways it doesn't. Both types of discrimination are objectionable: they both treat applicants as members of a group rather than as individuals. Both are illegal. The distinction between them is unlikely to seem important to you if you're black, well qualified and jobless. Furthermore, that distinction is risky, because it offers racists a dangerous intellectual refuge for their bigotry.

But the difference is important, because it's the difference between racism that helps the racist and racism that is ultimately self-defeating. A racist boss who turns down black workers even though he could quickly establish their competence will eventually take a hit to the bottom line. In other words, taste-based discrimination is not only miserable for the victims, it is expensive for the bigots.

Statistical discrimination is different. If done cleverly, it could improve profits, which makes it more worrying because it is more likely to endure than dumb prejudice. That is why I have chosen to use the discomfiting term 'rational racism', rather than the more anodyne-sounding 'statistical discrimination' – I want to drive home the point that it will not go away if we don't do something about it.

If you want evidence of enduring statistical discrimination, it's not hard to find, because although racial statistical discrimination is just as illegal as taste-based discrimination, non-racial statistical discrimination is often legal and overt. An insurer will consider your age and your sex when deciding how much to charge for car insurance, and if you're a young man, you'll pay more than your twin sister. That's not because the insurer dislikes young men; it is because the insurer knows that young men tend to be bad risks on the road. Much as we usually find sexism and ageism objectionable, we somehow accept that careful and careless drivers will be lumped together into crude groups, because it's not practical for an insurance company to follow every seventeen-year-old boy around and judge his individual driving skill and sense of responsibility.

This disparity is not going to go away of its own accord, and that's the difference between rational racism (or rational sexism, or rational ageism) and taste-based discrimination. If the chauvinist owners of a car insurance company decided to offer generous discounts to men because they hated women, we would confidently expect them to be put out of business by rivals who employ rational actuaries. Bigotry is expensive in a sufficiently competitive market, but rational discrimination can be profitable.

Unfortunately, while the forces of competition should eventually triumph over taste-based discrimination, there are few reasons to think it will happen quickly. Those on the receiving end still suffer in the meantime. Imagine a company with racist managers who simply don't like to employ black workers, whether they're capable or not. If the choice they face in hiring a new employee is between a smart black worker and a less smart white worker, they will employ the dumb applicant and let the smart applicant go to work for a non-racist (or less racist) competitor. That is not a profitable strategy.

Yet that is not much comfort to the black applicants. Even in the best-case scenario, when there are many non-racist firms around and so blacks will earn as much as equally qualified white counterparts, black applicants still have to face the indignity of unjustified rejection if they encounter a racist firm. If there are relatively few non-racist firms around – or, worst of all, if all firms are racist but some are more racist than others – black workers will suffer lower wages as well as routine humiliations. It's true that market forces will funnel profits towards the less racist firms, and racist managers will eventually fall foul of irate shareholders or the bankruptcy courts – but the racists might be hurt far less than their victims, so you shouldn't hold your breath waiting for it to happen.

To find out who suffers most from bigotry, we turn yet again to Gary Becker. He used a simple mathematical model to get a sense of the likely balance of effects. His estimates suggested that while discrimination hurt the income of both the racist and the victim, how serious the economic effects were depended on the size of the minority group relative to the majority. In America, only 12 per cent of the population classify themselves as black or African American; that means even modest discrimination by whites would have serious economic effects on blacks. By the same token, even serious bigotry from the white majority would not damage white incomes very much, and competitive pressures could take a long time to favour the more enlightened companies. Becker contrasted the situation with the apartheid regime in South Africa, where the blacks who were ruthlessly discriminated against made up around 80 per cent of the population. As well as being a moral outrage, that was very bad news for South Africa's economy – much more significant than the effects on the US economy of the more modest discrimination suffered by the smaller proportion of African Americans. Becker argues that this is one of the reasons why apartheid was eventually dismantled.

What Becker's analysis did not deliver was a compelling account of how much racism was taste-based, and therefore vulnerable to erosion by market forces – nor how quickly that might happen. It's possible, though, that we can get a clue from looking more closely at the data from Bertrand and Mullainathan's experiment. CVs with black-sounding names fared no worse when sent to federal contractors than they did at private companies (but no better, either). Since government agencies are those most protected from the competitive forces that penalise taste-based racism, there are two possible conclusions we might tentatively draw, and both are depressing. One possibility is that taste-based discrimination is pervasive, but competitive forces are too weak to be having a noticeable impact on it. The other possibility is that most of the racism in the American jobs market is profitable and could therefore go on for ever.

Discrimination can hurt minorities in two ways: directly, by denying them opportunities; and indirectly, by sapping the incentive they have to study hard and aim high. The indirect effect is insidious and probably even more serious in the long run. Think back to Roland Fryer's classroom experiment: 'The purple workers would say, "I'm not investing because you won't hire me," and the employers would respond, "I didn't hire you because you weren't investing."' That sort of statistical discrimination would discourage any rational student from bothering to study.

Or think of the categories apparently adopted by the recruiters approached by Bertrand and Mullainathan's fake applicants: 'white and good', 'white and mediocre', 'black'. What is the rational response to such prejudice? If you're white, study hard and make sure your CV looks great. If you're black, don't bother.

Not all discrimination has this effect. There is some evidence, for instance, that educated women suffer less discrimination than uneducated women. It is not surprising, then, to see that women do so much better than men at school. But when it comes to race, both rational racism and taste-based discrimination are reducing the incentive for black students to get qualified. Rational racism becomes self-perpetuating, while taste-based discrimination inflicts a further double penalty: it reduces the chance of getting a good job, but also encourages blacks to get less education and thus lowers their income even if they find non-racist employers.

And it's not as if discrimination is the only obstacle faced by young African Americans today. So, too, is the difficulty of making good from poor beginnings. The green and purple workers started the experiment on an equal footing, but African Americans have never had a level playing field. As Roland Fryer put it to me, 'Suppose that in 1964, when the Civil Rights Act had passed, there was no discrimination. But there would still have been differences in wealth, in income, in where people lived. It's only been two generations since then. Things don't move that quickly.'

Along with Steven Levitt, the co-author of *Freakonomics*, Ronald Fryer has extensively studied the education of young African-American kids to see how serious a handicap results from a deprived start in life. They found that black children start off at a disadvantage not because they're black, but because they are more likely to start from a difficult family background. Their families tend to be poorer, for instance, and have fewer children's books in the home. Adjust for those characteristics and the difference between kindergarten students disappears. 'Black children and white children with similar family background characteristics start school at similar levels of achievement,' Fryer and Levitt wrote in an article in *Education Next* in the autumn of 2004. The differences some commentators naïvely put down to race are in fact due to differences in class, health, parental education and wealth. There is a huge gap between black kids and white kids arriving at kindergarten, but it is not a racial gap; it is a social one.

Yet even that limited form of equality does not last. Black kids fall behind white kids with a similar background after just a few months at kindergarten, and the disparity continues to widen over time, until the difference between the average black student and the average white student becomes the difference between the average fourth-grader and the average eighth-grader. Could this simply be the result of bad schools? At first, Fryer and Levitt thought so, but as their research progressed they had to abandon even this explanation. A more convincing reason is that the kids are rational: knowing that they will face a hostile job market, just as the purple workers knew they were facing a hostile job market, they do not bother to study.

If that were the only thing holding back African-American students at school, it would be worrying enough: the iron logic of underachievement is all the more difficult to break because it makes rational sense. But there is yet another example of rationality creating a self-perpetuating vicious circle for African-American students, one that is as disturbing – and controversial – as rational racism from employers. It is the phenomenon of 'acting white'.

Democratic National Convention, Boston, Massachusetts, July 2004

Barack Obama's keynote address to the Democratic National Convention propelled him overnight from being the little-known junior senator from Illinois into a media sensation, and anointed him as the great young (black) hope of the Democratic Party. It also brought the phrase 'acting white' firmly into the American consciousness: 'Children can't achieve unless we raise their expectations and turn off the television sets and eradicate the slander that says a black youth with a book is acting white.'

'Acting white' is the controversial idea that studious black kids are regarded as traitors to the race and systematically pilloried by their peers, or perhaps by their parents or other role models. It is a modern example of an older school of thought: that what is really holding back African Americans is African-American culture. That's a hard thing even to say. When the young black economist Glenn Loury delivered a speech in 1984 to veterans of the civil rights establishment, he argued that racism was no

longer the problem: black society's own frailties were. By the end
of the speech, Martin Luther King Jr's widow, Coretta Scott
King, was sobbing quietly.

Controversial as the idea is, it struck Roland Fryer as worth
investigating. To Fryer, as to Loury and to Obama, it made perfect sense to take the possibility of 'acting white' seriously. He
came from a background that was hardly conducive to academic
achievement. Fryer reckons that eight out of ten of his close
family either died young or spent time in jail. Many of his family
produced or dealt crack cocaine, and his cousin was murdered.
Fryer decided to go to college almost by accident. When he was
fifteen, his friends wanted him to go with them on a burglary,
but he cried off, having lost his nerve after being harassed by
white police officers earlier that day. His friends did the burglary
and ended up in jail; Fryer decided to study. Far from being a
source of pride, his newfound academic enthusiasm simply
seemed to be a threat to those who should have supported him.
In an emotional conversation with the writer Stephen Dubner,
Fryer recalled his own father's response to his scholarship to the
University of Texas: 'I don't care how much education you get or
how successful you become, because you'll always be a nigger.'

That bitter reaction was in stark contrast to the encourage-
ment Fryer received from his colleagues at Harvard. Fryer
recalled to me that when Dubner's article exposed Fryer's past to
anyone who picked up the *New York Times Magazine*, 'I didn't
know what my colleagues would think. But the response was one
of being embraced. For the first time in one's life I thought, I can
be myself.'

Wait a moment, though. It might be politically astute for
Barack Obama to condemn 'acting white'. And the 'acting white'
idea, that studious black kids – like the young Glenn Loury or
the young Roland Fryer – are being held back by the disapproval
of those around them, clearly matched Roland Fryer's own experience of growing up. But where's the proof? Various academics
had examined the phenomenon of 'acting white', pinning it

down as a tendency for studious or smart students to be bullied or lose out on friends to a greater extent if they were black than if they were white. However, serious quantitative research, which investigated how popular the more and less successful students actually were, suggested that 'acting white' was simply a myth.

Fryer was not so sure. The previous researchers hadn't considered the basic incentives of the kids being scrutinised. If a researcher with a clipboard comes up and asks you if you have any friends, are you really going to tell him the truth? 'Asking twelve-year-olds how popular they are is tantamount to asking them how much sex they're having,' Fryer has remarked. 'You're going to get an answer, but it's probably not going to be the right one.'

Fryer instead used a survey of ninety thousand students that asked each student to name her friends. Instead of judging a student's popularity by how many friends she claimed to have, he looked at how many other kids had that student on their lists. His results were crystal clear: white kids with good exam results find themselves on a lot of other students' lists of friends. But black kids (and Hispanic kids, too) have more friends if their exam results are middling. Acting white is not a myth.

So much for the proof that this phenomenon exists. What do we make of it? Using 'acting white' as a term of abuse looks like quintessential irrationality. Those who acknowledge it usually blame it on cultural factors. If you're on the left, the 'acting white' slur is the response of a scarred psyche to a racist society. If you're on the right, you might prefer to speak of a victim complex. It takes an economist to realise that the ostracism inherent in 'acting white', while tragic, is perfectly rational.

Here's why. To a typical white student, studying hard does not offer an escape route from the society that surrounds him. His parents, extended family and peers are holding down the kinds of job that come from an education. But as long as African Americans remain disadvantaged and clustered together in ghettos, a black student who studies hard is acquiring the ability to escape from poverty, crime and deprivation – and from those around him. That may not be popular. People don't like to see their friends developing escape plans; even the option to escape makes us nervous.

To reach for an analogy, would you tell an employer that you were training to acquire the skills to switch industries? Say you're a receptionist at an advertising agency, but you're taking night classes in law. Your boss might accept your decision with a shrug, but he's certainly not going to include you in his long-term plans for the department. When he has an internal promotion to hand out, you can bet you won't be near the top of the list, but when there's a compulsory redundancy to be made, you just might be. He knows that you could be on your way out any time you wanted to be. Your option to escape means you can't be relied upon.

Far from being a distinctively African-American phenomenon, it is common for deprived minorities to distrust those who are neglecting community-specific interests in favour of skills valued on the global market place. Fryer points to analogues of 'acting white' in communities as diverse as the British working class (that certainly matches my experience at school), Italian immigrants in Boston's West End, the Maori of New Zealand, and the Burakumin, traditionally Japan's lowest caste. His favourite example is the young child from Catalonia in Spain. Does he learn Catalan, a language spoken and valued only by locals, thus signalling that he'll be a member of the local community for life? Or does he learn computer programming, which is useful in Catalonia but useful everywhere else, too? The latter choice is an escape route, and even if the escape route is never taken, the fact that it is there indicates that the computer geek from Catalonia is not entirely to be trusted. Like a rational employer choosing not to promote the receptionist who is training to become a lawyer, the rational Catalan child will choose not to become best buddies with the programming enthusiast.

The whole sorry stigma of 'acting white', which at first seems to be no more and no less than a cultural disease, turns out to emerge from Von Neumann-style mathematics as unavoidably as the poker bluffs of Chapter Two.

So far, this chapter has painted a grim picture. First, racism can be rational – meaning that while it is appalling, it is profitable for employers. Second, rational racism makes it rational for black kids to study less. Third, the logic of a disadvantaged group rationally sticking together means that those kids who study anyway will be punished for it by their own peers. This is a miserable story, but identifying problems is a first step towards establishing solutions. Since there are so many forces holding back young blacks, no single solution is going to deal with them all. Still, there are some things we can say.

The first is that bureaucracies need to fight harder than most against racism, because they are more prone to it than are firms who face fierce competition. To the extent that racism is taste-based – that is, pure bigotry – private companies are shooting themselves in the feet when they allow racist managers free rein. Competitors will note and exploit biased hiring procedures, snapping up neglected talent. It may take a while, but it is one force we can identify for sure that works against racism. For a government department, no such luck. It's not enough to wait for bigoted departments to go out of business, because they never will. Education and racially enlightened hiring policies are, therefore, all the more important, and given the success of some government agencies in promoting minority employees, such policies can be very successful.

Rational racism – statistical discrimination – needs to be fought in a different way. It can be profitable, and rational firms don't stop doing profitable things unless you change their incentives. One way to do that is to change the statistics: if employers had confidence that black applicants had been given the opportunity to go to a good school, that would discourage them from trying to use statistics to discriminate. Naturally there are plenty of obvious reasons to improve the schools to which black kids have access – but this is one that is not often recognised.

Since blacks are locked into a spiral of negative incentives, we need to work out how to change those incentives. Affirmative action (or positive discrimination) programmes are often thought to dampen the incentives of minority groups to work hard. If you're going to get the job anyway through some affirmative action programme, why work? A badly designed programme certainly could have that effect, but it doesn't have to. Instead, affirmative action could make the difference between a young black kid giving up because he thinks he has no chance, and striving on because he realises that he does have a chance if he studies. Not all affirmative action programmes are alike; what matters is what impact the programme has on incentives. Given the complexities, I am not sure what a successful affirmative action programme would look like, but I am sure that randomised trials, 'Moving to opportunity' style, could pick out some success stories.

Roland Fryer, who was recently appointed 'chief equality officer' of New York City's education department, has also been thinking about more direct incentives. What about paying kids to read? Or paying them more if they get better grades? He has secured the funding to run a big randomised trial with tens of thousands of kids, of all races. Some kids will be paid for their own achievements – say, two dollars to read a book. Others won't be paid at all. Still others will be put into groups and everyone in the group will be paid if the group does well.

This idea is horrifying to conventional wisdom. Psychologist Barry Schwartz attacked Fryer in an op-ed piece in the *New York Times*: 'The assumption that underlies the project is simple: people respond to incentives.'

The trouble, Schwartz continued, was that psychologists had found circumstances in which that wasn't true. He suggested that what schools do instead is rekindle the intrinsic joy of learning; this is inspiring material for an op-ed article, but offers no practical help whatsoever.

Despite what Schwartz implied, Fryer had never made the *assumption* that students would respond to a cash incentive. Instead, he thought it was a possibility worth investigating with a rigorous trial. Schwartz also failed to mention Fryer's suspicion that individual incentives wouldn't work, but group incentives would. The group incentives are exactly the ones that would fight against the problem of 'acting white'. But that's just a theory. The proof will come when the trial has been done. For my money, it's got to be worth a try.

You might reasonably expect that 'acting white' would be a bigger problem in ghettos than in less segregated areas. So you would think it's unequivocally good news that segregation of blacks from non-blacks has been falling sharply since 1970 and is now at its lowest levels since 1920. But things don't seem to be that simple. Recall the research from the last chapter by Lawrence Katz, Jeffrey Kling and Jeffrey Liebman, which showed that while the many benefits of moving from the ghetto to nicer neighbourhoods were significant, improved exam results for children – at least in the short term – were not among them. Roland Fryer's database of school friendships backs this up: it shows that under the surface of apparently integrated schools are highly segregated networks of friends, and that the isolation of hardworking black students is greater in mixed schools than in heavily black schools. Other researchers, surprisingly, failed to find evidence that blacks did worse in segregated areas than when integrated.

That leads to a very pointed question indeed: do ghettos offer advantages to the people who live in them? The obvious answer is 'no', and back in the 1970s, when segregation was at its recent height, Glenn Loury's doctoral thesis argued for that view. His high-octane mathematics showed that, even in the absence of any discrimination at all, as long as people tended to cluster together by race an initial disadvantage for blacks could be perpetuated for ever. To adopt the jargon beloved of social scientists, blacks were at an ongoing disadvantage because they didn't have enough 'social capital' – a catch-all technical term meaning anything from political connections to local support networks. 'Low social capital' meant simply that African Americans were locked in poor neighbourhoods with bad schools, high crime and a peer group that condemned academic success.

On the other hand, minority groups might conceivably benefit from self-segregation because it surrounded them with a supportive community. For example, and it is a trivial but telling example, Kerwin Charles has studied not only imprisonment's effect on marriage markets (as we saw in Chapter Three) but car-pooling. He found that if you are black and you want to share a car with someone on the way to work, you'd better live in a black neighbourhood. Another example: when Bertrand and Mullainathan sent out their black- and white-named CVs, the ones with black names suffered less discrimination from the employers who were based in largely black areas of Chicago.

So what is the answer? Does an ethnic enclave provide support or simply isolation? Economists Ed Glaeser, David Cutler, and Jake Vigdor analysed some fine-grained data on ethnic segregation and quality of life. They concluded that Loury was right to fear for the inhabitants of African-American ghettos, because living in such ghettos damages your quality of life in many ways, from your chances of getting a job to your prospects of doing well at school.

But they also found that ghettos create winners as well as losers: there is a certain kind of person who thrives despite segregation. Such people live near, but not in, the ghettos. They are connectors, bridge-builders, members of minority groups who live outside the ghetto and link it to the outside world. Vigdor believes that such people are entrepreneurs benefiting from selling services into the segregated community, or employing its members to produce something for the wider world. The importance of bridge-builders and social connectors is now well known. The sociologist Mark Granovetter showed, as an example, that many people found out about new job openings not via close friends, who tended to know exactly the same things they did, but through acquaintances who could link them to news from other communities.

What Cutler, Glaeser and Vigdor showed that is encouraging is that these social connectors, members of an ethnic minority who lived near but not in a ghetto, were not only doing very well for themselves but were growing in number. That has to be good news. It is also rational: if it is profitable to act as a bridge between an ethnic enclave and the rest of the world, small wonder that more and more people are seeking out that role.

Glaeser and Vigdor also confirmed that the fall in segregation was being driven by the growth of new, more integrated communities. Those communities were dynamic, with rapidly growing black populations and rapidly growing economies. Places that showed little improvement between 1990 and 2000 included Detroit and New Orleans. Places that showed a marked fall in segregation included boom towns such as Las Vegas, Phoenix and Austin. In other words, segregation was not being eroded because the old ghettos were becoming integrated, but because more and more African Americans were finding jobs and homes in traditionally white communities.

Just as market forces may eventually undermine taste-based discrimination, so the impetus of economic growth in dynamic cities is providing an unexpected solution to the age-old problem of segregation. The question then becomes how to get more of that dynamism, and in more places. How do you help city economies thrive? We'll hunt for answers in the next chapter.

Seven

The world is spiky

I want to be a part of it – New York, New York.

– 'New York, New York,' lyrics by Fred Ebb

Manhattan, New York

Pity the hardworking residents of New York City. 'Our dollar looks the same as the better-known US version, but it doesn't go nearly as far here as anywhere else,' grumbles the New York-based financial journalist Daniel Gross, who goes on to provide some rough-and-ready calculations. For a New Yorker to buy or rent a home similar to those readily available elsewhere in the United States would cost an extra 14 per cent of her income. Higher taxes add up to almost 6 per cent of income; high prices for utilities, groceries and other basics cost another 4 per cent. Then there are lifestyle costs. These are much harder to compare because, as Gross points out, New York is 'a city with the best of everything'. But he gamely tots up the prices of cultural experiences such as good seats at a baseball game or dinner at a nice restaurant, and shows that they are twice those of comparable activities in Minneapolis. The bottom line: a New York dollar is worth 61.2 cents. Now, it's true that New York wages are higher than the national average, but only by about 15 per cent. The real purchasing power of the typical New Yorker is only about three-quarters of what it would be if he or she lived somewhere else in the United States.

Somewhere like Rock Island, Illinois, perhaps. Gross points out that Rock Island offers a far more advantageous combination of low prices and high-ish wages. Now, clearly nothing is stopping anyone moving from Manhattan to Rock Island, or preventing immigrants or new college graduates from choosing to put down roots in Rock Island in the first place. But they don't. Since we can assume these are rational people, that tells me we can also assume that Rock Island must really suck. (Sorry, Rock Islanders, it's nothing personal. I know nothing about your town – except that you evidently can't pay New Yorkers to live there.) Since some rational people prefer an expensive New York to a cheap Rock Island, New York must be offering them something that money cannot buy – or more accurately, something that money can buy only indirectly.

Whatever that is, it seems to be something that tends to be in greater supply the bigger a city gets. Ed Glaeser, the Harvard-based economist who specialises in the study of cities, crunched numbers from across the United States and found that Gross's findings about New York apply to most large cities: while average earnings are higher in larger cities, the cost of living is higher yet. As a rule of thumb, each doubling of city size raises wages by 10 per cent but raises prices by 16 per cent.

So what is going on here? Why do people live in tiny apartments in places like Manhattan, panicking over mortgage payments or rent, when they could instead have a spacious home in Rock Island? They could sell up and move to a sprawling ranch out in the wilderness, or to a cheap city such as Detroit, where you could pick up a house for sixty thousand dollars. They don't. Is there a rational explanation?

Yes, there is. And the explanation is more important than simply explaining the demography of Rock Island. It tells us about what really happens in successful cities: innovation. This chapter is about trying to understand how, why and whether there is anything we can or should do to make cities more successful and more innovative. But make no mistake, new ideas of any kind are, ultimately, what cities produce. Indeed, the reason why people live in big and thriving cities is also the reason why you're reading this book – in the sense that I might otherwise never have come to be in a position to write it.

Washington, DC, April 2004

I first met Stephen McGroarty in a windowless meeting room in one of the World Bank's quieter office buildings. He stood out immediately among the earnest, bookish, charisma-free World Bank staff. He had a huge, full-face smile; he was full of ideas that he wanted to share first and evaluate later; he was exuberant, a real person, a people person. His enthusiasm was so tangible that you got the feeling he was within an inch of giving somebody in the meeting a hug. I was bowled over immediately.

Stephen is a good friend these days, but that's not the only reason I have to be grateful that I bumped into him. When I met him, I was busily failing to interest publishers in my proposal for a book called *The Undercover Economist*. But Stephen, an experienced publisher himself, was bursting with enthusiasm for my book idea. Actually, he was bursting with enthusiasm for pretty much everything: Guinness, the 18th Street Lounge, my baby daughter, the latest seminar he'd been to. 'This is so hot!' he exclaimed, waving my rolled-up proposal in the air. Sadly, it wasn't – until he cheerfully advised me exactly how to change it. A few weeks later, it was on the publication track.

Now, my friendship with Stephen feels pretty special. Of course, it isn't. (Sorry, Stephen.) This is the sort of thing that happens when you live in a city. You meet an interesting person at a party, or get introduced to them in the street or at a business meeting. You discover some connection, some shared interest or friend. You keep the connection going; perhaps it turns into a firm friendship, perhaps a more businesslike, cordial acquaintance. Perhaps the connection leads to a job offer or a deal. More likely, it is just making you a smarter person, because both of you are learning from each other every time you meet. That is important but hardly remarkable, because there is always something to learn from other people. And where do other people live? In cities. I was lucky to bump into Stephen, but if I'd lived and worked in a small town instead, luck wouldn't have come into it. By their very nature, small towns cannot offer the same opportunities to meet such a variety of people. (As the new-media pundit Jeff Jarvis commented after bumping into Rupert Murdoch on a Manhattan street, 'Who needs a network when you have New York?')

It is one of those rationally self-reinforcing trends we've met so often in the last two chapters. Not only do cities allow people to learn from one another, but the people who have most to gain from that process – people who depend on making connections and on the skills they can learn from watching others, anyone from restaurateurs to investment bankers – are the people most likely to be drawn in by the big cities.

The idea that a successful city is a kind of University of Life, a place to learn from others, has implications well beyond the fact that Manhattan is expensive and Rock Island is not. If that is the reason – or even one important reason – why people flock to cities, it implies that large cities should be hives of intellectual activity and innovation. That is an idea that was championed by Alfred Marshall, the intellectual leader of the Cambridge University economics department and the author of a textbook that was to bring economics into the twentieth century, *Principles of Economics*. Writing in 1890, Marshall was firmly convinced that dense clusters of industry were natural breeding grounds for new ideas:

Great are the advantages which people following the same skilled trade get from near neighbourhood to one another. The mysteries of the trade become no mysteries; but are as it

were in the air, and children learn many of them unconsciously. Good work is rightly appreciated, inventions and
improvements in machinery, in processes and the general
organisation of the business have their merits promptly discussed: if one man starts a new idea, it is taken up by others
and combined with suggestions of their own; and thus it
becomes the source of further new ideas.

Marshall's idea was intuitive, and, as we shall see, contains more
than a kernel of truth. It identifies vibrant cities as the ultimate
source of innovation and progress, fundamental to civilisation.

But Marshall's analysis also suggests a problem. If ideas are
just 'in the air', then when I learn something just by hanging
around other people, they don't get paid for that no matter how
valuable the experience is to me. I might value a lesson learned
at fifty or a hundred or a thousand pounds, but the teacher will
not be paid – and if the teacher is rational, that means that there
will be fewer lessons offered than there should be. In this
respect, ideas are not like, say, hot dogs. If I am willing to pay
two pounds for a hot dog and hot dogs cost a pound to make,
ship and cook, then you can bet that a free market will get that
hot dog to me for a price somewhere between two pounds and
one pound. With an idea there is no such guarantee.

For example, when I learned how to write a decent book proposal and where to send it, all Stephen McGroarty got in
repayment from me was a pint or two of Guinness, and possibly
the vague sense that I owed him a favour. Another example: after
I knew my book was to be published, I started to make a habit of
attending book talks to pick up some tips for the forthcoming
promotional tour. It cost me nothing at all to receive a lesson in
how to give a book talk from James Surowiecki, author of *The
Wisdom of Crowds*, at my local bookshop. It's hard to imagine
how he might try to charge soon-to-be authors to hear his book
talks while letting mere potential buyers of his own tome
through the doors for nothing.

Neither service is as easy to package and market as a hot dog. That means there exist potentially publishable authors with lousy proposals and potentially eloquent authors who are insufficiently skilled in the art of book talks, but there isn't anyone with two pounds in their pocket and an unfulfillable desire for a hot dog.

These are what economists call 'externalities' or 'spillovers'. Usually we think of externalities as being 'negative'. A classic example is traffic: when nobody has to pay to drive on the roads, the roads are too congested; people drive more than they would if they were charged for the cost of delays they were causing to others. But just as important, perhaps much more important, are 'positive externalities' – nobody has to pay for book talk lessons from James Surowiecki, so he gives out fewer lessons than he would if he were fairly rewarded. This particular positive externality is called, for an obvious enough reason, a 'knowledge spillover'. Knowledge spillovers sound wonderful, but as we learned on Hackney Downs in Chapter Five, they are only wonderful if they happen. Without fair payment for all these implicit lessons, many potential teachers and role models will rationally retire to the country, or stay in with the PlayStation in the evenings. If the biggest cities are hotbeds of underpriced education lessons, shouldn't we be subsidising them, for exactly the same reasons we should be taxing people according to how much they congest the roads?

Let's hold on a minute, though. All I've given you so far as evidence for positive externalities and knowledge spillovers are a couple of anecdotes about my first book. You might understandably be sceptical about whether this amounts to much – positive externalities are invisible, after all, and consequently hard to measure. But there is a way we can try to put a cash figure on the invisible benefits of living in a dynamic city. It's a topic that dominates many a dinner-party conversation, and one that I introduced at the very start of this book: house prices.

Hackney, London, 2006

There's plenty to like about living in London, including the company of friends, decent cafés and a choice of interesting jobs to do – or at least, to apply for. But you may recall from this book's preface some aspects of my neighbourhood that I'd be keen to move away from: my local amenities include a 'massage parlour', a kebab shop, a fried-chicken joint, betting shops and junkyards. Clearly, the externalities of living in cities are a mixed bag. How does one weigh the negative against the positive? That's simple. Ask an estate agent.

So I did. I asked one of the most successful local estate agents, Anne Currell, what sort of local features might really bring down the value of a house. She suggested 'massage parlours', kebab shops, fried chicken joints, betting shops and junkyards. Our house prices are therefore a great measure of the extent to which my neighbours and I must value the positive externalities of living close to more desirable London amenities, because the house price is a summary of everything potential buyers think is likely to make them happy or miserable. How much value do we place on that local crack den, say, when compared against an extra bedroom and a shorter commute? That kind of judgement is, as many of us know from experience, a complicated one. Currell told me of one case where a beautiful house lost several possible buyers when it became clear that the pub two doors down might gain a licence to stay open late. People weren't keen on the noise of revellers, the stink of stale beer, and the emptying of bottle bins in the early hours. These negative externalities were remarkably local: a similar home a couple of doors further away was unaffected, and rationally so. Currell estimated that the loss to the nearer seller was 5 per cent or so; with the house being valued at about a million pounds, that's about fifty thousand quid. Meanwhile, people buying houses in the next street paid more, not less, for convenient access to a pub.

The estate agent's motto 'location, location, location' sums up the simple reality that what's around a house determines its price (and its rental value) more than the size and quality of the house itself. As long as the housing market is fairly competitive, with many buyers and sellers scrambling to get the best deal, then the rent payable on a flat is a good measure of how much that flat's surroundings are worth. Externalities, in a city, are almost everything; and just as an aerosol spray can reveal a laser beam, house prices or rents make these invisible externalities visible.

The idea of using rents to measure the externalities in cities was proposed by Robert Lucas in 1985. Lucas was speaking, appropriately enough, at the prestigious Marshall Lectures, named in honour of Alfred Marshall. At the time, Lucas was world renowned for his study of monetary economics and the business cycle. But rather than talking about the subjects that had made him famous, he instructed the Cambridge dons on the implications of Marshall's theory of innovation. Lucas titled his lectures 'On the Mechanics of Economic Development'. He wanted to know why some countries grow rich while others stay poor. And he emphasised an idea from his Chicago colleague, Gary Becker: 'human capital' – education, training and skill – is important.

When, in 1959, Becker first proposed the idea that people invested in education and training the way they might invest in a business or the stock market, even other economists were scandalised. Education was thought to be its own reward, and have nothing to do with a rational investment in one's own productivity. But Becker's view later became the consensus; as he remarked to me, no politician can get elected these days without talking about the importance of building human capital. By the time Lucas discussed the idea in his Marshall Lecture, it was widely accepted.

Lucas, however, had a new take on human capital and its importance for development. He thought that one of the most important ways in which countries grew rich was through human capital spillovers – or, to use Marshall's more elegant phrase, the very knowledge 'in the air'. Countries that somehow created an environment in which smart, well-educated people could learn from one another would tend to grow rich. (This is an idea we'll return to right at the end of the book.) But what might that learning environment be? Cities, of course.

It was almost as an afterthought in his speech that Lucas turned his attention to the problem of measuring knowledge 'in the air'. 'What can people be paying Manhattan or downtown Chicago rents *for*,' he asked, 'if not for being near other people?'

Like much good economics, it was a bold, brilliant and over-simplified idea. Yes, Manhattan rents are the price you rationally pay for being near other people, but perhaps not just because you expect to learn from them. How much of big-city rents can we really attribute to payments for lessons at the University of Life?

Let's start by considering the possible objection that, instead of the kind of knowledge spillovers that Lucas was talking about, high city rents instead represent access to such things as the opera or museums or a variety of nice restaurants. That's certainly true to an extent – but I'd argue that for most people the difference in the cost of living is so high that 'cities are fun' is only part of the story. For instance, renting a nice two-bedroom flat in Greenwich Village might easily set you back five thousand dollars a month. A similar-sized place in Rock Island would be closer to five hundred a month. The difference is $150 a day. Just how often do people plan on going to the opera anyway? Sure, Manhattan's restaurant scene is better than Rock Island's, but if Manhattan residents are really paying for access to restaurants then they are paying $150 to their landlord for every evening his nicely located place puts them close to a decent restaurant. You'd need to eat out an awful lot to make these figures seem halfway plausible.

I admit, by living in a more downmarket area of New York you can enjoy some of the benefits of the city at a lower price, but only by accepting high crime, painful commutes and awful schools. Residents of smaller towns don't need to brave these terrors to get cheap rents.

Another reason to doubt the idea that high city rents represent access to cultural amenities is that most of the cultural amenities have their own price tags. True, nobody except your landlord can charge you for the pleasure of the Manhattan skyline or the buzz of walking down the street, but would you really pay $150 a day for that buzz? As for the owners of restaurants and theatres, they are well aware that if they provide a high-quality product in cities, they can charge a high price for it over and above the rent you pay to your landlord.

These are common-sense justifications for the view that high city rents are more about learning everything the city can teach than about access to good Vietnamese takeaways. And there is solid evidence to back up the common-sense view. Ed Glaeser found it by looking not at rents but at wages. We've seen that the high wages in big cities do not compensate workers for the higher prices – but from the perspective of the firms who pay these wages, the high salary expense is perfectly real. The New York dollar might be worth only sixty-one cents to a New Yorker, but to the firm employing her, a dollar is a dollar. So why do those firms put up with paying such high salaries when they could move to small towns and hire workers more cheaply there? Cities might be a lot of fun, but that doesn't explain high city wages. The only rational justification is that workers in big cities are more productive in some way.

There are three possible reasons why that might be. The first is that New Yorkers and Londoners are just smarter than rural hicks and that is why they earn more. All big-city folk are secretly convinced this is true, but it isn't. When you compare like with like – say, a pair of accountants, one in New York and one in Rock Island, but each with a professional qualification and five years' experience – then the wage gap only shrinks a little. It's possible that the two accountants are different in ways that the statistics just can't measure, but you would expect the attempt to make a like-for-like comparison would go a long way to closing the gap. It doesn't.

A second explanation is that the New York accountants are more productive not because they're inherently smarter, but because they happen to be lumped together within walking distance of one another, which saves on the time and trouble of organising meetings. But wage patterns don't support that idea. Looking at individual workers who move from the city to the country or vice versa, you'll find that wages don't change moving either way: move a New York lawyer to Rock Island and he keeps the wage he had before. (Actually, movers in either direction get a small one-off pay rise. That's no surprise: people offered pay rises are more likely to move.) That suggests the New York wage premium is not about saving on taxi fares, nor a payment for being smart.

Here is what is really going on. Whenever workers are in big cities, their wages grow faster. Move to the country and you keep your higher wage, but the rate of growth slows down. Move back to the city and the pay rises start to mount up again. The real city wage premium is not actually paid to people who work in cities, but to people who did work in cities for long periods of time, whether or not they still do. There is one simple explanation for this pattern: when people are in cities, they are getting smarter quickly because they are learning from one another. Lucas and Marshall were quite right: learning really is invisibly hanging 'in the air' in cities. And looking at how wages change allows you to see the invisible.

But the world is changing. Marshall was writing less than a decade after the invention of the telephone; even Lucas was speaking several years before the development of the World Wide Web, and could scarcely have imagined Facebook or the BlackBerry. Are ubiquitous, cheap and powerful new communications technologies eroding the special advantages of cities? And if so, will cities continue to be centres of learning in the future as they have been in the past?

Lake District, November 2006

Much of this book was written in the British Library in central London, but I am typing these words up in the scenic Lake District, a five-hour drive away. It is an appropriate place to contemplate the much-discussed death of cities. After all, if cities are all about the spread of knowledge, then modern technology, which allows knowledge to be transmitted over long distances, is surely making them a phenomenon of the past. A famous study by economists Adam Jaffe, Manuel Trajtenberg and Rebecca Henderson provides some more fascinating direct evidence of knowledge spillover in cities. Studying the official records at the Patent Office, they found that patents that cited an earlier invention were between two and six times more likely to originate in the same city as the 'parent' patent than you would expect if ideas spread effortlessly around the world. But that study was carried out at the end of the last century. Digital technology, the whole purpose of which is to spread ideas effortlessly around the world, has progressed enormously even since then. So the knowledge spillover effects of cities, and thus their *raison d'être*, must be on the wane. Right?

It is not difficult to tell stories that appear, at first sight, to support this idea. After all, what have I done since I arrived in the Lake District a few days ago? I have been engaged in a knowledge-intensive activity: researching the economics of cities. The mere fact that I am able to do this suggests that the economics of cities are changing. I have better access to academic research here than in the British Library (or at least cheaper – the Internet charges there are outrageous). Here on the slopes above Lake Windermere, with access to online versions of the top journals, I can read almost any academic paper I could want. I also easily and cheaply reached Adam Jaffe at his home in Massachusetts, having found his contact details on the Internet. I dropped him a quick e-mail and called him for a chat the next day.

In short, what I seem to need to do my knowledge-intensive work is a wireless signal, a mobile phone and a quiet spot – something in much greater supply here in the Lake District than in London. Small wonder that many commentators are arguing that digital technologies are making cities things of the past. But there's an often-overlooked thing to remember here: commentators like me are not necessarily the best people to judge whether modern communication is making cities obsolete. The writers, academics and consultants who get so excited about these changes are exactly the people whose lives have benefited most quickly and immediately from them. So we need to think a bit harder.

I put the idea that cities are becoming irrelevant for innovation to Adam Jaffe. 'Poppycock,' he responded. His own work suggests that the geography of knowledge is becoming more concentrated, not less. In fact, few economists believe that information technology is going to kill off cities and the local concentration of knowledge they provide.

To see the reason, consider a world where it is expensive to move stuff around: muddy roads, horse-drawn carts, highwaymen, and other problems mean that long-distance trade is prohibitively costly. In such a world, it would be rational to produce most goods locally. There would be few big cities because it would be expensive to move food to them and expensive to move manufactured goods away from them to pay for the food. That is why cities have always been dependent on the best possible transport network; all roads lead to Rome.

Now imagine that it gets easier to move things around. The cities can grow. More food is shipped from further away, the city produces more specialised manufactured products, and can then sell them to distant customers. The 'death of distance' doesn't make the world flatter, it makes it spikier, with evermore activity taking place in big cities. When transport costs fall, rational people don't spread out into the countryside, they cluster together in cities, or at least in suburbs. Historically, that has been true for transporting basic goods such as food, and for transporting people, including commuters. Is it also true for transporting ideas?

It seems so. The more knowledge-intensive an industry is, the more that industry is concentrated in a small area. Industries that use particularly skilled workers also tend to cluster together. Looking at the location of over four thousand commercial innovations, developed all over the United States, economists have found that over half came from just three areas: clusters of innovation in California, New York–New Jersey and Massachusetts. Industries were concentrated there, high-technology industries even more so, and actual innovations were concentrated most of all. The effect is even more dramatic within a particular field. Almost half of all computing breakthroughs were developed in California. Almost half of all American pharmaceutical innovations were invented in New Jersey, a state with less than 3 per cent of the US population. It's a spiky world.

And it makes sense that the world should be getting even spikier. Contrast two of the world's leading companies, Exxon and Microsoft. Old-economy Exxon has operations across the planet, drilling, refining and selling petroleum products. New-economy Microsoft can dominate the global market for software from a campus on the outskirts of Seattle. Most high-tech companies are concentrated in a small number of innovative hot spots. Admittedly, Silicon Valley is not as compact as Manhattan, but Silicon Valley firms are now reaching across the global economy from one small site in a way that even the sugar and garment industries of New York were not able to do.

The world economy is ever more composed of two sorts of highly transportable goods. There are those that can be produced in one place and shipped anywhere very cheaply; even shop displays are now being assembled in China and transported intact to distant cities all over the world. Other 'goods' are even easier to transport: they are instructions for making a new drug or a new designer handbag. The physical product may or may not be made locally, but it is the instructions that have the true value.

Either way, the transportability of these goods means that local clusters of industry – London's financial markets, Italy's fashion houses, Seattle's software companies – are larger and more important than they were when transport costs were higher. While many of the products we consume come from the other side of the world, they do not come from telecommuters in converted farmhouses. They come from distant cities.

Apart from these easily transportable products, there is the rapidly growing service sector. Its growth is partly the result of an apparent paradox: more jobs tend to be created in industries that are *not* enjoying productivity improvements. Cars are made by robots, but restaurant meals are still served by humans, blood tests are still performed by nurses, and taxis still have drivers. We have become so effective at manufacturing that these days we spend all our time creating services for one another. And while you can get a haircut or consult a doctor even in a very small town, if you want to see the top stylist or be treated by the best neurosurgeon – or, just as important, if you want to learn from these experts – you will have to seek out a big city. Advanced city economies spend a little effort producing 'weightless' products that will be consumed the world over, and a lot of effort taking in one another's washing. We've become so good at producing those manufactures that they're becoming a marginal factor in jobs and income, even if a major factor in the quality of our lives. Far from being the mark of decadence, our booming service economy is a symptom of economic sophistication.

Anyone who believes that communications technologies will kill off cities believes implicitly that these technologies are a substitute for face-to-face contact. According to this view, instead of having coffee with someone I will phone them or write an e-mail, or even download information from their website without engaging in any two-way communication.

But that is an assumption well worth questioning. What if these communication technologies are not substitutes for face-to-face contact at all, but instead encourage them? For instance, as I write, I can see that my friend Seamus McCauley is in central London. This is thanks to a service called 'BuddyPing', which lets you track anyone over the Web – with their permission – via their mobile phone. On his blog (of course) Seamus comments:

> One of the things that now strikes me about BuddyPing is what a mockery it makes of my delusion that I don't see some people I like because they're too far away. On my list of friends are just two people more than seven leagues from my current location. Good lord, we could all be in the same pub in half an hour if we downed tools right now and just got on with it.

I know that Seamus often puts this idea into practice, and if I were in London I could join him, signing up to receive a text message whenever he ventured within a mile of my location. Far from being a substitute for a face-to-face meeting, a high-tech service such as BuddyPing could be the only reason that the meeting happens at all. But when I'm up in the Lakes, it's of no use to know exactly where in London Seamus is. The technology has increased the benefit of being in London, not reduced it.

Within any given relationship, more communication now takes place through digital channels. At the same time, these digital channels make it easier to meet new people, to maintain old relationships, and to arrange to meet up. To put it in the economic jargon, digital communications might just as easily be a complement of face-to-face meetings as a substitute for them. And if digital technology is a complement of face-to-face meetings, it is also a complement of the cities that make such meetings easier. Cities were always great places to bump into interesting people, but modern technology turns serendipity into something more like a guarantee: thanks to the Internet and your mobile phone, you don't just hope to meet interesting people in a city, you can scarcely avoid them.

The BuddyPing technology is an example of how communications technology helps people meet face-to-face. Other everyday examples are the impromptu mobile-phone call ('I was just in the area and wondered if you had time to pop out for coffee' – much easier, quicker and less intrusive than knocking on the door) and the get-together arranged through e-mail or social networking technology, such as Facebook. When I was at college, back in the days when mobile phones were brick-heavy curiosities, you would meet a friend by walking across town in the hope of finding her in. Often you would fail and leave a hopeful note on her door. Even that flawed system would have been unworkable in London. But e-mail and mobile phones have made it easy to arrange to meet people in these larger cities. Where once they were too big to work well, now they are easier to manage. A look at the data supports this argument. In both the United States and Japan most phone calls are made to people who live or work just a few miles away. As for e-mail, a recent study of its use and productivity concluded that the most productive employees were not the ones who sent and received a lot of external e-mail, but the ones with the largest network of e-mail communications *inside* the company.

New technology also helps you pick the right people out of a big crowd, meaning that when you do meet people face-to-face you enjoy it – or profit from it – more than you would have done. Yes, the Web makes it is easy to exchange e-mails with Viggo Mortensen fans all over the world; but it also makes it much easier to find the Viggo fans *in your own city* and meet up to discuss the great man over a beer. On niche dating sites – from SeniorPeopleMeet to BBW Datefinder, for 'Big Beautiful Women' and their admirers – you can meet people with tastes to match yours.

Don't tell me that Internet dating is supposed to be a substitute for face-to-face contact. And if face-to-face contact is the aim, what's the point in this new ability to make connections if the people you connect with live hundreds of miles away? In all of these cases, the high-tech, distance-free forms of communication help your social life much more if you live in New York than if you live in Nebraska – with the possible exception of the (real) online dating site FarmersOnly.com.

Communications technology also seems to stimulate more local collaboration. Just look at jointly written academic papers. In the 1960s, economists rarely produced joint work (just 12 per cent of published articles in the top economics journals had two authors) but by the 1990s joint work was more common than not. And while many of these new papers were written by collaborators from different states or even different countries, half of them were written by collaborators who lived and worked near to one another. More long-range communication does not mean less local communication.

And even those long-range collaborations strengthen the importance of cities. Since the 1980s, business air travel – which was supposed to have been wiped out by faxes, cheap phone calls, e-mail and video-conferencing – has grown 50 per cent faster than the US economy as a whole. Like friendships, business relationships can be maintained and arranged using communications technology, but this simply encourages more meetings in person. And what sort of travel is air travel? It is a journey from one city to another.

It's true that modern communications technology is allowing some forms of work that once had to be done in the city to be done in the countryside. But as we've seen, it also allows the most efficient suppliers – be they New York advertisers, London financiers, Milanese designers or Bangalore's software engineers – to reach anywhere in the world. It makes cities more manageable, unlocking their diversity as a source of friendship and of business, and encourages global travel that links one city to another. Throw in the increasing importance of the service sector, and the fact that services are more varied and high quality in cities, and the rational conclusion is inescapable: cities are likely to enter a new golden age.

New York, 1920s

We've seen how cities are hubs of innovation and learning, and the foundation of all modern economic development. But this chapter and the last have also been peppered with occasional references to struggling cities, such as Detroit and New Orleans – about which I'll have more to say in a moment. Clearly, not all cities are equal in terms of bringing benefits to their residents. So what sort of city is the most successful and the most innovative, and what sort is the most likely to spiral into the rationally self-reinforcing decline that we'll examine in the next section?

Jane Jacobs (we met her in Chapter Five) thought she had the answer in the person of Mrs Ida Rosenthal, a Manhattan seamstress who tailored dresses for affluent customers in the boom years before the Great Depression:

> She was dissatisfied with the way the dresses she made hung on her customers. To improve the fit, she began experimenting with improvements to underclothing and the result was the first brassiere. . . . Mrs Rosenthal dropped dressmaking to devote herself to manufacturing, wholesaling and distributing brassieres.

Jacobs then describes 3M's move from abrasives to unsuccessful sandpaper (the glue didn't work) to all kinds of adhesives and thus 'shoe tape, electrical tape, acetate tape . . . acetate fiber tape, cellophane tape, printed cellophane tape, plastic tape, filament tape, sound-recording tape' and 'sandblasting stencils, automotive adhesives, industrial adhesives'.

For Jacobs, the essence of innovation was cross-pollination, the leaping of an idea from one industry to another, or the generation of a whole new industry. It was supported by the city environment and the diverse set of services such an environment provided. Mrs Rosenthal could probably not have succeeded without being able to rely on various 'shippers, sewing machine suppliers, box makers, textile suppliers, bankers and so on'. Outsourcing is not as modern a phenomenon as some would have you believe.

If we want to understand how the most successful, innovative cities work, it's important to establish whether Jacobs was right. She believed that innovative cities were ones that were home to all sorts of different companies, cheek by jowl. The proximity of different industries was the sort of thing that had created the brassiere and countless other business ideas.

Not everyone sees innovation that way. The business guru Michael Porter, writing thirty years after Jacobs, also recognised the importance of ideas jumping from one company to another. But he thought the most productive type of city was one where all the companies were similar, all learning from one another and using a deep pool of specialised local expertise to make many tiny improvements in similar processes: winemaking, tailoring or developing medical equipment.

Alfred Marshall himself, who had strongly emphasised the role of cities in innovation, had a different view from both Jacobs and Porter. While they both pointed to small, competing companies, Marshall thought that innovation would be quicker in large, dominant ones. It was almost as though he could see a hundred years ahead to the age of near-monopolists such as Google, Microsoft and Intel. His reasoning was simple: if ideas spill over from one person to another, or from one team to another, then small companies will be reluctant to invest too much in producing new ideas because they will soon be copied by competitors. A titan like Microsoft could hire large numbers of smart people and have the confidence that the ideas they were sparking in one another were more likely to remain in-house. Big firms such as Microsoft could afford to spend more money and devote more employee time to research, so such firms should be centres of innovation.

A group of four economists, once more including Ed Glaeser, put together a set of data designed to try to establish which of these three views is correct. Should we expect a city like Seattle, with big, powerful companies such as Starbucks and Microsoft, to do well – Alfred Marshall's view? Or a city like Boston, home to a cluster of small firms that all operate in the medical services industry, as Michael Porter argues? Or a city like Los Angeles or New York, each with several competitive industries (where even the biggest companies have big competitors) allowing for the transfer of ideas from one to another, as Jane Jacobs claimed?

Glaeser and his colleagues looked at 170 American cities over three decades, and compared the fortunes of each industry depending on its setting. Some industries were growing quickly, of course, and others were in decline, but whenever an industry was concentrated in a city at first, it tended to decline more quickly than elsewhere, or grow more slowly than elsewhere. Industries seemed to thrive in a diversified city environment and wither away in company towns. Both Porter and Marshall would predict the reverse: strength builds strength, according to their theories, so that a traditionally dominant industry should grow even faster. Jacobs, at least according to this evidence, wins the argument.

Porter and Marshall seem to have been wrong to believe that innovative strength came from specialisation. However, Glaeser and his colleagues did find support for Porter's and Jacobs' faith in competition. They believed that small firms, fighting for survival, were more likely to innovate. Indeed, the fastest-growing industries were also those in cities where more firms were competing with one another.

Nor is this the only sense in which diversity is good for cities: immigrants seem to boost the productivity of cities, too. In the

US cities that enjoyed an increasing share of foreign-born residents between 1970 and 1990, the wages and house prices rose for US-born citizens in the same cities. The chain of causation seems to run from diversity to productivity rather than the other way around, and the most plausible explanation is that cultural diversity, one way or another, makes cities more productive.

Unlikely as it might seem, then, colossal, diverse cities such as New York and Los Angeles, far from being relics of a bygone age, are the likely innovative powerhouses of the future. The real estate market in Manhattan and similar hot spots backs up that view. But for some other cities, it is a sadly different story.

New Orleans, Louisiana, 29 August 2005

By midday on the day Hurricane Katrina made landfall, the city was in desperate trouble. The levees had been breached and much of the city was already under water. The disaster unfolded with the world watching.

But for those who had been paying attention to New Orleans, behind the charming tourism scene and before the camera crews arrived, it was evident that the city had been in a desperate state for years. When Katrina hit, over a quarter of the city's population lived beneath the poverty line and nearly three-quarters of its state schools were rated 'unacceptable' or were under 'academic warning' from the state of Louisiana. In 2004, university researchers persuaded the New Orleans police to head into the city one afternoon and shoot off a quick seven hundred blanks – without provoking a single call to report the shootings.

New Orleans is not the only once-great city that has been struggling. Baltimore, Buffalo, Cleveland, St Louis, Pittsburgh and Philadelphia all shrank in every decade from 1950 on. In the United Kingdom, Liverpool lost almost half its population between 1937 and 2001. But the quintessential emblem of urban misery is surely Detroit, a city that has lost more than half its people since 1950 and whose population has declined faster than anywhere else in the United States. Next to faded glories such as the Masonic Temple of Detroit lie decrepit warehouses or vast abandoned lots. While there are still wealthy suburbs, it seems that land in Detroit's city centre is so valueless that it might as well be left fallow.

Real estate economist Joe Gyourko, with Ed Glaeser, explicitly recognised this decay when they began circulating a paper with the subtitle 'Why Does Anyone Still Live in Detroit?' (Perhaps because of a belated outbreak of tact, they eventually removed the subtitle.) After all, being stuck in Detroit is not like being stuck in North Korea or Zimbabwe. It is easy to move to where the weather is better, the skies are broader, and there are jobs galore. Why didn't everyone leave?

The answer is that houses in Detroit, St Louis and other fading cities are cheap. Gyourko estimates that a house that would cost at least eighty thousand dollars to build could be picked up for much less than that in much of Detroit, where the typical house price is around sixty thousand dollars and many homes are cheaper still. 'There's no builder who would build those today,' Gyourko told the *New York Times Magazine*. The acres of derelict land next to Detroit's Masonic Temple are testament to that.

But because the houses last for many decades, the price can fall and fall until it is low enough to suck people into failing cities. The housing stock in pre-Katrina New Orleans, for instance, was far older than the national average: just one in ten houses had been built in the previous twenty-five years, compared with one in three nationwide.

It is not hard to see what kind of person is rationally attracted by a city with cheap houses but no good jobs: people who have already retired, or people with few skills, or people whose skills were once in demand but have fallen out of favour because of technological change or global competition. For those people, the likely alternative to a cheap house and no job is an expensive house in a more dynamic city, but still no certainty of a good job. Sixty thousand dollars wouldn't buy a broom closet in Manhattan, but highly skilled people value the opportunities provided by a dynamic city, even though the cost may be high. Hedge fund partners don't move to Detroit to save on rent.

The result is yet another rationally self-reinforcing trend, this time a vicious circle: struggling cities attract people with low skills, which means that they are unlikely to create the sort of exuberant innovation seen in more successful cities; and the more that modern economies depend on people with skills, the more serious and insuperable these disadvantages are likely to become.

That might explain the apparently heartless reaction of many urban economists to the devastation of New Orleans. They saw struggling cities as a trap: deprived people with limited opportunities would be sucked in by the attraction of cheap housing, and find themselves surrounded by other deprived people with limited opportunities. The destruction of New Orleans was, without doubt, a disaster, but the two hundred billion dollars or so the government seemed to be mobilising for compensation and rebuilding provided an opportunity to create something better than before.

Yet plans to rebuild New Orleans as it was before were simply plans to rebuild the trap and pay victims to move back into it. Glaeser was aghast: he argued that the money should be spent not on the city but on the citizens. A generous handout to everybody who was displaced by the hurricane would give them the opportunity to rebuild their lives anywhere they chose – which might include New Orleans but didn't have to. Other economists agreed. They were far more interested in the people who had once lived in New Orleans than in the abstract concept of the city itself. Steven Landsburg, writing in *Slate*, reckoned that there was enough money earmarked for reconstruction to pay eight hundred thousand dollars to each family of four, no strings attached. George Horwich, a Purdue-based economist who studied the recovery of Kobe after its appalling earthquake in 1995 (the death toll was in excess of six thousand people, over three times more than were killed by Hurricane Katrina), made a similar argument. He felt that the city was almost certainly finished and that the victims of the hurricane should have the freedom to choose how to spend any compensation they received. 'Don't make them go back to that pit,' he told me.

The same political process that wanted to pack hurricane victims back into New Orleans stands foursquare behind a planning system that tries to keep people out of popular cities such as San Francisco, Boston and New York – or, indeed, out of the great European cities such as London. This isn't smart, but could there be a rational explanation behind it?

Back in 1970, the price of a house anywhere in America – even a flat in Manhattan – was not much more than the cost of building it. Now, zoning restrictions are preventing new homes being built. Ed Glaeser argues that there is no reason why even Manhattan cannot support more people: today's apartment buildings are actually smaller and lower than those erected in the 1970s. They needn't be. But instead of prompting the building of more flats, the surging demand to live in successful cities such as Boston and New York is being choked by high prices: Glaeser and Gyourko calculate that more than half the value of a flat in Manhattan can be directly laid at the feet of the planning officers, wielding zoning regulations to keep a stranglehold on supply. Gyourko reckons the regulatory 'tax' in Manhattan from zoning restrictions is at least $7,500 per person per year, taking the form of higher rents and mortgage payments. Since Manhattan prices have ballooned since he completed his research, the true figure is probably more like $10,000. In London, strangled by a long-standing 'green belt' policy that severely restricts building on the city's outskirts, a similar calculation applies.

Such zoning restrictions are dangerous. Unnecessarily high

prices for homes in Manhattan and London risk robbing those places of their diversity: they make it hard for immigrants to live there (Los Angeles is a more popular destination) and hard, too, for young people. So why do these restrictions exist?

It's not hard to see why one powerful pressure group rationally resists any attempt to weaken the restrictions – they directly benefit existing landlords and homeowners. It's a lot harder to understand why these zoning restrictions are widely supported by environmental campaigners. If you price people out of Manhattan they are going to live in Las Vegas instead – a booming city, where the price of a home is still only two hundred thousand dollars – and that is not the kind of thing any environmentalist should be encouraging. Dense cities like New York are not only Universities of Life: they are also good news for the environment.

That will come as news to many people, including my mother-in-law, who lives in the Lake District and is convinced that cities are choking concentrations of profligacy, pollution and waste. And she has a point. Per square mile, cities certainly do produce more pollution. But per person, the story is different. Manhattanites go shopping for their groceries on foot. They live in tiny flats and have little space to accumulate clutter. They use public transportation much more than other Americans, consume petrol at the tiny rate that the rest of America did before the Great Depression, and travel past countless homes and offices using the world's most energy-efficient mode of mass transport: the lift. Find eight million rural Americans and try to fit them into New York with all their possessions, and the games rooms, garden sheds, SUVs and lawn furniture would be piled up far higher than the Empire State Building. The journalist David Owen confessed that when he moved from New York to a small town, his electricity bills increased almost tenfold – even without air conditioning – and he went from owning no cars to owning three. His memorable conclusion: Manhattan is 'a utopian environmentalist community'.

Given how environmentally friendly cities are, how fundamental they are to innovation and economic growth, and how likely they are to play an increasingly important role in the future, you would expect politicians to cherish them. Earlier in this chapter, I suggested that because knowledge spillovers are the opposite of problems such as congestion, there is as good a case for subsidising people to live in cities as there is for taxing them away from road use. I wasn't joking. Without such a subsidy, people who have many unpaid lessons to teach will right now be living in isolated areas and unable to teach them to anyone but a couple of neighbours.

But we certainly don't see that kind of subsidy – quite the reverse. Not content with trying to keep people out of London and New York with tight planning restrictions, governments in rich countries seem very keen to suck as much money as possible out of cities and spray it over rural areas. One notorious example: in 2006 New York State received $2.78 per person in counter-terrorism grants, while rural Wyoming received $14.83 per person. Of course, New York is a target for terrorists and Wyoming probably is not, but that doesn't seem to matter: rural areas tend to be favoured by both the rhetoric and the electoral systems of most democracies.

Similar politics are in play in Europe. The European Union's infamous Common Agricultural Policy is often lambasted in the United Kingdom for unfairly distributing money to the French. Yet the much more dramatic redistribution is from urban areas to rural ones. The EU doles out forty-nine billion euros in agricultural subsidies, and imposes trade tariffs so that consumers pay over fifty billion euros in higher prices for food – but only one in twenty EU citizens is a farmer and the sector's economic contribution is even smaller. In the United Kingdom, Londoners pay £1,740 per person more in taxes than they receive in public services, despite the fact that many Londoners are poor; the southeast of England, far less poor but much more rural, pays much less. And most other regions receive a hefty subsidy: the average resident of largely rural Wales, for example, enjoys £2,870 more public spending than he or she pays in taxes.

What could possibly be happening? To answer that question, we need to look at the logic of politics.

Eight
Rational revolutions

Nashville, Tennessee, 3.30 a.m., 8 November 2000

The Vice-President of the United States, Al Gore, was on his way to a rain-soaked crowd in the centre of Nashville to make the speech no politician ever wants to give, conceding the presidency to George W. Bush. Gore had already called Bush to concede privately, sure that he had lost the state of Florida by fifty thousand votes. Then the messages started coming in over Gore's pager: he wasn't tens of thousands of votes behind, he was a few thousand. Make that a few hundred. Maybe he wasn't behind at all. Oh, to have eavesdropped on the telephone call in which Gore called Bush again and told him that he'd changed his mind: the election was too close to call after all.

In the end, Bush's official margin of victory in Florida was just 537 votes. By winning that state he also won the closest presidential election in US history, and surely that record won't be broken anytime soon. Floridians who considered voting for Gore but decided to watch TV or take a drive to the mall instead must have been kicking themselves.

Or perhaps not. Let's say you lived in Florida and you wanted

Al Gore to win. Would your vote have made the difference? It's incredibly unlikely. Just how unlikely is hard to say, but whichever way you look at it you had very little chance. In retrospect, many commentators concluded that the close result showed that a single vote was important. That's nonsense. In retrospect, there was zero chance you could have cast the deciding vote because if you had showed up and voted for Gore, he would have lost by 536 votes instead of 537.

It is more sensible to ask how likely your vote is to prove crucial in an election that appears to be neck-and-neck in the polls. In six-million-voter Florida, with the polls showing a fifty–fifty race all the way, the chance that your vote would in fact end up making the difference is about 1 in 300,000. (For more detail, see the note to this sentence at the end of the book.)

One in 300,000 isn't a big chance. So should you, a hypothetical Gore stay-at-home, really be kicking yourself? That depends on how badly you wanted to see Gore win. And that depends on a thought experiment you may find hard to stomach: putting a monetary value on your vote. I'm not saying that you would have sold your vote if Dick Cheney turned up on the doorstep and started peeling off the banknotes. All I'm trying to do is compare how strongly you felt about the election versus all the other things to care about in the world. So imagine for a moment that you had cast the deciding vote that put Gore in the White House. How good would that have made you feel? As good as a luxury holiday in Barbados? Better than a new Lexus? (Be honest, now. *A new Lexus*.) Let's say it would have made you feel better than a holiday, but not as good as a new car. How much is that – about $3,000? Or try another thought experiment: suppose you were caught out of town and somehow became aware that your vote would decide the election. How much would you have paid for a private jet to get yourself to the polling station?

Perhaps you're indignantly thinking more along the lines of $300,000 than $3,000. Maybe so. But for me, however you frame the thought experiment, $3,000 seems like a lot. Sure, I've been upset about seeing the wrong guy win an election – but I'd be more upset about losing $3,000. With a $3,000 preference for Gore, it wouldn't have been rational to cast your vote, because it would have been so unlikely to make the difference. Given the chance that your vote would have made a difference is 1 in 300,000, then the expected value of your vote is one cent: $3,000 for the time it would make the difference divided by the 300,000 times that it wouldn't. It's hardly surprising if a one-cent expected pay-off fails to divert many people from the joys of the sofa. And if you insist you'd rather have seen Gore in the White House than an extra $300,000 in your current account (are you sure?), your vote was still worth only a buck. Even if you're the kind of person who likes buying lottery tickets, these are terrible odds.

Anyway, this whole scenario is rigged to maximise your chances of casting the deciding vote. There won't be an election as close as Florida for many years, and most voters don't live in Florida, either. In a more normal election or a more typical state – say, strongly Democratic New York – the chance that your vote would make a difference is very close to zero, and the expected pay-off is far less than one cent. The economist Steve Landsburg goes so far as to suggest that if you want to change politics, you would be better advised to buy a lottery ticket with the intention of spending the proceeds on lobbying.

Let's summarise. In the closest presidential election in history, in the state with the closest race, even the most passionate partisan would have been a fool if she thought it was worth voting with the expectation that her vote might be the one that made the difference. Of course, lots of people do vote. Does that mean that voters are fools? Not quite. It means that voters don't vote with the expectation that they'll influence the election result.

We vote because the process of voting itself makes us feel good. Perhaps we want the satisfaction of being able to decorate our car with one of those bumper stickers that read 'Don't blame me, I voted for Gore' – or we want to avoid the pangs of guilt we imagine we'd feel when seeing those stickers on other people's cars. We might vote because we want to feel that we have done our duty. I think most people recognise that this is what really goes on when we choose to vote; what they don't recognise is what that implies for the choices we make in the voting booth.

Here's the striking implication: because the chance of any individual's vote making any difference to the result is tiny, the benefits of turning an uninformed vote into an informed vote are also tiny. Rationally speaking, why bother?

Contrast the voting decision with, say, buying a new car. If you buy a particular model of car in the mistaken belief that it's reliable and gives great mileage, your mistake is likely to cost you dearly. If you voted for George Bush in the mistaken belief that he would champion your right to marry your same-sex partner, your mistake cost you absolutely nothing, because your vote did not decide the election. Therefore, faced with the choice of researching a new car or researching a new political platform, the rational person reaches for *Consumer Reports*, not a manifesto. The rational choice view of politics tells us that typical voters will be ignorant – rationally ignorant.

As an example of that ignorance, 41 per cent of Americans believe that foreign aid is one of the two largest items in the federal budget; in fact, spending on foreign aid is about fifty times smaller than social security or the defence budget. The typical US voter is absurdly ignorant of how much her government spends on aid. But is she irrationally ignorant? No. If she votes foolishly as a result, that vote costs her precisely nothing. She might try to educate herself because she finds the facts inherently interesting, or because she wants to look smart at dinner parties, but certainly not because it will equip her to vote in a way that will get her the policies that she wants.

This rational ignorance of voters opens the doors to a reversal of a well-known dictum by that most logical of creatures, *Star Trek*'s Mr Spock: the needs of the many, Spock said, outweigh the needs of the few. As we shall see in the next section, the unfortunate reality of politics is often that the needs of the few outweigh the needs of the many. We'll see why that seemingly illogical reversal of Spock's dictum is exactly what we would expect from rational voters on the rampage, and examine the rational reasons that explain which types of 'few' are best able to exploit the rest of us.

This US government programme is a surefire vote-winner: take $1.9 billion away from a large group of voters; then give just over $1 billion to a much smaller group of voters; then throw away the rest. Would you vote for it? It turns out that Americans do just that, time after time.

Of course, the programme is generally presented in a different light, as a defence of American jobs in the sugar industry from unfair foreign competition. Smug European readers, please note: European sugar producers enjoy a similar deal.

Anyone who understands a bit about how the economy works will tell you that trade barriers on sugar are a terrible idea. They raise costs for American producers who use sugar in their products, such as sweet manufacturers and refiners of biofuels. They raise costs for American consumers. They reduce demand for American products abroad, because the dollars that foreign sugar producers would have received, had they not been shut out, would have eventually been spent buying American products. (This chapter is about politics, not trade barriers, so I'll not try to explain the reasoning here. If you're doubtful, you might look at Chapter Nine of my book *The Undercover Economist*.)

Of course, trade barriers *do* benefit US sugar producers: cane growers make about $300 million from these trade restrictions, and sugar beet growers about $650 million. There are only about fifty thousand workers employed by the industry, and if they shared evenly in the benefits then they would each be making about twenty thousand dollars from the trade restrictions. In fact, the benefits are yet more concentrated than that.

A US government report found that over a third of the benefits of the sugar support programme in 1991 went to just thirty-three sugar-cane farms; if the pattern holds for more recent sugar support efforts, that would be about ten million dollars per big farm. All this costs each US citizen about six dollars, of which about three are wasted and three go to agribusiness.

As I promised, Mr Spock's dictum is reversed: the few are exploiting the many. Three hundred million people are losing from the protection for the sugar industry, and fifty thousand are gaining, with most of the gains going to a very small elite.

That seems an extraordinary and irrational outcome for a democratic society to produce, but the apparent paradox should not be quite so confusing. As we've seen in earlier chapters, individually rational behaviour does not necessarily lead to a socially rational outcome. As a voter, you can be excused for being rationally ignorant of how you're being fleeced by the sugar industry: why bother making the effort to understand the issue and find out which candidates at the next election are opposed to sugar subsidies? You might be seething with righteous indignation, but your vote would likely have no effect whatsoever. Even if it did penetrate your rational ignorance that sugar tariffs are costing you six dollars a year in higher grocery bills, how much do you care? Would you change your vote as a result? Remember the split-the-bill problem back in Chapter Four, where small shareholders had no rational incentive to discipline greedy managers. In that sense voters are a little like small shareholders in a country.

There are millions of voters who lose from tariffs protecting the sugar industry, but not one of them will rationally expend any effort trying to do something about that.

On the other hand, if you're one of the fifty thousand sugar workers whose livelihood heavily depends on the sugar tariffs, you'd certainly care. Carol Campbell, a widow from Belle Glade, south Florida, loses sleep every time Congress discusses allowing foreign sugar imports – as well she might, since she has worked in the sugar industry for over thirty-five years. Remember, Bush's margin of victory was 537 votes. There are nearly ten thousand people like Carol Campbell in Florida and you can bet that they'll be voting for the candidate who promises to protect their jobs. We can rationally disregard the chance that one vote will sway the election, but having ten thousand votes in the bag becomes a bit more interesting. And protectionist politicians don't just want the guaranteed votes from sugar industry workers, either. They also want the cash from the sugar lobby, which contributes about three million dollars to politicians every time there's an election.

There are about three hundred million people in America who consume some sugar. If they each sent one cent to a counter-lobbying effort, they could match the sugar lobby's spending dollar for dollar – and with a much larger potential voter base to mobilise, they would surely succeed in having the subsidies abolished and saving themselves six dollars a year. They never will do this, however, because it wouldn't be rational. One of those cute university lab games nicely illustrates why.

Texas A&M University, College Station, 1986

A class of twenty-six students were offered the chance to make some cash by their professor. Each student was given a secret ballot with two options. The first option was the selfless one: any student ticking option one would secure a pay-out of two dollars, to be shared equally among the group – about eight cents each. The second option was the selfish one: any student ticking option two simply received fifty cents for himself, while the group got nothing. All students would do better if all students chose option one: the payments from everybody else's generosity would far outweigh the loss of the fifty-cent pay-off. Still, each student would do better by keeping hold of his fifty cents and hoping everybody else was more generous.

Unlike America's hapless sugar consumers, the students had plenty of opportunity to discuss their predicament before making their choices. They all professed their intention to cooperate and choose option one, of course. Yet their attempt to coordinate in wringing cash from the professor failed about as completely as it could have. Twenty-two out of twenty-six did the selfish thing and chose option two – the equivalent of an ignorant vote or an apathetic lobbying effort – hoping that somebody else would pick up the slack. One of the ringleaders was disgusted. 'I'll never trust anyone again as long as I live.' And did he choose the selfless option one? No. 'Oh, I voted two.'

As this experiment shows, what you choose for yourself is not the same as what you choose to share with others – especially when your decision is made anonymously. You'd happily spend five pounds on a meal for yourself, but imagine trying to decide what to contribute to a meal that you'll split with nine unidentified strangers. You won't actually meet the strangers; you'll just get a lunchbox with your share of the meal. If you spend five pounds, you'll see fifty pence of the benefit and these total strangers will each get fifty pence's worth of extra food, too. It's not rational to contribute anything, unless it makes you feel good to spend money on strangers. This is a flipped-around version of the split-the-bill problem.

In fact, because each individual has no incentive to contribute, it's likely that all ten of us together might spend less on lunch for ten than any would have spent on lunch for himself. That is exactly what we see in the sugar industry: a few people with much to gain are willing to spend more in total than their three hundred million victims.

You might think that it would be in somebody's interest to get all the lunching strangers organised and committed to sharing the bill fairly; it might also be in somebody's interest to get together some organisation to campaign on behalf of sugar consumers and solicit all those one-cent donations. But this doesn't solve the problem: it simply shifts it from the question of who will pay to buy lunch or lobby for free trade in sugar to the question of who will get everybody organised. The total benefits of being organised are large, but the benefits for any one member of the group are pretty small. Saying 'get organised' solves nothing.

The curious logic of rational politics, then, is the exploitation of the many by the few, because a few citizens each with a lot to gain will fight, campaign and lobby much harder than millions of citizens each with very little to lose.

It's not just any old 'few' that can get it together to exploit the many, though. We do not see, for example, organisations such as 'Friends of Tim Harford' – a small organisation if ever there was one – campaigning for a six-million-pound government subsidy towards research for my next book. That would be just ten pence from each citizen of the UK. I'm not greedy – I'd settle for the six million. Would you fight to prevent the loss of ten pence? Clearly something is missing from any theory that could raise my hopes of succeeding with such an organisation. Two things, in fact: the exploitation must be easy to hide; and the apparent beneficiaries must genuinely stand to benefit. The first condition is generally not hard to satisfy; we'll soon see that the second is surprisingly strict.

Just suppose for a moment that I had a friend in high places who managed to siphon six million pounds a year of taxpayers' money into my personal bank account. In a country that possesses a moderate degree of effective opposition and freedom of the press, we would not expect this policy to survive for long – not because the policy has many losers and few gainers, but because it's so cheap for the losers to figure out what's going on. Some investigative journalist or rival politician could explain the scandal so succinctly that even the most rationally ignorant voter would get the point.

Trade barriers such as sugar subsidies also rob the majority and favour a small pressure group, but less blatantly. It takes effort to work out what trade barriers really do, because it's counter-intuitive to hear that exposing American jobs to foreign competition is good for ordinary Americans. The US sugar lobby takes full advantage of the confusion. You could explain in a twenty-second TV spot why it's bad for the Prime Minister to be diverting taxpayers' money to his friend Tim, but good luck making the case for free trade in a sound bite. That's a major reason why trade barriers are a popular way to siphon cash to pressure groups: they are deliberately confusing, just as the stock option plans described back in Chapter Four are deliberately confusing.

So much for the need to make sure the exploitation isn't blatant enough to pique the interest of rational voters. But the lobbyists also have to be sure that benefits from their lobbying will remain within a well-defined interest group. That is not always so easy. For example, you might expect the National Association of Estate Agents to lobby for a subsidy for estate agents. Assume the NAEA's lobbyists could put together some hypothetical package that dished out ten thousand pounds a year to every estate agent at the expense of taxpayers or consumers, but managed to hide the details of the deal so that those taxpayers and consumers didn't notice. The problem would be that anyone could get into the estate agency business and pick up the ten-thousand pound subsidy. The phone book would be full of underemployed estate agents, the ten-thousand-pound subsidy just barely compensating for the fact that there aren't enough customers to go around. So this would not be a package for which the rational estate agent would campaign very hard.

Industries that are difficult for newcomers to break into – that have high barriers to entry, in the jargon of economics – are more likely to find it rational to campaign for subsidies. But even high barriers to entry are not in themselves enough, if the industry is booming. Suppose existing out-of-town superstores such as Tesco successfully lobbied for a government subsidy. It would do them little good, because new rivals would be willing to climb the entry barriers, pick up the subsidy, and watch their investments pay off in a growing market.

In contrast, it's rational to campaign for subsidies if you're in an industry that's expensive to enter and has poor long-term prospects, such as the car or steel industry. No new competitor is going to pay to build huge factories to enter a declining industry, even if it is getting handouts. A tariff or subsidy might make the plants profitable enough to run once built, but not profitable enough to cover the costs of building a new factory. Politically, this is perfect: the trade barriers protect a small, tightly knit group of people with a lot to gain, but those benefits don't leak away to countless upstart competitors.

Agriculture is another tempting target for lobbyists, for a similar reason – it's impossible for outsiders to seek to cash in on a subsidy by creating some new agricultural land, because there's only so much good agricultural land in the country. A farm subsidy will raise the value of the land, and agribusinesses can either keep the land and collect the subsidy, or sell the land to competitors at a profit. Either way, the financial advantage of the lobbying effort stays with the farm lobby, which is why it's politically rational to subsidise farming in rich countries. Interestingly, the agribusiness sector in the United States contributes about fifty million dollars to each election campaign, while estate agents don't show up on the contribution charts.

You have probably worked it out for yourself by now, but we have all the elements in place to resolve the puzzle at the end of the last chapter: why, in rich countries, are rural areas subsidised by urban areas?

The first reason is that many rural subsidies offer a clear benefit to rural residents but a concealed cost for city dwellers. Universal service obligations for phone, mail and utilities such as power are one example. These services are much more expensive to provide for people who live in the countryside; they know this and they complain vehemently when faced with plans to close down so much as a village post office. And well they might: these are big benefits provided to a tightly defined group of people. City folk are picking up the tab with higher prices, but they are richer and more numerous (the United States is 80 per cent urban, the United Kingdom about 90 per cent) and they barely notice.

The second reason is that the subsidy does not encourage many people to pile in and collect it. In the last chapter, I explained why cities were so important and such attractive places to live, and were growing ever more so. Against this background of relative rural decline, it would take a huge subsidy to attract many people away from the cities. Rural lobbies can be fairly sure that subsidies will not be slurped up by latecomers, and that is why the lobbyists work so hard.

The position of rural areas relative to cities has not always been what it is in rich, early twenty-first-century economies. At other times, and in other places, the situation of rural dwellers has been different and so the theory of rational politics points to a very different outcome. When an economy is rural and most of the population is involved in farming, the same logic that makes farming a good target for subsidies in a rich country – that farmland does not appear or disappear, it just becomes more or less profitable – is also logic that makes farming a good target for taxes in a poor rural economy. That is another illustration of the anti-Spock dictum: the needs of the few outweigh the needs of the many.

We don't have to look too far back in time for an example. Africa is rapidly urbanising today, but back in the 1960s and 1970s African countries had ostensibly democratic regimes and almost completely rural economies. As the theory of rational politics predicts, those rural areas suffered badly. In 1970, for example – a fairly typical year – peasant farmers in Nigeria received less than half the international price for their palm oil or cocoa, and barely more than a third of the international price for cotton or peanuts. Senegalese peanut farmers received even less than a third of the market price. In other African countries there was a similar story.

What was going on? The low prices were paid by government agricultural boards, most of which pre-dated independence. Economist Robert H. Bates showed that although these agricultural boards were legally obliged to use their powers to stabilise the price of crops, this hardly ever happened. Instead, the boards sold the crops on international markets for a handsome profit. A Ghanaian government investigation in 1967 noted:

> The evidence before us suggests that the [Cocoa Marketing Board] used the profits obtained from its monopoly cocoa operations to . . . provide funds for the dance band, footballers, actors and actresses, and a whole host of satellite units and individuals . . . The CMB's area of operation . . . involves a staff which would have appeared absurd only ten years ago.

A somewhat less blatant approach was to use the cash to make loans to industrialists at half the market rate. Such cheap loans were, naturally, hotly demanded and could be handed out to favoured groups.

From a rational politics viewpoint, this is not so different from US sugar tariffs and other conventional trade barriers. Through the agricultural boards, governments were engineering market conditions that creamed profits away from many small players and delivered them to a few large players with far more political influence. In many African countries of the time, there were fewer than a thousand manufacturing firms in total. Whole industries might be represented by a single monopolist. In contrast, there were many hundreds of thousands of farms – 800,000 in Ghana, 400,000 in Zambia, 2,500,000 in Tanzania. Half of all Ghanaian farms were under four acres. And when the farmers were big players – in Kenya, half the farms were over four hundred acres – the farmers received much better prices.

There is one big difference between the African agricultural boards of the 1960s and 1970s and trade barriers in rich countries today: the effect on the victims was much greater. Most US citizens don't notice higher prices for sugar and sweets that add up to six dollars a year, but the African peasant farmers were giving up roughly half their earnings. They certainly noticed, but they were still held back by the collective action problem that confounded the students of Texas A&M. In a well-functioning democracy, they would simply have voted for an opposition party, but where politics was crooked, a lot more effort was required. In Ghana, exploited peasant farmers formed an opposition party; the government responded by offering cheap loans to farmers who belonged instead to the governing party. Beatings and assassinations are also alleged to have been commonplace. Other African governments similarly tended to do all they could to make it more difficult for the exploited masses to organise politically.

The blatant corruption of the agricultural boards has improved in the last couple of decades, partly because of pressure from international agencies, but also because so many rural farmers rationally responded by flocking to the cities, where people were getting cheap food at their expense. Unfortunately, the tendency to repress exploited masses has not faded to the same extent. Readers of my previous book, *The Undercover Economist*, may recall some similar observations from my visit to Cameroon, an African nation in which few observers have much confidence in the credibility of elections. I found in Cameroon, as Robert Bates found in the Africa of the 1960s and 1970s, policies that were very profitable for a few people – government bureaucrats, the police – but not for the majority.

The difference between such policies and the handouts to pressure groups in more democratic countries is not their fundamental structure – because Western governments also distribute cash to concentrated interest groups – but the fact that the redistributive politics can be far more brazen. In a dictatorship or quasi-dictatorship, you don't need to hide the fact that you're fleecing the masses, because there's even less they can do about it.

Sometimes, though, dictatorial leaders can push too far. It's time to look at what rational choice theory can tell us about revolutions.

Fobbing, England, 1381

When a tax collector arrived at the Essex village of Fobbing to collect the third oppressive poll tax in four years, the villagers threw him out. Soldiers arrived the next month; the villagers threw them out, too. Before long, Wat Tyler of Kent was leading a mass revolt and two armies of furious peasants were marching on London, burning tax registers and records as they went. The force from Essex was camped at Mile End, just east of London, on 12 June. The next day, the Kentish band arrived unexpectedly at Blackheath, at the southeast border of London. Some of the capital's poor joined the rebels, who roamed through the city at will, burning Highbury Manor, which was the King's Treasurer's residence, and the Savoy Palace, which was the home of the powerful nobleman John of Gaunt. They overwhelmed the Tower of London. They executed the King's Treasurer and the Archbishop of Canterbury.

The teenage King Richard II met Wat Tyler and the mob at Smithfield in east London. Tyler set out his demands: an end to the authority of feudal lords other than the King, an end to the poll tax, work based on freely agreed contracts rather than feudal obligation, and cheap rent of land. A contemporary chronicler reported, 'To this the King gave an easy answer, and said that he should have all that he could fairly grant, reserving only for himself the regality of his crown. And then he bade him go back to his home, without making further delay.'

The King's promises reassured the rebels and they dispersed (but not before Tyler himself was killed in a brawl with the

Mayor of London). Later, the King broke every promise; his army toured the rebel villages, executing the ringleaders. Wat Tyler should have realised that a king can change his mind.

Revolutionary masses sometimes acquire temporary power. Wat Tyler's peasant army used a local difficulty as a focal point that helped them coordinate their efforts, solving the 'get organised' problem I outlined earlier in the chapter. At other times the temporary power comes about because the repressive armies of the elite are temporarily weakened or distracted by war, or because a foreign army lends a hand. Sometimes the masses are empowered because a war has just finished: they are the armed forces, so they still have their weapons and training.

The point is that it is no good for the revolutionaries to demand lower taxes, a welfare state or a higher minimum wage. These policies may suit them, but they can be reversed when the revolution has lost some of its steam. It's a tricky problem: the embattled elites may genuinely want to offer concessions to save their skins. The rebels may genuinely want to accept the offer, because it avoids the potentially dangerous chaos that would ensue from the ultimate solution of putting the elites to the sword. But the rebels cannot be sure that the promises will be kept.

Revolution, then, bears a strong resemblance to the kidnapper's dilemma. The hostage is taken; the kidnappers have temporary power. But how to cash in – how to swap the hostage for the ransom or for safe passage? As Woody Allen put it:

The FBI surround the house. 'Throw the kid out,' they say, 'give us your guns, and come out with your hands up.' The kidnappers say, 'We'll throw the kid out, but let us keep our guns, and get to our car.' The FBI say, 'Throw the kid out, we'll let you get to your car, but give us your guns.' The kidnappers say, 'We'll throw the kid out, but let us keep our guns – we don't have to get to our car.' The FBI say, 'Keep the kid.'

Jokes aside, the problem is one of credibility. The kidnapper wants to release the hostage, if the hostage could believably promise not to testify against him; the hostage would happily comply, but neither of them can think of a way to make that promise binding. Even as profound a thinker as Tom Schelling, attempting to apply insights from game theory to the problem facing the hostage and kidnapper, concluded that these problems are just inherently hard to solve.

Far better, then, to avoid the situation coming to such a head – and according to the economists Daron Acemoglu and James A. Robinson, the way to do so is called 'democracy'. Revolutions rarely come out of nothing, and embattled elites who have imminent reason to fear being placed in the thorny position of kidnap victims should rationally cede some power if by doing so they can save their skins.

Acemoglu and Robinson recall the inspiring words of British Prime Minister Earl Grey, advocating reform in 1831: 'There is no-one more decided against annual parliaments, universal suffrage and the ballot, than I am. My object is not to favour, but to put an end to such hopes and projects.'

Way to go, Earl Grey! He added: 'The principle of my reform is, to prevent the necessity of revolution . . . reforming to preserve and not to overthrow.' Of course, Earl Grey – who was nervous about the growing unrest in Britain at the time – could have placated revolutionaries with whatever policies they desired. But rational revolutionaries would have learned from Wat Tyler's mistake and would not find such promises credible.

But why would democratic institutions, such as universal suffrage or the separation of powers, provide any more of a credible commitment? After all, if the current institutional set-up can be overturned by force, force can be used to reverse it. There are coups as well as democratic revolutions in the world.

Yet the institutions do matter. In part, this is a matter of the difficulty in coordinating to overthrow them: no doubt each peasant in fourteenth-century England felt frustrated with his lot, but he was hardly likely to march on the Tower of London by himself. The uprising led by Wat Tyler's peasants against King Richard was a once-in-a-generation piece of coordination. Such coordination is difficult both for revolutionary peasant mobs and for counter-revolutionary coup leaders, and that means that whether the institutions are democratic or dictatorial, they will tend to last.

Another reason why political institutions often last is that many people in society invest in a particular way of doing things. A democracy contains pressure groups and political parties; a dictatorship contains cliques and private armies. Either one will tend to last because powerful people have made their decisions expecting that it will. In both respects, political institutions are all in the mind: people rationally invest in them if they expect them to last and do not if they do not. They will rationally defend them only if they expect others to do likewise. Confidence in the permanence of political institutions, whether democratic or dictatorial, is self-justifying.

This, then, is the basic model of rational revolutions. There are two players in the 'game': the rich elites, who take the role of potential kidnap victim; and the poor masses, who take the role of potential kidnapper. The masses want different economic policies from the elites – say, an end to the poll tax, free contracts for labour, and cheap rent of land. If they are sufficiently indignant and are able to get themselves organised, the masses can rise up and demand greater democratic rights. They do this because they rationally foresee that promises of different economic policies are not credible; only a chance in political institutions will do. Or elites may realise an uprising is likely and offer reform to forestall it. Again, new policies are not credible but new institutions might be.

The elites might even end up being pleased about the credibility the new system provides. Thomas Schelling argues that the ability to make a binding promise can be very useful. If you doubt that, imagine trying to get a mortgage in a country where the courts never enforced debt collection. You'd never be able to promise to pay the money back, and so a rational bank would never lend you the money in the first place. Without credibility, both you and the bank are worse off. The point might be best illustrated by what, in retrospect, seems to have been a particularly important example.

Holland, 1688

A curious invitation arrived at the court of William of Orange, the Dutch ruler, and his wife, Mary Stuart, daughter of King James II of England: please invade England and seize the throne. The invitation came from English power-brokers representing both parliamentary parties, Whig and Tory, who were disturbed at James II's efforts to extend his powers. The invitation was duly accepted, the Dutch army that landed in England in late 1688 was quickly joined by English parliamentarians, and James II fled to France before battle was joined.

It was the second time in forty years that parliamentarian armies had booted out the monarch, and this time the parliamentarians insisted on a new constitution that would protect the rights of merchants and the landed gentry, if not of ordinary citizens. William and Mary were in no position to argue with a constitution that handed many powers to Parliament; anyway, in retrospect, such a constitution was hugely advantageous to them.

Before William and Mary took power, revenue had been a serious problem for the kings and queens of England. The problem was not weakness but strength: with Parliament impotent, nobody would believe royal promises to pay back loans. Whenever there was a temporary shortage of cash, the Crown sold royal lands. Elizabeth I sold off a quarter of hers to fund her war with Spain. That ate away at her revenue base and future monarchs had to sell at an ever-faster rate.

The King still had near-dictatorial powers, so turned

elsewhere for revenue. One handy source was the creation of artificial monopolies: the King would sell the sole right to sell spirits in east London or to trade tobacco from the West Indies. Such royal monopolies were hugely lucrative and sold for high prices; the most famous beneficiary was the East India Company. But the monopolies were disastrous distortions of the economy, and they took place over the protests of Parliament (which was itself full of moneyed interests).

An alternative way of raising revenue was the 'forced loan'. For instance, in 1617, James I, Elizabeth's successor, agreed a loan with London bankers of one hundred thousand pounds. It was to be repaid after a year with 10 per cent interest. Yet at the end of the year the King paid only the interest and then demanded that the loan be renewed. It was several years before any more interest was paid. Eight years later James I unilaterally reduced the interest rate but still didn't make any payments. Five years after that he finally returned the principal. This was very handy: the budget deficit in 1617 was thirty-six thousand pounds, so the delinquent King was able to cover a large chunk of that simply by confiscating interest payments. Such forced loans were common.

After 1688, William and Mary were unable to play such games because they were under much closer scrutiny from a Parliament with many new powers. Royal monopolies were banned, as were forced loans. The fact that Parliament had successfully dethroned two intransigent kings meant that these new powers were treated with respect by the Crown.

You might think that such constraints were a disadvantage for William and Mary, but not at all. Suddenly able to make credible promises to repay debt – because Parliament wouldn't let them default – they were quickly able to borrow huge sums of money. The Crown's debt expanded from about a million pounds in 1688 to almost seventeen million pounds nine years later, almost half the size of the economy itself.

The delighted William and Mary spent the money on war

with France, while merchants and bankers in England were so happy with their newly secure property rights that interest rates were falling, from 14 per cent in the early 1690s to 6–8 per cent before 1700, and much lower still after that. Limits on their power turned out to magnify it dramatically, a point that Schelling would have understood perfectly. The new credibility produced a 'win–win' situation, unless, of course, you were French.

Douglass North and Barry Weingast, the economists who advanced this explanation, concluded that the effect of the Glorious Revolution was that 'while France slumped towards bankruptcy, England strode into the Industrial Revolution'.

But that is a story to be told more fully in the next chapter.

Nine

A million years of logic

Imagine compressing the last million years of human history into just one year. Three thousand years would pass each day, or two years each minute. On this compressed timescale, our ancestors first used fire sometime in the spring. Despite this early breakthrough, new ideas were slow to arrive on the scene. Until late October, our ancestors were still wielding the most basic stone tools; humans biologically like ourselves, *Homo sapiens*, appeared around mid-November. About 19 December, the beginnings of civilisation were visible: cave paintings and burial sites. It wasn't until 27 December that there was much evidence of sewing needles, spear-throwers, or the bow and arrow. We don't know much about our economic prehistory, but we do know that it was a story with all the action packed into the final scene.

But economic growth didn't simply shift into a different gear once we entered recorded history. Zoom in on those last few days and you'll see that the rate of innovation and growth continued to speed up. The world economy was ten times larger at the end of 30 December than twenty-fours hours earlier, a time span bridged by the epic rule of the Egyptian pharaohs. Imperial

China lasted for most of 31 December, during which time the Roman Empire rose and fell, and Europe then moved through the Middle Ages. Meanwhile, the size of the world economy increased in size another ten times between the start of New Year's Eve and 7.30 p.m., the time Columbus discovered the Americas. Growth then became faster still, and the world economy grew tenfold again between 7.30 p.m. and 11.20 p.m., when the First World War began.

That growth was astonishing by historical standards, but puny by the standards of the twentieth century, because in the last forty minutes – the rest of the twentieth century – the world economy expanded tenfold yet again. If current growth rates are sustained, the next tenfold increase will be completed by about twenty-five past midnight.

There might not seem to be any rational explanation as to why economic growth took off in such a dramatic way. If you credit anything, I suspect you'd be inclined to point to the people who embody scientific and technological genius: Galileo and Curie, Newcomen and Edison. But leaving it at that would make the take-off a matter of pure luck: luck that we live after such brilliant minds and not before them, and luck that their achievements fell upon a fertile culture that was open to innovation.

It won't surprise you to hear that I disagree. In this final chapter, I will argue that the stellar economic growth of the past two centuries is not a matter of luck at all. Neither is the pattern of growth across the globe. Whether you look closely at individual innovators or step back and survey the broad sweep of economic growth all the way back to the Palaeolithic era, you find a common thread: neither progress nor stagnation is an accident. Both rapidly growing economies and stuttering ones are full of individuals rationally responding to the incentives they face.

This is a detective story, and as it takes us further and further into the past it will necessarily become speculative. I'll begin by looking at the work of an economist who tried to recreate old technologies in an effort to work out how much richer we have really become – a surprisingly difficult question. Then I'll uncover evidence to show that the moment of 'take-off', the Industrial Revolution, wasn't based on scientific genius at all, but rather on rational, carefully planned responses to simple economic incentives.

The search for economic incentives then leads us to ask why some countries were fertile ground for an economic revolution. I argue that the answer lies in the age of European exploration and conquest – not, as is often believed, because the exploitation of Africa and the New World directly enriched Europe, but because the trading opportunities empowered a merchant class with a strong interest in creating laws and institutions that provided incentives for economic growth. Speculative stuff, as I say, even if it is based on some ingenious work. Still, I do not want to finish this book by proclaiming all the answers, but by showing that economists are asking the right questions.

Before we start our journey into the past, though, perhaps you're thinking that it's hard to estimate economic growth for all of human prehistory and much of human history. You'd be correct. So perhaps you're also thinking that this tale of incredible growth acceleration sounds a bit wild-eyed. You'd be wrong.

In fact, my estimate of growth is conservative because it does not take full account of the way that the quality of products is improving. When economists try to compare our material standard of living with that of our predecessors, they have to calculate the extent to which prices have changed. A dollar in 1900 bought more than a dollar today – but how much more? It's an impossible comparison, because we don't spend our money on the same things as we did in 1900. For example, if you flip through an old mail-order catalogue from the US retailer Montgomery Ward, you'll discover that a bicycle cost 260 hours' wages for the typical worker in the late nineteenth century, but just 7.2 hours' wages in 2000. But silver spoons cost more hours of labour today than they did in 1900. Which inflation rate should you use? It depends on whether you are buying bicycles or spoons.

More difficult yet, what about products that were not available at any price in 1900? Lifesaving drugs such as penicillin are simply not captured in the official economic statistics. As far as our standard measures of income growth since 1900 are concerned, those drugs might as well not have been invented.

The economist William Nordhaus tried to show just how important these new products were by considering one example, the cost of illuminating a dark room. Prehistoric man would have had to chop logs or gather deadwood to light his cave. How long would that have taken? How much light would it have produced? Nordhaus chopped logs and burned them in his own fireplace, measuring the dim, flickering light they gave off with a light meter. What about Roman oil lamps? Nordhaus bought one – alleged to be a genuine antique – and rigged it up with a wick. He filled it with cold-pressed sesame oil. Twenty pounds of logs burned for a little more than three hours, but an eggcup of oil burned all day, more brightly, and far more controllably. This was a sensational improvement, if nothing compared with the lightbulb and the LED.

Nordhaus's experiments suggest that as far as light was concerned, economic growth had been underestimated not by a factor of two or three but ten thousand times over. A modern lightbulb, illuminating a room from 6 p.m. until midnight every night for a year, produces the same amount of light as thirty-four thousand candles from the early nineteenth century. In the early nineteenth century, earning the money to buy thirty-four thousand candles would have taken an average worker all year. When I remind myself to turn off unnecessary lights, I am saving light that would have taken my grandfather's grandfather all his working hours to provide. For me, the saving is too small to notice.

Not every product has enjoyed such a spectacular trans-
formation. Food, for example, and the technology to produce it,
has developed more slowly. Nordhaus himself reckoned that
about a third of the modern economy has gone through
improvements similar to the illumination sector's. Yet even leaving the Nordhaus effect completely aside, and relying totally on
the conservative estimates of the official statistics, the picture of
an incredible growth acceleration remains.

The income of the richest countries today is around fifty
pounds per person per day. Subsistence income – that is, the
income that most people have relied on for most of history – is
about fifty pence a day, a sum that will provide food, rudimentary shelter, and almost nothing else. The halfway point between
today's living standards in the United States and those of
1,000,000 BC (or 100,000 BC, or 10,000 BC, since little changed)
is as recent as 1880: income per head increased tenfold, to about
ten dollars a day, in the entirety of the existence of humankind
running up to AD 1880, and it has increased another ten times in
the 127 years since then. Remember that these figures do not
even make allowances for the Nordhaus effect.

Of course, we do not have any persuasive way of measuring
income in prehistoric times. But we can be fairly sure that for
most of human history, it was roughly zero. During recorded history, zero income growth has been the norm until recently. The
only economic growth has been population growth. For example, real wages in England fluctuated – AD 1300 was a tough
time, 1450 was pretty good – but did not show any long-term
improvement between 1215 (Magna Carta) and 1800. Whenever
the economy boomed, the boom showed up in more people
rather than as richer people.

But by that measure, the prehistoric economy never did
boom. The population of our distant ancestors, *Homo erectus*,
grew very slowly, around 0.03 per cent per century. Things did
speed up, but that's not saying much: population growth was still
just 2 per cent per century in the first millennium AD. Things are

different in the modern world: in the 1960s, population growth was as high as 2 per cent, not per century, but per year. And unlike our predecessors, we're combining more people with richer people. While prehistoric growth was 0.03 per cent per century, modern growth is 4–5 per cent a year. Something changed. What? It's time to start our journey into the past by visiting the cradle of the Industrial Revolution.

Coalbrookdale, Shropshire, England, 1709

Abraham Darby arrived in Coalbrookdale with a mission in mind: to produce cheap iron using coal – in the form of coke – as a fuel. His success was foundational to the Industrial Revolution, allowing the production of cheap iron and so enabling the construction of railways, steamships and industrial machinery, not to mention the famous iron bridge built by Darby's grandson near Coalbrookdale. A stroke of genius? A triumph for Darby's Quaker work ethic and practical British entrepreneurialism?

Hardly. Economic historian Robert Allen points out that Darby's pivotal invention was a simple response to economic incentives. Existing iron smelters used wood; it did not need an Einstein to think of chucking coal in the furnace instead. What it required was a supply of the world's cheapest coal to make the project worthwhile, and that is exactly what Coalbrookdale's mines provided. Once he worked out that the economics were viable, Darby simply commissioned researchers to experiment, solve the technical problems, and make his project a reality. And even after Darby's invention was tried and tested, it did not spread to mainland Europe, for the simple reason that Europe's coal was too expensive; most of it was shipped over from Newcastle in England anyway. Coke smelting in France or Germany was technologically possible, but just not profitable for 150 years.

This seems like an unusually straightforward case, but on closer inspection the same turns out to be true of many of the Industrial Revolution's technological advances. Cotton-spinning machinery, for example, did not require any scientific knowledge, just a careful process of development and experimentation plus a little creativity: legend has it that the spinning jenny was inspired by a traditional medieval spinning wheel that fell over and kept spinning while lying on the ground. The inventors of spinning machines such as the spinning jenny and the water frame launched serious research programs; they knew exactly what they hoped to achieve, and just needed to solve a series of modest engineering problems.

They expended this considerable effort rationally – and those in France or China rationally did not – because the financials added up: Allen's calculations show that British workers were at that time the most highly paid in the world, whether measured against the price of silver, of food, of energy, or of capital. That meant that they were big consumers of imported cotton, but also that a labour-saving device would pay dividends. In Britain, a spinning jenny cost less than five months' wages, while in low-wage France it cost more than a year's wages. It was cheap French labour that accounted for the machine's slow take-up on the continent, not the superior scientific ingenuity or commercial acumen of the British.

That was even more true of the steam engines. They were, unusually for Industrial Revolution technology, based on an actual scientific advance: Galileo discovered that atmosphere had weight and so could exert pressure. Yet the practical invention took place in Britain, not in Galileo's Italy, and again, the reason was neither genius nor an entrepreneurial culture but the fact that labour was expensive and fuel was incredibly cheap. Allen calculates that, in terms of thermal units per hour, wages in Newcastle in the early seventeenth century were perhaps ten times higher than those in continental cities such as Paris and Strasbourg. Labour in China was even cheaper. By the same reckoning, London wages were three times higher than those in continental cities and six or seven times those in Beijing. It's no surprise that the steam engine, a device for replacing labour with coal, was a British invention.

All this shows that many of the important innovations of the Industrial Revolution were calculated and deliberate responses to high British wages and cheap British coal. The cheap coal was an accident of geography, but the wages weren't. Our historical detective story leads us to another question: why were wages so high?

We heard about part of the answer at the end of the previous chapter: the politics of the Glorious Revolution. While Britain was moving towards a freer society with more respect for individual property at the end of the seventeenth century, most of Europe – the other exception was Holland – was moving in the opposite direction under the Habsburgs and the Bourbons. With the British and Dutch governments restrained from arbitrarily taxing anyone who looked invitingly rich, or from banning competitors to a favoured monopolist, British and Dutch entrepreneurs were far more willing to invest their capital. A society with more capital investment and more entrepreneurship is also a society that is likely to enjoy higher wages. Adam Smith, writing in 1776, commented:

> In all countries where there is tolerable security, every man of common understanding will endeavour to employ whatever stock he can command in procuring either present enjoyment or future profit ... In those unfortunate countries, indeed, where men are continually afraid of the violence of their superiors, they frequently bury and conceal a great part of their stock ... This is said to be a common practice in Turkey, in Indostan, and, I believe, in most other governments of Asia. It seems to have been a common practice among our ancestors during the violence of the feudal government.

Smith might also have mentioned the French, because France was rapidly becoming more absolutist at the time. One indication is the population of cities, which we know from Chapter Seven is a sound guide to prosperity. Economists Bradford DeLong and Andrei Shleifer have used city populations to chart the effects of absolutism in political rule. In 1500, Paris was Europe's largest city, and the great (and relatively free) Italian city-states of Naples, Milan and Venice were the only other cities with populations over one hundred thousand. By 1800, London was almost twice as large as Paris, Amsterdam was doing well, and other cities under British rule such as Dublin, Manchester and Edinburgh were rapidly growing. Twelve of Europe's fifty-six largest cities were in the British Isles. Oppressive monarchs created regimes in which the cities were leached of life, while in freer areas, the cities boomed.

Even without the cities, we would have expected higher wages in countries that enjoyed freedom from arbitrary taxes. The fact that cities prospered in free nations simply magnified wages and created conditions ripe for the innovations of the Industrial Revolution. But can we say something about why England and Holland had freer governments than France, Germany and Spain? It seems that here the rational historian hits bedrock. DeLong and Shleifer blame 'politics, luck and even theology' and I have not seen a better explanation, at least not one quite so succinct.

But if there is no rational explanation for the freedom of English and Dutch economic institutions, there is a rational account of why small differences between those institutions and those of the absolute monarchies became magnified.

The account comes from Simon Johnson, now chief economist of the International Monetary Fund, along with Daron Acemoglu and James Robinson, whose idea of rational revolutions we encountered in the last chapter.

Europe started to become decisively richer than China

between AD 1500 and 1800, as opportunities to trade with the New World opened up; but this was not a pan-European phenomenon. It was confined to the nations that engaged in the Atlantic trade: Spain, Portugal, France, the Netherlands and England. Eastern European countries missed out. Atlantic port cities grew explosively; Mediterranean port cities did not. That might not seem puzzling: hauling slaves from Africa to the Americas and shipping gold and sugar to Europe was a profitable business, so it's no surprise that the trading nations prospered and wages rose. But the problem with that explanation is that the volume of trade just wasn't large enough to fuel such economic growth. The domestic economies of Western Europe were at least twenty-five times bigger than their commodity trade with the rest of the world. So what was going on?

Acemoglu, Johnson and Robinson argued that the chief contribution of Atlantic trade was indirect. It realigned the politics of Western European countries and offered new opportunities to a growing trader class. It strengthened them and thereby also strengthened the things they valued: strong property rights, the rule of law, and modest, predictable taxes. (The slaves, of course, had a different experience.)

For example, the English Civil War was won with the help of the Earl of Warwick. He had made a massive fifty thousand pounds in the year before the Civil War as a privateer, trading across the Atlantic and seizing booty from the Spanish and Portuguese. He threw both his funds and his military experience behind the parliamentarians. Parliament itself was funded by taxes on the Atlantic trade, and profits from it. Then during the Glorious Revolution of 1688, English merchants contributed around eight hundred thousand pounds to William of Orange's war fund; this was a huge sum, about 2 per cent of the size of the English economy and enough to equip almost twenty-five thousand soldiers for a year. Similarly, Dutch merchants funded the war of independence that freed Holland from Spanish rule.

Acemoglu and his colleagues aren't able to produce an

account of why England and Holland had a stronger merchant class in 1500 than did France or Spain – we are back to DeLong and Shleifer's 'politics, luck and even theology'. What they do show is that the Atlantic trade dramatically strengthened the merchant class wherever it existed. Where it did not, the profits from trade accrued to the monarch – to the eventual disadvantage of Spain and France.

Not everyone will buy this account of the ultimate cause of the English and Dutch commercial revolutions, and the subsequent Industrial Revolution. But whether you do or not, you should be persuaded that economic institutions have been hugely important for the dramatic economic growth I described at the beginning of the chapter. Rationally, that would make sense. These institutions provide incentives for rational entrepreneurs to invest, trade and develop new business ideas. With those incentives comes wealth; without them, misery.

That does sound plausible, but simply establishing a correlation between wealth and property rights does not make a cast-iron case about the direction of causation. There is an alternative explanation: rich countries have respect for property rights, well-functioning courts and the rest, because they can afford them. I think this alternative is the wrong explanation – and I think it is the brutal history of colonialism that provides the proof, as we are about to see.

Siaya District, Kenya, July 2004

Jeffrey Sachs, perhaps the world's most famous development economist, is visiting villagers who live their lives firmly in the grip of poverty. What he sees is 'grim, but salvageable'. Disease is common. Malaria is dangerous for young children, and everyone knows about anti-malarial bed nets and would like to use them. Yet only two out of two hundred villagers can afford them. Aids has spread through the adult population; most households contain orphaned children. The soil is badly depleted, and the farmers cannot afford new breeds of tree designed to fix nitrogen in their fields. Siaya District is several hundred miles from the sea, and some distance even from the capital, Nairobi, making it difficult to transport goods to market, and particularly hard to reach the global markets supplied by countries with better transport links. Poverty, argues Sachs, is evidently compounded by geography.

Sachs and various colleagues had already produced a series of academic papers arguing that poor countries are poor in part because of their geographical disadvantages. Diseases such as malaria devastate their economies; poor soil cannot be replenished for lack of funds; long distances from potential markets make it difficult to compete with China and the Asian Tigers, which can simply put their goods on a container ship and send them across the Pacific. The statistics seem to back them up: tropical, landlocked countries tend to be poor. Being poor, the argument goes, they cannot afford the wonderful economic institutions we have in rich countries such as fair courts, property registers and a banking system.

That view of the world is persuasive; the only trouble is, it seems to be false. Granted, Sachs makes a strong case for supplying the money to help fight malaria and buy those nitrogen-fixing trees. Granted, also, if someone – anyone – could fix the roads and get the electricity running reliably, Kenya would do better. But is its geography actually why Kenya is poor? No, for two reasons.

First, geographic isolation is not an insuperable barrier to economic success. America and Australia were once utterly isolated, but both are now rich, and America is the market from which everyone else's isolation is measured.

Second, malaria is an unlikely candidate for being a cause of underdevelopment. It kills young children, not adults who have grown up with the disease. Fighting malaria will save children's lives, so it's desperately worth doing. But it probably will not bring economic growth. From the narrow perspective of economic growth, Aids is a more dangerous disease because it kills economically productive young adults, but Aids is a recent epidemic and Africa has been poor for generations. In any case, these diseases can be fought by countries with the resources to do so: malaria used to afflict Australia, Israel and the Panama Canal Zone, but no longer.

Furthermore, non-tropical diseases can be deadly, too. In the United States, merely living in a city brought a serious risk of disease, even in the early twentieth century. Around 1900, life expectancy of city dwellers was a decade less than for those who lived in the countryside. But the United States grew rich anyway, and the urban diseases were stamped out.

Yet I don't wish to dismiss the economic significance of malaria. There is one thing malaria did very effectively: it killed adults who did not grow up with the disease and who did not have access to mosquito nets, drugs or even knowledge about how it spreads. In short, it killed European settlers; by doing so, it created incentives to crush economic growth in tropical areas, and changed the course of history.

Leiden, Holland, 1617

Fleeing persecution in England, a small group of highly religious people were finding that life in Leiden was not much better. There were few jobs to be had, their savings were being eaten away, and the morals of the congregation were being tempted 'by evill examples into extravagence and dangerous courses'. The leaders of the community decided that they would cross the Atlantic to the New World, where there were opportunities for all, millions of natives with souls to save, and few lascivious Dutch. So it was that the Pilgrim Fathers came to . . . Guyana, on the northern borders of Brazil.

Or so it might have been. But settlers in Guyana were twice as likely to die as settlers in North America. The Pilgrim Fathers, after debating the issue, and very worried about the risks of tropical disease in Guyana, decided to set sail for New England instead.

They are not the only settlers who were kept out of the tropics by fear of disease. The British authorities used to deport convicts to the American colonies, but after independence that was no longer an option. The Beauchamp Committee was established in 1785 to decide where to deport the convicts to instead; Gambia was a possibility and so was Southwest Africa, but in the end the deadly local diseases were thought to pose an unacceptable risk, even to convicted criminals. (On a large expedition led by a Scottish explorer from Gambia to Niger just ten years later, every single European died.) Mortality rates in African colonies were typically 40 or 50 per cent in the first year. As well as swaying the consciences of the penal authorities, all these facts were well known to potential migrants from the European colonial powers, who much preferred to settle in the safer climes of what would eventually become Australia, Canada, New Zealand and the United States.

Instead of trying to send colonial settlers to areas with fearsome tropical diseases, Europeans took the even more brutal yet selfishly rational decision to establish the slave trade in such places and set up abusive economic systems designed to exploit the land and people or scrape up as much gold and ivory as possible in the shortest time. Economists Daron Acemoglu, Simon Johnson and James Robinson therefore argue that it was history, rather than geography, that shaped the wealth of nations, because of the differing institutional legacies of colonialism. The settler-based colonies – New Zealand, Canada, the United States and Australia – became independent with a decent set of political institutions, designed to respect private property and uphold the law. The plantation economies became independent with a political system designed to suck out every penny of short-term gain and funnel it to the guys in charge. Since political and economic systems are hard to change, the systems these former colonies have today bear a strong family resemblance to the systems they had at independence. There are no prizes for guessing which institutions promote economic growth.

The direct effects of today's tropical diseases are trivial for the economy, if not for the people bitten by mosquitoes, while yesterday's diseases are a major cause of today's poverty because they scared away serious efforts at colonisation. But how much credence can we lend to this somewhat reductive analysis of complex historical trends? It would be helpful to be able to construct a laboratory experiment to test the effects of colonisation on the modern economy.

As luck would have it, something very close to such an experiment exists in the shape of the Pacific islands. Each island has its own colonial history and enjoyed the benefits and suffered the costs of settlement by different colonial powers, starting at different times and lasting for differing periods. If this really were a laboratory experiment, you would want some omnipotent researcher to plonk down colonists on different islands at randomly selected times. And that is – sort of – what happened. How? The answer is blowing in the wind (sorry). Until the late eighteenth century, sailors had no idea what their longitude – their east–west position – was. They could, however, easily work out their latitude by measuring how high the sun rose at noon. If a ship's captain wanted to land on a Pacific island, he would sail around Cape Horn at the tip of South America, then sail due north until reaching the correct latitude, then due west across the Pacific until bumping into the island in question. Trying to steer a diagonal route, north-west, risked overshooting the island, which with a scurvied crew and the water barrels running dry would be no joke.

Because of this cumbersome procedure, a Pacific island that happened to lie on a latitude with a good, reliable breeze from the east was more likely to be discovered, then to be used regularly as a stop for water, and then to be colonised. Guam, for example, is on the main east–west sailing route across the Pacific. It was discovered by Ferdinand Magellan back in 1521, and spent over four hundred years as a colony. Other islands, although they enjoyed equally fertile land and idyllic beaches, were less likely to be stumbled upon by sailors. Since the relationship between islands and prevailing breezes is random – the strength and direction of winds affected the likelihood that an island would be discovered and then colonised early, but the winds didn't have any connection with how attractive the island was as a colony – it provides the natural experiment necessary to work out whether colonial regimes are good or bad for growth.

Economists James Feyrer and Bruce Sacerdote worked all this out. They gathered careful data on the modern wealth, colonial history and weather patterns of eighty small islands, and they concluded that the islands that were easy to reach because of the prevailing winds back in the sixteenth and seventeenth centuries are wealthier today. An extra century of colonial rule increased per-capita incomes by 40 per cent and reduced infant deaths by 2.6 per hundred births.

Needless to say, the wealth brought by colonial rule did not usually benefit the original inhabitants of the colonies. While Australia leapt from being perhaps the poorest place in the world to perhaps one of the richest in just a couple of centuries, that impressive record is a little tarnished by the fact that most of the original inhabitants died of smallpox. The positive impact of colonialism on present-day wealth is interesting not because it is cause for celebration, but because of what it tells you about how countries grow rich. And it's not true that rich countries have good institutions because they can afford them. These inventive papers on the colonial era strongly suggest that the institutions came first, and then the economic growth.

*

The further back in time we go, the more we must speculate about what the economic institutions might then have been. Archaeologists can see new tools and technologies in the archaeological record, but beyond the most obvious distinctions between urban and rural, institutions do not leave physical traces. The last few pages of this book, then, are going to be the most wildly speculative of all. I won't apologise for that: we've come a long way together and now we deserve some fun.

Our first speculative question: how did our ancestors kill off the Neanderthals? The Neanderthals had survived for over two hundred thousand years, including through the brutal European winters of the last ice age. They were large and strong and they had big brains, too, but for some reason they lasted just a few thousand years once modern humans arrived in Europe about forty thousand years ago. Since they were competing for the same resources, the obvious conclusion is that *Homo sapiens* was simply better adapted to European life and drove the Neanderthals to extinction. But that's a hard case to make. After all, *Homo sapiens* had evolved in Africa and the Neanderthals had spent two hundred thousand years adapting to Europe. They were hairy and tough. Some – though not all – palaeobiologists think that they used language and had the same brainpower as the humans with whom they competed.

The fascinating speculation that emerges from a rational view of history suggests that the Neanderthals were missing out on an important economic institution, one whose value to rational beings we explored in an earlier chapter: the division of labour.

Division of labour is all-pervasive for humans. As I've said before, my trusty cappuccino is the product of many hands: the miners who dug the coal to generate the electricity to power the espresso machine; the farmers who grew the coffee beans; and those who raised the dairy cows, not to mention the inventors of electricity, steel refining, paper cups and the rest. The market – that is, many people all trading one thing for another – ensures that the cappuccino is made as inexpensively as can be. Even primitive societies use trading to allow people to spend more time doing and practising what it is they are relatively good at, and less time bumbling around outside the limits of their competence.

Division of labour may mean one family trading with another, or even one community trading with another quite far away. Even forty thousand years ago, human settlements were using stone tools from other regions and wearing seashell ornaments far from the sea. Early humans also had homes with different spaces set aside for different uses, possibly a sign of specialised crafts. This would have been a big help: cerebral types could have stayed home and made fishing hooks while the hairy brutes went out to hunt mammoth.

Adam Smith saw 'the propensity to truck, barter and exchange' as being part of human nature, and indeed a quality that set men apart from other animals: 'Nobody ever saw a dog make a fair and deliberate exchange of one bone for another with another dog.'

In this respect, for all their brainpower, Neanderthals appear to have been more like dogs than humans. There is no sign in the archaeological record that they ever traded. That would have been a big disadvantage. Computer-based simulations show that 'the propensity to truck, barter and exchange' could easily have allowed humans to wipe out Neanderthals in a few thousand years, even if the typical Neanderthal were faster, stronger, and perhaps smarter too.

But the division of labour might have been even simpler than that. Perhaps the most important trades were not between coastal villages and settlements near flint seams, but – as we saw in Chapter Three – between men and women. Today's simple hunter–gatherer societies divide tasks between the sexes. Men hunt big game and not much else; women hunt small animals, gather berries and nuts, make clothes and look after the kids. Early humans, too, seem to have divided up jobs between hunters and gatherers, presumably along the same lines.

Neanderthals, apparently, did not: men, women and children all behaved like human males, hunting reindeer and mastodons.

So much for the past. Now what about the future?

Economists are typically wrong about the future, but few have ever been as spectacularly, famously and lucklessly wrong as Thomas Malthus. A fellow of Jesus College, Cambridge, and a parson at Okewood Church, near Albury, Malthus produced his most famous work in 1798: 'An Essay on the Principle of Population'. He offered two 'postulata': 'First, That food is necessary to the existence of man. Secondly, That the passion between the sexes is necessary and will remain nearly in its present state.'

In other words, people will always need to eat and they'll never stop having kids. Next, Malthus suggests: 'Population, when unchecked, increases in a geometrical ratio. Subsistence increases only in an arithmetical ratio.' His presumption was that population would always be checked by the limits on people's ability to grow enough food for themselves. In the absence of technological progress, long-run population growth would be zero after the human species had filled its ecological niche, as it is for non-human animals. Malthus, no fool, knew that human technology was always improving, so population would also grow. But he assumed that technology would improve 'in an arithmetical ratio' – 10, 20, 30, 40, 50, 60, 70 – while population would grow geometrically – 2, 4, 8, 16, 32, 64, 128 – which meant that sooner or later – 64, 128 – people would run out of food.

The implication of Malthus's analysis is not apocalypse, but the more prosaic conclusion that while potential population growth could be geometric, actual population growth will be arithmetic as human fecundity constantly bumps against the steady progress of human technology. As we discovered at the beginning of this chapter, that has been true for most of human history – until 1798. At the very moment he advanced his thesis, the evidence began to accumulate that he was wrong.

Malthus didn't anticipate the pill, which conclusively separated 'the passion between the sexes' from the birth rate. But that isn't where he went wrong. His mistake was to assume that technology progresses arithmetically.

It wasn't until 1993 that an irrepressibly inventive economist, Michael Kremer of Harvard, published the most elegant exposition of exactly what went wrong for Malthus – and right for humanity. Never short of chutzpah, Kremer promised a model of economic growth 'from one million BC to 1990'; he offered a million years of human history in one equation.

Kremer's model, simply stated, is that any old caveman is as likely to invent something useful as any other caveman. Once Fred Flintstone invents something – fire, the wheel, free jazz – then that invention is available to everybody. Perhaps the invention would take a bit of time to spread, but with a million years of history to play with, who cares about that? The basic insight here is that an idea can be used by everyone. If you take Fred's flint axe then he doesn't have a flint axe any more; but if you take the idea of making a flint axe from him, that doesn't mean he'll forget the trick. That would mean that inventions are more useful when the population is larger. Back in 300,000 BC, Fred's idea would only be enjoyed by one million people. Today, the wheel makes life easier for six billion of us.

If that story is true, it also gives us Kremer's equation: the rate of technological progress is proportional to the world's population. Assuming one really brilliant idea per billion people per year, then the million-strong *Homo erectus* population in 300,000 BC would have been coming up with one such idea every thousand years. By 1800, the dawn of the Industrial Revolution, with a billion people in the world, the innovation rate would have risen to one stunning idea every year. By 1930 it would be one world-changing idea every six months. With six billion minds on the planet we should now be producing this kind of idea every two months. Such ideas could be anything from double-entry book-keeping to crop rotation.

It's an absurd, grotesquely oversimplified model; it also fits the data perfectly. Kremer suggests simply taking population growth as a measure of technological progress: the faster the human population is able to grow, the more advanced technology must have become. It turns out that these eminently Malthusian assumptions fit very nicely indeed, at least until 1960 and the pill. The world of 1960 had about twice the number of people and twice the population growth rate as the world of 1920, which had about twice the number of people and twice the population growth rate of the world of 1800, which had about twice the number of people and twice the population growth rate of the world of 1500 – and so on, right back into the Stone Age. True, we're not really sure what the population was back in one million B.C, but archaeologists and palaeontologists have been making well-established, educated and independent estimates that existed long before Kremer and his one-equation model of prehistory. They are the best we have, and they match the model unnervingly well.

The end of the last ice age provides a bit of extra evidence in favour of the idea that big populations are good for innovation. As the glaciers retreated about eleven thousand years ago, draining into the oceans, a narrow isthmus was submerged. It had once joined Tasmania to mainland Australia; now the seas had drowned it, cutting off Tasmania and a tiny place called Flinders Island.

Only fifty miles long, Flinders Island must have been a tough place to eke out an existence. But a few dozen islanders clung on for thousands of years, finally dying out in about 5000 BC. We can extrapolate from Kremer's ideas about large populations being more prone to brilliant ideas, and speculate that small populations are more vulnerable to collective amnesia: slowly but surely, it seems the Flinders Islanders forgot the tricks and tools that had allowed their ancestors to prosper, and being such a tiny community there simply were not enough people to generate fresh ideas.

Across the Bass Strait in Tasmania, a civilisation of a few thousand people was also struggling. Archaeologists tell us that the Tasmanians were going backward technologically, forgetting how to make boats and how to fish. The Tasmanians might have been expected to do well: with only a few thousand of them and an island the size of Ireland to expand across, a climate similar to the northeastern United States, and plenty of fertile land, they had a promising natural setting. From a natural resource point of view, they should have done well, with lots of space to grow into.

Kremer's explanation of why they struggled is the only one that makes much sense. Coming up with new ideas was always going to be hard with a population of a few thousand. They did not expand to fill Tasmania, and by AD 1500 the population density of the Old World (Europe, Asia and Africa) was a hundred times greater than that of Tasmania.

Mainland Australia's larger population – perhaps two hundred thousand – continued to advance, but very slowly. There is scant evidence that they invented very much beyond the boomerang; no match for the technology being developed in the Old World by a population of nearly half a billion people. When Eurasians, personified by Captain James Cook, finally decided to colonise Australia, the gap in technology was so great that there was nothing the indigenous population could do to resist.

Meanwhile, the Americas, with a pre-Columbian population of about fourteen million, were doing better, possessing a population density ten times greater than Australia's. Several American civilisations were formidable, highly organised and capable of building cities that are still admired today. But fourteen million brains are not as smart as four hundred million brains, and by the time Europe made contact with America, the former's technological advantage was overwhelming.

Poor Malthus. He seemed justified by a million years of human history, and wrote his essay at exactly the time he was about to be clearly proved wrong. Human beings always have been constrained by the progress of technology, but before 1798 technological progress was so slow that it was impossible to distinguish between arithmetical progress and geometrical progress. After all, slow is slow. Geometrical advances only become fast when the base of the geometrical progress reaches a certain size.

Consider the difference between a hundred pounds in a bank account earning a pound a year (arithmetical), and a hundred pounds in a bank account earning 1 per cent a year (geometrical). After a thousand years the geometrical account would be two thousand times larger, and growing two thousand times faster, but for the first few years the difference in growth rates would be mere pennies. While the difference is initially trivial – probably imperceptible – it eventually becomes impossibly large. As Malthus was writing, the world's population was about to reach one billion, and the combined inventive power of a billion minds was about to prove that technology does not grow at an arithmetical rate.

It remains to be seen whether Malthus will have his revenge, and global warming, overfishing, soil erosion, or the end of oil will eventually outwit human technology and bring living standards crashing back down to subsistence levels. So far there is little sign of that. Most commodity prices, for example, fell throughout the twentieth century, suggesting that despite ever-higher demand, better technology was winning the day.

For now the evidence supports Ted Baxter's strategy. Baxter, the pompous newsreader from *The Mary Tyler Moore Show*, planned to have six children in the hope that one of them would solve the population problem. It seems he had the right idea.

And for the rest of us? I hope I've convinced you over the course of this book that human beings are pretty smart. Our rational behaviour often backfires socially – witness the racism of Chapter Six, the crime of Chapters One and Five, and the environmental problems we face today. But our rational behaviour can also produce wonders. The more of us there are in the world, living our logical lives, the better our chances of seeing out the next million years.

Acknowledgements

A glance at this book makes it clear that it is based on the discoveries of a large number of talented researchers. I am very grateful to them for offering pointers, answering e-mails, and, frequently, allowing me to interview them at some length. They include Robert Axtell, Gary Becker, Stefano Bertozzi, Marianne Bertrand, Darse Billings, Simon Burgess, Bryan Caplan, Philip Cook, Frank Chaloupka, Kerwin Kofi Charles, Andre Chiappori, Gregory Clark, Daniel Dorling, Lena Edlund, Paula England, Marco Francesconi, Roland Fryer, Paul Gertler, Ed Glaeser, Claudia Goldin, Joe Gyourko, Daniel Hamermesh, George Horwich, Adam Jaffe, John Kagel, Matthew Kahn, Michael Kell, Mark Kleiman, Jeff Kling, Alan Krueger, David Laibson, Steven Landsburg, John List, Steven Levitt, Glenn Loury, Rob MacCoun, Enrico Moretti, Sendhil Mullainathan, Victoria Prowse, Daniel Read, Peter Riach, Jeffrey Sachs, Saskia Sassen, Thomas Schelling, Thomas Stratmann, Philip A. Stevens, Jake Vigdor, Yoram Weiss, Justin Wolfers, Peyton Young and Jonathan Zenilman.

Equally talented and equally generous with their expertise or comments were Lee Aitken, Sam Bodanis, Dominic Camus, Anne Currell, Stephen Dubner, Chris 'Jesus' Ferguson, Patri Friedman, Mark Henstridge, Diana Jackson, Howard Lederer, Philippe Legrain, Dave Morris, Seamus McCauley, Giuliana Molinari, Frazer Payne, William Poundstone, Greg Raymer, Romesh Vaitilingam and David Warsh.

Every day at the *Financial Times* brings me new ideas, but I particularly wish to thank my colleagues on the leader writing team, David Gardner, Robin Harding and Alison Smith; my *FT Magazine* editors, Isabel Berwick, Rosie Blau, Pilita Clark, Graham Watts and Michael Skapinker; Chris Giles and Martin Wolf; and Lionel Barber and Dan Bogler for so quickly agreeing to give me some time to write this book. I am also grateful to the *Financial Times* for allowing me to use my articles as the basis for some sections of this book.

Beyond the *FT*, David Plotz of *Slate* and Elisabeth Eaves, Dave Ewalt and Michael Noer of *Forbes* improved articles that served as preparation for writing this book. The amazing production crew of *Trust Me, I'm an Economist* all deserve a medal, but Simon Chu, Gabi Kent and Lindsay Shapero particularly helped me develop ideas that have ended up here. And since this book could not have been written without *The Undercover Economist*, everyone I thanked there I thank again – especially Paul Domjan, whom I did not thank quite enough, I feel.

At Random House, Doubleday, and Little, Brown, thanks to Tim Bartlett, Kerry Chapple, Diana Fox, Steve Guise, Maya Mavjee and Tim Rostron. Sally Holloway, my agent, kept all of us in line.

Eleneus Meulengracht and Venetia Strangwayes-Booth of Venetia's on Chatsworth Road made me excellent coffee. This turned out to be very important.

I'd also like to thank the nameless hero who knocked Reginald Jones's knife away on Fifteenth Street; that turned out to be important, too.

Tim Bartlett, David Bodanis, Paul Klemperer and Andrew Wright read and commented on every word of the manuscript and improved it immeasurably. I particularly wish to thank Andrew, who read each draft and still managed to produce fresh ideas every time.

Writing a book is an emotional marathon as much as an intellectual one. So most of all I want to thank my long-suffering and incredibly wonderful wife, Fran Monks.

Notes

Introduction

xi By comparing public data: Leigh L. Linden and Jonah E. Rockoff, 'There Goes the Neighbourhood? Estimates of the Impact of Crime Risk on Property Values from Megan's Laws,' NBER Working Paper No. 12253, May 2006, www.publicpolicy.umd.edu/news/rock off.pdf.

1. Introducing the logic of life

1 'The moms in my set': Caitlin Flanagan, 'Are You There God? It's Me, Monica,' review essay, *Atlantic*, January/February 2006.

2 For boys the rate climbed: Reuters, 'Rates of Oral and Anal Sex on the Increase among Adolescents, Young Adults,' 9 May 2006, www.medscape.com/viewarticle/532034.

2 I sought advice from: Interview with Professor Zenilman, February 2006.

2 One recent study of sex education: Kaiser Family Foundation, 'Sex Education in the US: Policy and Politics,' www.kff.org/youth-hivstds/3224-02-index.cfm, 2003, reports that 91 per cent of schools offer sex education, and of these, 96 per cent raise awareness of HIV and 84 per cent offer advice on preventing pregnancy.

3 Certainly, the evidence suggests: Centers for Disease Control and Prevention, National Youth Risk Behavior Survey, www.cdc.gov/HealthyYouth/yrbs/pdf/trends/2005_YRBS_Sexual_Behaviours.pdf. There are mixed indicators, though: anal sex, which is not safe, is also on the rise from low levels.

3 That real economist: Jonathan Klick and Thomas Stratmann, 'Abortion Access and Risky Sex among Teens: Parental Involvement

Laws and Sexually Transmitted Diseases,' FSU College of Law, Public Law Research Paper No. 175, 3 October 2005, available at ssrn.com/abstract=819304.

4 The only explanation: One query with Klick and Stratmann's research is that gonorrhoea has for years been strongly concentrated in the African-American population, while Klick and Stratmann only find their results stand up strongly for white and especially for Hispanic teenagers. (They speculate that Catholic Hispanic teenagers are more worried than black teenagers about the prospect of confessing to their parents that they want an abortion. Perhaps.) In principle, though, their statistical method should cope with this problem.

5 A young economist: Andrew M. Francis, 'The Economics of Sexuality,' draft paper, 1 March 2006.

5 'Oh my God': Stephen J. Dubner and Steven D. Levitt, 'The Economy of Desire,' *New York Times Magazine*, 11 December 2005.

8 It is true that economists: An economics textbook will offer a different definition of rationality, based on mathematical axioms. The maths, too, is foundational to the way economists write their academic papers: It makes the equations work. But the axioms are not important for the purposes of this book.

9 *Homo economicus* or 'economic man': Classical scholars will recognise that *Homo economicus* actually means 'economic human' – but since the name is usually used to describe a weird psychopathic accountant, nobody seems to complain about sexism here. For a discussion of homo economicus and his origins, see Joseph Persky, 'The Ethology of Homo Economicus,' *Journal of Economic Perspectives* 9, no. 2 (spring 1995).

11 That it's bad for you: For a summary with links to research, see Tim Harford, 'When Moms Work, Kids Get Fat,' *Slate*, 30 September 2006, www.slate.com/id/2150391/.

11 Smoking rates have fallen dramatically: According to the WHO Tobacco Atlas, www.who.int/tobacco/statistics/tobacco_atlas/en/, smoking among adult men in the United States fell from 52 to 26 per cent between 1965 and 1999, and for women from 34 per cent to 22 per cent. In the United Kingdom, the fall was from 61 to 28 per cent among men and 42 to 26 per cent among women, between 1960 and 1999.

12 To one group of subjects: Amos Tversky and Daniel Kahneman, 'The Framing of Decisions and the Psychology of Choice,' *Science* 211 (1981): 453–58.

14 'I was a sports card dealer': Telephone interview with John List, January 2007.

15 That's why Professor List: John A. List, 'Does Market Experience

Eliminate Anomalies?', *Quarterly Journal of Economics*, February 2003.

16 On another occasion: Uri Gneezy and John List, 'Putting Behavioral Economics to Work: Testing for Gift Exchange in Labour Markets Using Field Experiments,' *Econometrica* 74, no. 5 (September 2006): 1365–84, rady.ucsd.edu/faculty/directory/gneezy/docs/behavioral-economics.pdf.

16 I am oversimplifying here: For an economic model in which it is rational to pay an excess wage, see C. Shapiro and J. Stiglitz, 'Equilibrium Unemployment as a Worker Discipline Device,' *American Economic Review* (June 1984). The theory that high wages and high effort are a sort of gift exchange, rather than a response to economic incentives, originates with George A. Akerlof, 'Labor Contracts as Partial Gift Exchange,' *Quarterly Journal of Economics* 97 (1982): 543–69.

18 Kagel and Battalio put each rat: Telephone interview with John Kagel, 24 January 2005.

20 Battalio, Kagel and Kogut showed: Raymond Battalio, John Kagel and Carl Kogut, 'Experimental Confirmation of the Existence of a Giffen Good,' *American Economic Review* 81, no. 4 (September 1991).

20 A Giffen good is: The first written discussion of Giffen goods is in Alfred Marshall's definitive 1895 textbook, *Principles of Economics*.

21 'We should be fine here': Author interview with Gary Becker, September 2005. See 'It's the Humanity, Stupid: Gary Becker Has Lunch with the *FT*,' *FT Magazine*, 17 June 2006.

22 For example, three authors: William J. Bennett, John J. DiIulio, Jr. and John P. Walters, *Body Count: Moral Poverty – and How to Win America's War against Crime and Drugs* (New York: Simon and Schuster, 1996), p. 27, quoted in Steven D. Levitt, 'Juvenile Crime and Punishment,' *Journal of Political Economy* 106 (1998): 1157.

22 These are tough questions: Levitt, 'Juvenile Crime and Punishment'.

23 Levitt explained to me: Interview with Steven Levitt, April 2005.

26 'The best girls don't last': This comment is from a sex tourism website. I am not sure whether our reviewer meant 'transvestites' in the next sentence.

28 The risks prostitutes take: Paul Gertler, Manisha Shah, and Stefano M. Bertozzi, 'Risky Business: The Market for Unprotected Commercial Sex,' *Journal of Political Economy* 113, no. 3 (2005): 518–50.

28 Consider Staff Sergeant Matthew Kruger: Faye Fiore, 'Amid War, Troops See Safety in Reenlisting,' *Los Angeles Times*, 21 May 2006.

2. Las Vegas

36 'Real life consists of bluffing': Jacob Bronowski, *The Ascent of Man* (Boston: Little, Brown, 1974).

36 His feats of calculation: William Poundstone's *Prisoner's Dilemma* (New York: Doubleday, 1992) contains many such stories.

37 In the 1972 final: Two excellent sources on the history of poker and the great poker characters are Michael Kaplan and Brad Reagan, *Aces and Kings* (New York: Wenner Books, 2005), and David Spanier, *Total Poker*, new edition (London: High Stakes, 2002).

40 What was remarkable: For a discussion of the Von Neumann poker model, and explanation of the mathematics, see Chris Ferguson and Tom Ferguson, 'On the Borel and Von Neumann Poker Models,' *Game Theory and Applications* 9 (2003): 17–32, www.math.ucla.edu/~tom/papers/poker1.pdf.

41 'Posterity may regard': Quoted in Poundstone, *Prisoner's Dilemma*, p. 7.

42 'Great books': Quoted in Poundstone, *Prisoner's Dilemma*, p. 41.

43 'You've never seen so many': Kaplan and Reagan, *Aces and Kings*, p. 32.

46 The age of rational poker: My sources for the Chris Ferguson story include my conversations with Ferguson around the 2005 World Series of Poker; Kaplan and Reagan, *Aces and Kings*; and James McManus, *Positively Fifth Street* (New York: Farrar, Straus & Giroux, 2003). McManus was in Las Vegas to write an article for *Harper's* and ended up at the final table with Cloutier and Ferguson.

49 If I ask a large number: See James Surowiecki, *The Wisdom of Crowds* (Boston: Little, Brown, 2004).

50 Even professional footballers: Ignacio Palacios-Huerta, 'Professionals Play Minimax,' *Review of Economic Studies* 70, no. 2 (2003): 395–415, and Tim Harford, 'Keep Them Guessing,' *FT Magazine*, 17 June 2006.

50 It turns out that: See Steven Levitt and John List, 'What Do Laboratory Experiments Tell Us about the Real World?' (University of Chicago and NBER, 27 June 2006) for a survey. Detailed studies of the winner's curse include Douglas Dyer and John Kagel, 'Bidding in Common Value Auctions: How the Commercial Construction Industry Corrects for the Winner's Curse,' *Management Science* 42 (1996): 143–76; James Cox, Sam Dinkin and James Swarthout, 'Endogenous Entry and Exit in Common Value Auctions,' *Experimental Economics* 4, no. 2 (October): 163–81; and Glenn Harrison and John List, 'Naturally Occurring Markets and Exogenous Laboratory Experiments: A Case Study of Winner's Curse,' UCF Working Paper, 2005.

50 Camp David: The story is told in Fred Kaplan's history, *The Wizards of Armageddon* (New York: Simon and Schuster, 1983), and Robert Dodge's biography of Schelling, *The Strategist* (Hollis, NH: Hollis, 2006).

54 With his emphasis on communication: Christopher Rand, 'Profiles,' *New Yorker*, 25 April 1964, mentions the red telephone. Dodge, *The Strategist*, has the full story.

54 'Somehow or other': For more about Dulles and Eisenhower, see Schelling's Nobel Prize lecture, nobelprize.org/nobel_prizes/economics/laureates/2005/schelling-lecture.pdf, pp. 366–67. Schelling cites McGeorge Bundy's *Danger and Survival: Choices about the Bomb in the First Fifty Years* (New York: Random House, 1988).

55 'The timing was perfect': Schelling's autobiography, on the Nobel Prize website, nobelprize.org/nobel_prizes/economics/laureates/2005/schelling-autobio.html.

55 'The most spectacular event': Schelling, Nobel Prize lecture.

56 In his 1980 essay: 'The Intimate Contest for Self Command' was reprinted in Thomas Schelling's *Choice and Consequence* (Cambridge, Mass.: Harvard University Press, 1984).

56 'I imagine him sitting': The speaker here is Robert Topel. John Easton, 'Murphy's Law,' *University of Chicago Magazine*, November–December 2006, magazine.uchicago.edu/0612/features/murphy.shtml.

57 Perhaps it will not be surprising: Gary S. Becker and Kevin M. Murphy, 'A Theory of Rational Addiction,' *Journal of Political Economy* 9 (August 1988): 675–700.

58 Becker and Murphy found: Gary S. Becker, Michael Grossman and Kevin M. Murphy, 'Rational Addiction and the Effect of Price on Consumption,' *American Economic Review* 81, no. 2. (May 1991): 237–41.

58 Another researcher discovered: Pamela Mobilia, 'Gambling as a Rational Addiction,' *Journal of Gambling Studies* 9, no. 2. (June 1993): 121–51, www.springerlink.com/content/p347422531h91241/.

59 In other words: Philip J. Cook and George Tauchen, 'The Effect of Liquor Taxes on Heavy Drinking,' *Bell Journal of Economics* 13 (autumn 1982): 379–90.

59 Economists have also found: Henry Saffer, Melanie Wakefield and Yvonne Terry-McElrath, 'The Effect of Nicotine Replacement Therapy Advertising on Youth Smoking,' NBER Working Paper No. 12964, March 2007, www.nber.org/papers/w12964.

59 Kevin Murphy told me: Interview with Kevin Murphy, March 2007.

60 Schelling sometimes told a story: Dodge, *The Strategist*, p. 164.

60 Rather than reflecting and speculating: Some economists model the weaker half of the split personality as irrational, while others make

the weaker half rational but holding different preferences – usually impatient ones. I've stuck to *impatient* as shorthand for the weaker half. Game theory applies to a battle of wills between two rational opponents (here, in the same body) with different preferences. The alternative models where the addicted personality is irrational do not employ game theory. I'm grateful to David Laibson for clarifying the distinction in an interview in October 2006.

61   This impatient part of the brain: B. Douglas Bernheim and Antonio Rangel, 'Addiction and Cue-Triggered Decision Processes,' *American Economic Review* 94, no. 5 (December 2004): 1558–90. See also Helen Phillips, 'Hooked: Why Your Brain Is Primed for Addiction,' *New Scientist*, 26 August 2006.

61   Lower-tech experiments: Daniel Read and Barbara van Leeuwen, 'Predicting Hunger: The Effects of Appetite and Delay on Choice,' *Organizational Behavior and Human Decision Processes* 76, no. 2 (November 1998): 189–205, personal.lse.ac.uk/readd/predicting%20hunger.pdf. For the study of highbrow and lowbrow movies, see D. Read, G. Loewenstein and S. Kalyanaraman, 'Mixing Virtue and Vice: Combining the Immediacy Effect and the Diversification Heuristic,' *Journal of Behavioral Decision Making* 12 (1999): 257–73, personal.lse.ac.uk/readd/mixing%20virtue%20and%20vice.pdf.

62   One of the researchers: E-mail correspondence with Daniel Read, June 2007.

63   That public commitment: Dodge, *The Strategist*, p. 91.

63   A more sophisticated example: Richard Thaler and Shlomo Benartzi, 'Save More Tomorrow: Using Behavioral Economics to Increase Employee Saving,' *Journal of Political Economy* 112, no. 1 (February 2004): 164–87, part 2, gsbwww.uchicago.edu/fac/richard.thaler/research/SMarTJPE.pdf.

64   Who did the director: Interview with Thomas Schelling, November 2005. Also Dodge, *The Strategist*, p. 83.

65   Paul Klemperer: Paul Klemperer, 'What Really Matters in Auction Design,' *Journal of Economic Perspectives* 16 (2002): 169–89, www.nuff.ox.ac.uk/users/klemperer/wrm6.pdf. I devoted a chapter of my book *The Undercover Economist* to explaining the successes and failures of such mobile-phone licence auctions.

65   These men and women: These self-exclusion schemes don't always work. According to Jim Holt, 'The New, Soft Paternalism,' *New York Times Magazine*, 3 December 2006, the first person in Michigan to sign up for the state-run self-exclusion list was also the first to be arrested for violating its terms.

3. Is divorce underrated?

68 Economists at Columbia University: R. Fisman, S. Iyengar, E. Kamenica and I. Simonson, 'Gender Differences in Mate Selection: Evidence from a Speed Dating Experiment,' *Quarterly Journal of Economics* 121 (May 2006): 673–97. Also see their 2004 working paper on racial preferences, papers.ssrn.com/sol3/papers.cfm? abstract_id=610589.

70 But there is some suggestive evidence: Michèle Belot and Marco Francesconi, 'Can Anyone Be "The" One? Evidence on Mate Selection from Speed Dating,' IZA Discussion Paper 2377, October 2006.

71 'Who you propose': Interview with Marco Francesconi, October 2006.

77 Women are cautious: See Robert Wright, *The Moral Animal* (New York: Pantheon, 1994), for a discussion of evolutionary psychology, Robert Trivers's model and the experiments to explore it. The differences between male attitudes to sex and female attitudes can nevertheless be exaggerated. See Olivia Judson, *Dr Tatiana's Sex Guide for All Creation* (New York: Metropolitan, 2002), for a witty explanation of some of the subtleties.

77 Robert Trivers, the evolutionary biologist: R. L. Trivers, 'Parental Investment and Sexual Selection,' in B. Campbell, ed., *Sexual Selection and the Descent of Man, 1871–1971* (Chicago: Aldine, 1972), pp. 136–79.

78 In another experiment: Wright, *The Moral Animal*.

79 As ever, economists aren't satisfied: Guenter J. Hitsch, Ali Hortacsu and Dan Ariely, 'What Makes You Click? Mate Preferences and Matching Outcomes in Online Dating,' February 2006, MIT Sloan Research Paper No. 4603-06, SSRN: ssrn.com/abstract=895442.

79 The economist behind this idea: Lena Edlund, 'Sex and the City,' *Scandinavian Journal of Economics* 107, no. 1 (2005): 25–44.

79 She explained the implications: Interview with Lena Edlund, January 2007.

80 In New York: American Community Survey 2005 for New York City, factfinder.census.gov/servlet/STTable?_bm=y&-geo_id=1600 0US3651000&-qr_name=ACS_2005_EST_G00_S0101&-' ds_name=ACS_2005_EST_ G00_.

80 There are more men: Nationwide, there are very slightly more men than women aged twenty to thirty-four. See factfinder.census. gov/servlet/GRTTable?_bm=y&-_box_head_nbr=R0102&- ds_name=ACS_2005_EST_G00_&-format=US-30. Also see Census Brief: Gender 2000, www.census.gov/prod/2001pubs/c2k br01-9.pdf, figure 3.

80   Most people marry people: Data are from the US census, calculated and reported by Kerwin Kofi Charles and Ming Ching Luoh, 'Male Incarceration, the Marriage Market, and Female Outcomes,' working paper, table 2.

80   There are two million men: Department of Justice press release, 23 October 2005, www.ojp.gov/newsroom/2005/BJS06002.htm.

81   In New Mexico: These data are from Charles and Luoh, 'Male Incarceration,' table 1. The figures refer to the state of birth, not the current state of residence.

82   'Culture' is a poor explanation: It's possible that some sort of increasing social dysfunction or deprivation is simultaneously causing more young black men to behave badly and go to jail, and fewer black women to get married. But Charles and Luoh argue plausibly that the increase in incarceration rates is due to a change in sentencing policy rather than a change in behaviour.

84   It's a textbook case: Pierre-André Chiappori, Murat Iyigun and Yoram Weiss, 'Investment in Schooling and the Marriage Market,' working paper, September 2006.

84   Nowadays, four US women: Data from Claudia Goldin's 2006 Ely Lecture to the American Economic Association, published in *American Economic Review*, 2006, as 'The Quiet Revolution That Transformed Women's Employment, Education, and Family,' and Chiappori, Iyigun and Weiss, 'Investment in Schooling and the Marriage Market.'

85   Delaying motherhood means big income gains: Amalia Miller is the young economist behind this very clever research. Her working paper is available at www.virginia.edu/economics/miller.htm.

86   His employer was: Biographical details of Adam Smith are from James Buchan, *Adam Smith and the Pursuit of Perfect Liberty* (London: Profile, 2006).

86   But despite his travels: See David Warsh's superb *Knowledge and the Wealth of Nations* (New York: Norton, 2006), chapter 3.

86   'could scarce, perhaps': Adam Smith, *The Wealth of Nations*, book I, chapter 1, paragraph 3. Versions are available online, for instance at www.econlib.org/library/Smith/smWN.html.

88   His adoring wife: Stephanie Coontz, *Marriage: A History* (New York: Viking, 2005).

88   The roles were neatly reversed: 'Americans' Use of Time, 1965–6,' and 'American Time Use Survey 2003,' lecture notes by Yoram Weiss.

90   In the late 1970s: Gary S. Becker, *A Treatise on the Family*, enlarged edition (Cambridge, Mass.: Harvard University Press, 1993).

91   The only thing that would change: Becker, *A Treatise on the Family*, p. 334.

91 And sure enough: On divorce trends and the no-fault 'blip', see Becker, *A Treatise on the Family*, and Betsey Stevenson and Justin Wolfers, 'Marriage and Divorce: Changes and Their Driving Forces,' NBER Working Paper No. 12944, March 2007.

91 It became easy: Goldin, 'The Quiet Revolution.'

92 In the US, fewer than half: Lectures by Yoram Weiss, based on US current population surveys.

92 A close look at the statistics: Kerry L. Papps, 'The Effects of Divorce Risk on the Labour Supply of Married Couples,' IZA Discussion Paper No. 2395, October 2006, ftp.iza.org/dp2395.pdf.

93 The economist Betsey Stevenson: Betsey Stevenson, 'The Impact of Divorce Laws on Marriage-Specific Capital,' *Journal of Labor Economics* 25, no. 1 (2007): 75–94, bpp.wharton.upenn.edu/betseys/papers/IMSC.pdf.

94 One influential study: Jonathan Gardner and Andrew Oswald, 'Do Divorcing Couples Become Happier by Breaking up?,' *Journal of the Royal Statistical Society* 169, series A (2006), www2.warwick.ac.uk/fac/soc/economics/staff/faculty/oswald/jrssoct05.pdf.

94 That may sound a little abstract: Betsey Stevenson and Justin Wolfers, 'Bargaining in the Shadow of the Law: Divorce Laws and Family Distress,' *Quarterly Journal of Economics*, February 2006, bpp.wharton.upenn.edu/betseys/papers/Til%20Death%20%20MAY%2012%202005%20QJE%20FINAL.pdf.

95 And they are perhaps delayed indefinitely: Betsey Stevenson and Justin Wolfers, 'Marriage and Divorce: Changes and their Driving Forces'. Also Tyler Cowen, 'Matrimony Has Its Benefits, and Divorce Has a Lot to Do with That,' *New York Times*, 19 April 2007.

95 'We know there exists something': Interview with Justin Wolfers, June 2007.

95 'The man whose whole life': Adam Smith, *The Wealth of Nations*, book V, chapter 1, paragraph 178, www.econlib.org/library/Smith/smWN.html.

4. Why your boss is overpaid

97 Dilbert: This Dilbert cartoon was reprinted in Edward Lazear, *Personnel Economics for Managers* (New York: Wiley, 1998).

98 He reckoned that thirty thousand: Tim Harford, 'Odd Numbers,' *Financial Times*, 23 April 2005.

98 Levitt had also had a disagreement: Conversations with Steven Levitt and, separately, Stephen Dubner, March and April 2005.

100 Perhaps this was in deference: See, for instance, the work of Edward

Deci and his colleagues at Rochester University, psych.rochester. edu/SDT/theory.html.

100 It was also entirely correct: The Safelite case forms the basis for a famous paper by E. P. Lazear, 'Performance Pay and Productivity,' *American Economic Review* 90 (December 2000): 1346–61.

101 The Safelite case is unusual: Lazear, 'Performance Pay and Productivity,' p. 1359, based on National Longitudinal Survey of Youth.

101 Even when performance: The most famous take on this is Steven Kerr, 'On the Folly of Rewarding A, While Hoping for B,' *Academy of Management Journal* 18, no. 4 (December 1975): 769–83.

103 The economists in question: Alexandre Mas and Enrico Moretti, 'Peers at Work,' NBER Working Paper No. 12508, September 2006, www.nber.org/papers/w12508.

106 The economists who spotted: Edward Lazear and Sherwin Rosen, 'Rank Order Tournaments as Optimum Labor Contracts,' *Journal of Political Economy* 89, no. 5 (1981). Also Lazear, *Personnel Economics for Managers*.

106 In most tennis tournaments: On tennis tournament winnings, see for instance the Wimbledon website, aeltc.wimbledon.org/en_GB/ about/guide/prizemoney.html.

108 One study compared twenty-three firms: Robert Drago and Gerald Garvey, 'Incentives for Helping on the Job: Theory and Evidence,' *Journal of Labor Economics*, 1997, summarised in Lazear, *Personnel Economics for Managers*, p. 271.

110 'The salary of the vice president': Lazear, *Personnel Economics for Managers*, p. 226.

110 As the CEO of Walt Disney: 'Too Many Turkeys,' *The Economist*, 24 November 2005.

110 Since investors in Disney: 'Too Many Turkeys'.

112 The stock option revolution: Michael Jensen and Kevin J. Murphy, 'Performance Pay and Top-Management Incentives,' *Journal of Political Economy* 98, no. 2 (1990): 225–64.

114 That all sounds so satisfactory: I first heard this wonderfully perverse idea from Steven Landsburg, in his book *The Armchair Economist* (New York: Free Press, 1993).

116 Jensen and Murphy grumbled: Michael Jensen and Kevin J. Murphy, 'CEO Incentives – It's Not How Much You Pay, but How,' *Harvard Business Review* (May–June 1990): 225–64.

116 A CEO who captained: Brian J. Hall and Jeffrey P. Liebman, 'Are CEOs Really Paid Like Bureaucrats?,' *Quarterly Journal of Economics* 113 (August 1998): 653–91. The calculation is based on a survey by Sherwin Rosen.

116 In 2005: 'Executive Pay,' *The Economist*, 19 January 2006.

116 For instance, by the mid-1990s: Hall and Liebman, 'Are CEOs Really Paid Like Bureaucrats?,' pp. 654–5. To be more precise, they look at earnings of CEOs at the 30th and 70th per centile: these companies are just within the top and bottom thirds.

117 Sure, CEOs were paid: These statistics, and the definitive statement of the link between pay and firm size, are from Xavier Gabaix and Augustin Landier, 'Why Has CEO Pay Increased So Much?' NBER Working Paper No. 12365, July 2006, www.nber.org/papers/w12365.

117 There are other suspicious aspects: Lucian Bebchuk and Jesse Fried, *Pay without Performance: The Unfulfilled Promise of Executive Compensation* (Cambridge, Mass.: Harvard University Press, 2004), chapter 13.

117 Another is the 'backdated' option: For a good brief discussion, see James Surowiecki, 'The Dating Game,' *New Yorker*, 6 November 2006, www.newyorker.com/printables/talk/061106ta_talk_surowiecki.

117 Economists spotted the backdating trick: Erik Lie and Randall Heron, 'Does Backdating Explain the Stock Price Pattern around Executive Stock Option Grants?,' working paper (forthcoming, *Journal of Financial Economics*), www.biz.uiowa.edu/faculty/elie/Grants-JFE.pdf.

117 Backdating can be fraudulent: 'Walking the Plank,' *The Economist*, 19 October 2006, www.economist.com/business/displaystory.cfm?story_id = 8057657. Jobs was cleared of any wrongdoing in an internal investigation at Apple.

118 They granted backdated stock options: Richard Waters, 'Fresh Options Revelations Fail to Bite into Apple Share Price,' *Financial Times*, 30 December 2006.

118 But the odd options produce: Bebchuk and Fried, *Pay without Performance*.

120 A large shareholder: Marianne Bertrand and Sendhil Mullainathan, 'Are CEOs Rewarded for Luck? The Ones without Principals Are,' *Quarterly Journal of Economics* 116 (August 2001): 901–32.

5. In the neighbourhood

122 In the area carved in two: District of Columbia Metropolitan Police Department website, mpdc.dc.gov/mpdc/cwp/view,a,1239,q,543315.asp.

122 That isn't the only way: These data are from Neighborhood Info DC, www.neighborhoodinfodc.org/profiles.html. The area I refer to as 'Georgetown and Cleveland Park' is DC's third ward. 'Anacostia' is DC's eighth ward. The police districts are distinct from the electoral wards.

126 This striking demonstration: Thomas Schelling's original account of

the chessboard simulation is in his *Micromotives and Macrobehavior* (New York: Norton, 1978), chapter 4.

127 'A very small preference': Interview with Thomas Schelling, November 2005. Also see Tim Harford,'Lunch with the *FT*: The Game of Life,' *Financial Times*, 17 December 2005, www.ft.com/cms/s/585da744-6d24-11da-90c2-0000779e2340.html.

127 'If a white boy': Quoted in Schelling, *Micromotives and Macrobehavior*, p. 143.

132 'White pants – white bitch': A US Department of Justice press release, February 21, 2006, www.usdoj.gov/usao/dc/Press_Releases/2006_Archives/Feb_2006/06060 .html, summarises the evidence, which Reginald Jones accepted, entering an 'Alford' plea that asserted his innocence but accepted that enough evidence existed to convict him. Newspaper accounts include 'Horrific Attack, Heroic Rescue,' *Washington Post*, 7 July 2005, and 'Blood, Sweat, and Fear,' *FT Magazine*, 27 August 2005. I was one of the witnesses to the attack.

133 Jane Jacobs: Jane Jacobs, *The Death and Life of Great American Cities* (1961; reprinted New York: Vintage, 1992).

134 Two economists: Edward Glaeser and Bruce Sacerdote, 'The Social Consequences of Housing,' NBER Working Paper No. 8034, December 2000, papers.nber.org/papers/W8034.

135 The British ghettos are up: UK white population from the Office for National Statistics, www.statistics.gov.uk/cci/nugget.asp?id=273. Fact about people in high-rises is from an op-ed piece by the British geographer Daniel Dorling, published in the *Observer*, 25 September 2005. The original unedited version is at sasi.group.shef.ac.uk/publications/2005/Ghettos_observer_25_9_05.pdf.

136 Many of the eager consumers: See Richard Florida and Charlotta Mel-lander, 'There Goes the Neighborhood,' working paper, March 2007, for an exploration of the gays-as-pioneers thesis, creative-class.typepad.com/thecreativityexchange/files/Florida_Mellander_Housing_Values_1.pdf.

137 Hammond's computer creates: Ross Hammond, 'Endogenous Transition Dynamics in Corruption: An Agent-Based Computer Model,' CSED Working Paper No. 19, December 2000, www.brookings.edu/es/dynamics/papers/ross/ross.htm.

138 Anyone who doubts this: For Booth's map see, for instance, Peter Whitfield, *London: A Life in Maps* (London: British Library, 2006).

141 In 1994, selected residents: David Warsh, 'A Voucher Success,' *Boston Globe*, 22 May 2001.

143 'Even now, we can't': Lawrence Katz, Jeffrey Kling and Jeffrey Liebman, 'Moving to Opportunity in Boston: Early Results of a Randomised Mobility Experiment,' *Quarterly Journal of Economics* 116, no. 2 (May 2001): 607–54, www.nber.org/~kling/mto/mto_boston.pdf.

143   Over time, perhaps: Laurent Gobillon and Harris Selod, 'The Effect of Segregation and Spatial Mismatch on Unemployment: Evidence from France,' CEPR Discussion Paper No. 6198, March 2007, www.cepr.org/pubs/new-dps/dplist.asp?dpno=6198.

6. The dangers of rational racism

145   Some students at the University of Virginia: Roland Fryer, Jacob Goeree and Charles Holt, 'Experience-Based Discrimination: Classroom Games,' *Journal of Economic Education* 36, no. 2 (spring 2005): 160–70, www.economics.harvard.edu/faculty/fryer/papers/jece_2005pdf.

145   Then came the test itself: The test was, to be precise, two separate throws of a dice. An uneducated worker succeeded on a six, while an educated worker succeeded on a four–six. The employer would see whether the worker had passed both tests, just one test, or neither. The chance of an educated worker getting each result is 25 per cent, 50 per cent, and 25 per cent for good, middling and bad, respectively. For an uneducated worker, the chance is 1/36, 10/36 and 25/36, respectively – about 3 per cent, 28 per cent and 69 per cent. All of the students knew the way the test result was calculated.

147   'I was amazed': Interview with Roland Fryer, January 2007.

148   African Americans are not doing well: In his interview with Stephen Dubner of *New York Times Magazine*, Roland Fryer 'rattles off ' the statistics. See Dubner, 'Toward a Unified Theory of Black America,' 20 March 2005, www.nytimes.com/2005/03/20/magazine/20HARVARD.html?ei=5090&en=e9727ddcbbbd4431&ex=1268974800&partner=rssuserland&pagewanted=all. Other statistics are from the 1998 Council of Economic Advisers report, 'Changing America,' cited in Bertrand and Mullainathan, 'Are Emily and Greg More Employable than Lakisha and Jamal? A Field Experiment on Labor Market Discrimination,' working paper, 2004, www.economics.harvard.edu/faculty/mullainathan/papers/emilygreg.pdf, and from US Census Bureau: Jesse McKinnon and Claudette Bennett, 'We, the People: Blacks in the United States,' www.census.gov/prod/2005pubs/censr-25.pdf, figure 8.

149   Mullainathan spent his early childhood: Dana Wechsler Linden, 'Is Alfred Marshall Passé?,' *Forbes*, 17 October 2005, www.forbes.com/free_forbes/2005/1017/071.html.

150   Their researchers generated: Bertrand and Mullainathan, 'Are Emily and Greg More Employable than Lakisha and Jamal?' Some of the press coverage of Bertrand and Mullainathan's paper

suggested that this was the first time such a randomised trial had been carried out. That isn't true, although the Bertrand–Mullainathan study was on a particularly grand scale. The first researchers were British sociologists Roger Jowell and Patricia Prescott-Clarke, whose work, published in 1970, strongly influenced parliamentary debate at the time. Economists Peter Riach and Judith Rich, who have themselves carried out many such trials, survey the history of the method in 'Field Experiments of Discrimination in the Market Place,' *Economic Journal* 112 (November 2002): 480–518.

154   To find out who suffers: Gary Becker, *The Economics of Discrimination* (Chicago: University of Chicago Press, 1971). Also see Glen Cain, 'The Economic Analysis of Labour Market Discrimination: A Survey,' in Orley Ashenfelter and Richard Layard, eds, *Handbook of Labor Economics* (New York: Elsevier, 1986), chapter 13. Becker's Nobel lecture also contains a very brief summary of his analysis of discrimination.

154   In America, only 12 per cent: In the 2000 census, 12.3 per cent of the US population classified themselves as black or African American; 75.1 per cent classified themselves as white. See www.census.gov/prod/2001pubs/c2kbr01-1.pdf.

154   As well as being a moral outrage: 79 per cent of South Africa's population is black, 10 per cent is white. See encarta.msn.com/encyclopedia_761557321_3/South_Africa.html.

155   There is some evidence: Chiappori, Iyigun and Weiss, 'Investment in Schooling and the Marriage Market'.

156   'Black children and white children': Roland G. Fryer and Steven E. Levitt, 'Falling Behind,' *Education Next*, fall 2004, post.economics.harvard.edu/faculty/fryer/papers/falling_behind.pdf. The academic background is Fryer and Levitt, 'Understanding the Black–White Test Score Gap in the First Two Years of School,' *Review of Economics and Statistics* 86, no. 2 (May 2004): 447–64, post.economics.harvard.edu/faculty/fryer/papers/rest_vol86_2.pdf.

157   At first, Fryer and Levitt: Roland Fryer and Steven Levitt, 'The Black–White Test Score Gap through Third Grade,' *American Law and Economics Review* 8, no. 2 (2006): 249–81, pricetheory.uchicago.edu/levitt/Papers/FryerLevitt2005.pdf.

157   'Children can't achieve': The transcript of Obama's speech is widely available, for example at www.washingtonpost.com/wp-dyn/articles/A19751-2004Jul27.html.

157   When the young black economist: Loury's position today is not the same as his position in 1984 and his story is worth reading in its own right. See, for instance, Adam Shatz, 'Glenn Loury's about Face' *New York Times Magazine*, 20 January 2002, people.bu.edu/gloury/

NYT%20articles/Glenn%20Loury%27s%20About%20%20Face.
pdf. Also Robert Boynton, 'Loury's Exodus,' *New Yorker*, 1 May 1995,
www.robertboynton.com/articleDisplay.php?article_id=25.

158 'I didn't know what my colleagues': Interview with Roland Fryer,
January 2007.

159 However, serious quantitative research: See Roland G. Fryer,
'Acting White,' *Education Next*, winter 2005, post.economics.har-
vard.edu/faculty/fryer/papers/aw_ednext.pdf, for references. The
original 1986 academic study identifying 'acting white' as a problem
was by Signithia Fordham and John Ogbu. The economist Rob
Ferguson found supporting evidence. But James Ainsworth-Darnell
and Douglas Downey, and, separately, Philip Cook and Jens
Ludwig, found evidence that high-achieving black students were as
popular as high-achieving white students – perhaps more so.

159 'Asking twelve-year-olds how popular': Quoted in Beth Potier,
'Fryer Brings Mathematical Economics to Stubborn Racial Issues,'
Harvard University Gazette, 25 August 2005, www.news.harvard.edu/
gazette/2005/08.25/99-fryer.html.

159 Fryer instead used a survey: Roland Fryer, with David Austen-
Smith, 'An Economic Analysis of "Acting White",' *Quarterly Journal
of Economics* 120 (May 2005): 551–83, post.economics.harvard.edu/
faculty/fryer/papers/as_fryer_qje.pdf, and Fryer, 'Acting White'.

160 Fryer points to analogues: Roland Fryer, 'A Model of Social
Interactions and Endogenous Poverty Traps,' NBER Working
Paper No. W12364, post.economics.harvard.edu/faculty/fryer/
papers/cultural_capital_final.pdf, forthcoming in *Rationality and
Society*.

162 Not all affirmative action programs: Roland Fryer and Glenn Loury,
'Affirmative Action and Its Mythology,' *Journal of Economic
Perspectives* 19, no. 3 (summer 2005): 147–62.

162 Roland Fryer, who was recently: On Fryer's randomised trial,
Roland Fryer interview with author, January 2007. On his appoint-
ment by the New York City education department, see Jennifer
Medina, 'His Charge: Find a Key to Students' Success,' *New York
Times*, 21 June 2007.

162 Psychologist Barry Schwartz attacked Fryer: Barry Schwartz,
'Money for Nothing,' *New York Times*, 2 July 2007.

163 So you would think it's unequivocally: Edward Glaeser and Jacob
Vigdor, 'Racial Segregation in the 2000 Census: Promising News,'
Brookings Institution, April 2004.

163 Roland Fryer's database: Federico Echenique, Roland G. Fryer, Jr
and Alex Kaufman, 'Is School Segregation Good or Bad?' working
paper, January 2006, post.economics.harvard.edu/faculty/fryer/
papers/echen_fryer_kaufm.pdf.

163 Glenn Loury's doctoral thesis: Glenn C. Loury, 'A Dynamic Theory of Racial Income Differences,' in Phyllis Ann Wallace and Annette LaMond, eds., *Women, Minorities, and Employment Discrimination* (Lexington, Mass.: Lexington Books, 1977), pp. 153–86.

164 He found that if you are black: Kerwin Kofi Charles and Patrick Kline, 'Relational Costs and the Production of Social Capital: Evidence from Carpooling,' *Economic Journal* 116 (2006): 581–604. I wrote up the paper as 'Capital Idea,' *FT Magazine*, 22 July 2006, www.timharford.com/writing/2006/07/capital-idea.html.

164 Another example: when Bertrand: Bertrand and Mullainathan, 'Are Emily and Greg More Employable than Lakisha and Jamal?'

164 So what is the answer?: Jacob Vigdor, 'When Are Ghettos Bad? Lessons from Immigrant Segregation in the United States,' working paper, June 2006, trinity.aas.duke.edu/~jvigdor/cgv2006a.pdf.

165 The sociologist Mark Granovetter: Mark Granovetter, 'The Strength of Weak Ties,' *American Journal of Sociology* 78, no. 6 (May 1973): 1360–80, www.stanford.edu/dept/soc/people/faculty/granovetter/documents/TheStrengthofWeakTies.pdf.

7. The world is spiky

166 The World is Spiky: I stole this delightful title from Richard Florida's article with Tim Gulden in *The Atlantic*, October 2005.

166 'Our dollar looks the same': Daniel Gross, 'The Value of a New York Dollar,' *New York*, 6 November 2006.

166 The bottom line: Gross, 'The Value of a New York Dollar.'

167 Ed Glaeser, the Harvard-based economist: Edward Glaeser, 'Are Cities Dying?,' *Journal of Economic Perspectives* 12, no. 2 (spring 1998): 139–60.

169 'Who needs a network?,': Jeff Jarvis, 'Points to Forbes,' blog posting, www.buzzmachine.com/2007/04/23/points-to-forbes.

169 'Great are the advantages': Alfred Marshall, *Principles of Economics*, eighth edition (London: Macmillan, 1920), book IV, chapter 10, www.econ-lib.org/LIBRARY/Marshall/marP24.html.

170 Marshall's idea was intuitive: Marshall's idea was also mathematically convenient. David Warsh, *Knowledge and the Wealth of Nations* (New York: Norton, 2006), explains the mathematical appeal of Marshall's 'externalities' in chapter 7. Economists were starting to realise that contrary to the dismal predictions of Thomas Malthus, the world was getting richer rather than running out of everything. The explanation was 'increasing returns'. The world wasn't running out of food or energy or space. Instead, more people, more investment and larger firms made things cheaper. Marshall realised that if individual

firms enjoyed increasing returns to scale, the mathematics of modelling them would be formidably complicated, and logically the world would be dominated by monopolists. So he made increasing returns a matter of technological change 'in the air' – externalities – greatly simplifying the mathematics and preserving the basic idea of competition. The idea was the only way economists could really think about technological change until Avinash Dixit, Joseph Stiglitz and especially Paul Romer worked out how to model increasing returns and then technological change inside competitive firms.

173 The idea of using rents: Warsh, *Knowledge and the Wealth of Nations*, gives a great account of the Lucas lecture and its importance (chapter 18). The lecture was eventually published as 'On the Mechanics of Economic Development,' *Journal of Monetary Economics* 22 (1988): 3–42.

173 When, in 1959: Interview with Gary Becker, September 2005. See 'It's the Humanity, Stupid,' *FT Magazine*, 17 June 2006.

175 Ed Glaeser found it: Edward Glaeser and David Maré, 'Cities and Skills,' NBER Working Paper No. 4728, May 1994.

177 Studying the official records: It may be an underestimate because Jaffe and his colleagues eliminated cases where, say, an IBM patent cited an earlier IBM patent, because they weren't sure whether this sort of citation was just cheap talk or suggested some real inspiration from the earlier patent. But later work by Jaffe, Trajtenberg and Bronwyn Hall suggested strongly that self-citations indicated real innovative value and weren't cheap talk at all. The original paper is Adam B. Jaffe, Manuel Trajtenberg and Rebecca Henderson, 'Geographic Localization of Knowledge Spillovers as Evidenced by Patent Citations,' *Quarterly Journal of Economics* 108, no. 3 (August 1993): 577–98. I also interviewed Adam Jaffe in November 2006.

178 To see the reason: The canonical model of this argument is the paper that launched the so-called New Economic Geography, Paul Krugman's elegant 'Increasing Returns and Economic Geography,' *Journal of Political Economy* 99, no. 3 (June 1991): 483–99. This and many other Krugman academic papers are available at math.stanford.edu/~lekheng/krugman/index.html.

179 Looking at the location: David B. Audretsch and Maryann P. Feldman, 'R&D Spillovers and the Geography of Innovation and Production,' *American Economic Review* 86, no. 3 (June 1996): 630–40.

179 There are those that: Robert Wright, 'China Leads on Sorting of Goods Prior to Shipping,' *Financial Times*, 27 March 2007.

180 Apart from these easily transportable: Jane Jacobs discusses these points at length in two short books, *Cities and the Wealth of Nations* (New York: Random House, 1984) and *The Economy of Cities* (New

York: Vintage, 1969). Paul Krugman provides an updated discussion in the last chapter of *Pop Internationalism* (Cambridge, Mass.: MIT Press, 1996).

181 What if these communication technologies: Jess Gaspar and Edward Glaeser, 'Information Technology and the Future of Cities,' *Journal of Urban Economics* 43, no. 1 (January 1998): 136–56.

182 In both the United States and Japan: Gaspar and Glaeser, 'Information Technology and the Future of Cities'.

182 As for e-mail: Neil Gandal, Charles King III and Marshall W. Van Alstyne, 'Information Technology Use and Productivity at the Individual Level,' CEPR Discussion Paper No. 6260, April 2007 www.cepr.org/pubs/dps/DP6260.asp.

182 On niche dating sites: Alex Mindlin, 'On Niche Dating Sites, Many More Women,' *New York Times*, 26 February 2007.

183 Just look at jointly written academic papers: Gaspar and Glaeser, 'Information Technology and the Future of Cities'.

183 Since the 1980s: Gaspar and Glaeser, 'Information Technology and the Future of Cities'.

184 'She was dissatisfied': Jacobs, *The Economy of Cities*, p. 51.

185 The business guru Michael Porter: Michael Porter, 'Clusters and the New Economics of Competition,' *Harvard Business Review* 76, no. 6 (November–December 1998): 77–90.

186 A group of four economists: Edward L. Glaeser, Hedi D. Kallal, Jose A. Scheinkman and Andrei Shleifer, 'Growth in Cities,' *Journal of Political Economy* 100, no. 6 (December 1992): 1126–52.

186 Nor is this the only: Gianmarco Ottaviano and Giovanni Peri, 'The Economic Value of Cultural Diversity: Evidence from US Cities,' NBER Working Paper No. 10904, November 2004.

187 When Katrina hit: Jack Shafer, 'Don't Refloat: The Case against Rebuilding the Sunken City of New Orleans,' *Slate*, 7 September 2005, www.slate.com/id/2125810.

187 New Orleans is not the only: Ed Glaeser and Janet Kohlhase, 'Cities, Regions and the Decline of Tranport Costs,' Harvard Institute of Economic Research, Working Paper No. 2014, July 2003.

187 In the United Kingdom, Liverpool lost: Alan Beattie, 'Engine of Enterprise in the Push and Pull of Rural Desertion,' *Financial Times*, 7 August 2006.

188 Next to faded glories: A poignant portrait of Detroit is Daniel Pimlott, 'A Morbid Urban Safari,' *Financial Times*, 15 July 2006.

188 Perhaps because of a belated outbreak: The paper is now called 'Urban Decline and Durable Housing'. The story about the provocative subtitle is from a profile of Glaeser in the *New York Times Magazine*: Jon Gertner, 'Homo Economicus,' 5 March 2006.

188 'There's no builder': Gertner, 'Homo Economicus'.

188 The housing stock in pre-Katrina: My source for the age of New Orleans housing stock is Shafer, 'Don't Refloat'.

189 Glaeser was aghast: See Edward Glaeser, 'Should the Government Rebuild New Orleans, or Just Give Residents Checks?,' *Economists' Voice* 2, no. 4 (2005), article 4.

189 Steven Landsburg, writing in *Slate*: Steven E. Landsburg, 'Hurricane Relief? Or a $200,000 Check?,' *Slate*, 22 September 2005, www.slate.com/id/2126715/.

190 'Don't make them go back': Telephone interview with George Horwich, February 2006. In the end, some compensation was payable to residents who moved away from their original homes. It tended to be less generous; for instance, a federal programme would pay only 60 per cent of the value of a damaged home if the home-owner decided to leave Louisiana, but the full value of any damages, up to $150,000, for those who stayed to rebuild. See, for instance, Brett Martel, '$4.2 Billion for Hurricane Rebuilding Approved,' *Houston Chronicle*, 11 July 2006, www.chron.com/disp/story.mpl/hurricane/4039578.html.

190 Gyourko reckons: Interview with Joe Gyourko, December 2006.

191 His memorable conclusion: David Owen, 'Green Manhattan,' *New Yorker*, 18 October 2004.

192 One notorious example: 'Homeland Security Grants to New York Slashed,' *New York Times*, 31 May 2006.

192 The EU doles out: BBC News, 2 December 2005, news.bbc.co.uk/2/hi/europe/4407792.stm.

192 In the United Kingdom, Londoners pay: Oxford Economics, 'Regional Contributions to UK Public Finances', report and press release, 19 February 2007.

8. Rational revolutions

194 The Vice-President: Gore's retracted concession is detailed on news archives at CNN, archives.cnn.com/2000/ALLPOLITICS/stories/12/13/got.here/index.html, and PBS, www.pbs.org/newshour/media/election2000/election_night.html.

195 For more detail: For the maths behind the odds of 1 in 300,000 see Jordan Ellenberg 'Why Your Ballot Isn't Meaningless,' *Slate*, www.slate.com/id/2108029/ and accompanying equations at www.slate.com/Features/pdf/BayesianVote.pdf. Despite the title, Ellenberg's calculations show that your ballot *is* meaningless. Also see Steven Landsburg, 'Don't Vote: Play the Lottery Instead,' *Slate*, 29 September 2004, www.slate.com/id/2107240/. Landsburg's

alternative assumptions make it more likely that you would affect a fifty–fifty election and less likely you'd affect a less even race. The reason for the difference is that Landsburg assumes you know that a fifty–fifty election really is that close, while Ellenberg models the process of trying to judge how close the election really is. The disagreement is interesting but doesn't alter the conclusion: if you are thinking of affecting a presidential race, forget about it.

197   Contrast the voting decision: Bryan Caplan has the clearest explanation of this reasoning, for example in his essay for the Cato Institute, 'The Myth of the Rational Voter,' www.cato-unbound.org/ 2006/11/06/ bryan-caplan/the-myth-of-the-rationalvoter/, 6 November 2006, or in his book with the same title (Princeton, NJ: Princeton University Press, 2007). Caplan goes further than I do, claiming not only that voters are rationally ignorant but that they are 'rationally irrational' – they actually enjoy holding infantile views about politics, and know those views cost them nothing. Caplan's thesis is worth taking seriously. He might argue that voters should be bracketed with the clients of Mexican prostitutes from Chapter One: they are being silly but have no compelling reason to be sensible. In some instances, his thesis produces different implications from mine. However, I'd argue that 'rationally irrational' voters and 'rationally ignorant' voters are unlikely to behave differently in the examples I explore in this chapter.

197   As an example of that ignorance: my source for data on voter ignorance is Kaiser Family Foundation, www.kff.org/kaiserpolls/1001-welftbl.cfm, table 16. The size of foreign aid spending is from Samuel Bazzi, Sheila Herrling and Stewart Patrick, 'Billions for War, Pennies for the Poor,' Center for Global Development, 16 March 2007, www.cgdev.org/content/publications/detail/13232.

198   This US government programme: John C. Beghin, Barbara El Osta, Jay R. Cherlow and Samarendu Mohanty, 'The Cost of the US Sugar Program Revisited,' *Contemporary Economic Policy* 21, no. 1 (January 2003): 106–16, cep.oxfordjournals.org/cgi/content/abstract/21/1/106.

198   Smug European readers, please note: Quentin Somerville, 'Sugar Industry to Face Market Exposure,' BBC News, 22 December 2003, news.bbc.co.uk/1/hi/business/3309715.stm.

198   Of course, trade barriers *do* benefit: Daniella Markheim, 'Backgrounder: DR-CAFTA Yes, Sugar No,' Heritage Foundation, 2005, www.heritage.org/Research/TradeandForeignAid/upload/80814_1.pdf.

199   A US government report: US General Accounting Office report, cited in Douglas Irwin, *Free Trade under Fire* (Princeton, NJ: Princeton University Press, 2002), p. 61.

199   Carol Campbell: Susan Salisbury, 'A Bittersweet Struggle,' *Palm*

Beach Post, 29 August 2004, www.citizenstrade.org/pdf/palmbeach-post_floridasugar_08292004.pdf.

200 They also want the cash: Center for Responsive Politics, 'Sugar: Long-Term Contribution Trends,' www.opensecrets.org/industries/indus.asp?Ind=A1200.

200 A class of twenty-six students: The story is told by Avinash Dixit and Barry Nalebuff, *Thinking Strategically* (New York: Norton, 1993), chapter 4.

202 Saying 'get organised' solves nothing: The classic statement of this reasoning is in Mancur Olson's *Logic of Collective Action* (Cambridge, Mass.: Harvard University Press, 1965).

204 Politically, this is perfect: For more on this, see David Friedman, *Hidden Order* (New York: HarperBusiness, 1996), especially his chapter on 'Law and Sausage', a clear, quick explanation of the theory of rational politics. The argument originates with Gary Becker, 'A Theory of Competition among Pressure Groups for Political Influence,' *Quarterly Journal of Economics* 98, no. 3 (August 1983): 371–400.

204 Interestingly, the agribusiness sector: Center for Responsive Politics, www.opensecrets.org/industries/indus.asp?Ind=A. The real estate sector itself contributes a lot, which is what we'd expect, given the importance of planning laws for the value of land.

205 City folk are picking up: US Census Bureau; UK Office for National Statistics.

206 Economist Robert H. Bates: Robert H. Bates, *Markets and States in Tropical Africa* (Berkeley: University of California Press, 2005).

206 'The evidence before us suggests': *Government Statement on the Report of the Committee Appointed to Enquire into the Local Purchasing of Cocoa* (White Paper No. 3), Ghana, 1967. Quoted in Bates, *Markets and States in Tropical Africa*, p. 27.

206 In contrast, there were many: Bates, *Markets and States in Tropical Africa*, chapter 5.

207 Beatings and assassinations: Bates, *Markets and States in Tropical Africa*, pp. 106–10.

207 Readers of my previous book: Tim Harford, *The Undercover Economist* (New York: Oxford University Press, 2005), chapter 8. The argument itself comes from Mancur Olson, *Power and Prosperity* (New York: Basic Books, 2000).

208 'To this the King gave': Charles Oman, *The Great Revolt of 1381* (Oxford: Clarendon Press, 1906), pp. 200–3, 205, available at www.fordham.edu/halsall/source/anon1381.html.

209 Wat Tyler should have realised: Daron Acemoglu and James A. Robinson, *Economic Origins of Dictatorship and Democracy* (Cambridge: Cambridge University Press, 2006), p. 138.

209 'The FBI surround the house': The routine is captured on the album *Woody Allen – Standup Comic*.

210 Even as profound a thinker: Thomas Schelling, *The Strategy of Conflict* (Cambridge, Mass.: Harvard University Press, 1960).

210 'There is no-one more decided': William Easterly's review of Acemoglu and Robinson's book reminded me of this example. See *Economic Journal*, February 2007, for a collection of reviews, including Easterly's.

212 Holland, 1688: Sources include Acemoglu and Robinson, *Economic Origins of Dictatorship and Democracy*; Stephen Quinn, 'The Glorious Revolution of 1688,' *EH.Net Encyclopedia*, ed. Robert Whaples, 2003, eh.net/encyclopedia/article/quinn.revolution.1688; Douglass North and Barry Weingast, 'Constitutions and Commitment: The Evolution of Institutions Governing Public Choice in Seventeenth-Century England,' *Journal of Economic History* 49, no. 4 (1989): 803–32.

213 An alternative way of raising revenue: Details of the fiscal regime before 1688 are from North and Weingast, 'Constitutions and Commitment'.

9. A million years of logic

215 Imagine compressing: For the chronology I have relied on Eric Beinhocker's summary in *The Origins of Wealth* (London: Random House, 2007) and encyclopedias.

215 But economic growth didn't simply: For the Stone Age I am using population data from Kremer and assuming no appreciable increase in income per head. Michael Kremer, 'Population Growth and Technological Change: One Million BC to 1990,' *Quarterly Journal of Economics* 108, no. 3 (1993): 681–716. For modern population growth, see US Census Bureau, www.census.gov/ipc/www/idb. Data from after AD 1 are from Angus Maddison, the world's foremost calculator of historical economic data, at www.ggdc.net/maddison/Historical_Statistics/horizontal-file_10-2006.xls. I downloaded them in December 2006.

217 For example, if you flip: For this data and the example, I am relying on an old essay by J. Bradford DeLong for chapter 2 of his forthcoming book, *Slouching towards Utopia*. The essay has moved around but at the time of writing is available at econ161.berkeley.edu/TCEH/Slouch_wealth2.html.

218 The economist William Nordhaus: Nordhaus, 'Do Real-Output and Real-Wage Measures Capture Reality? The History of Lighting Suggests Not,' in Timothy F. Bresnahan and Robert J. Gordon, eds,

The Economics of New Goods (Chicago: University of Chicago Press, 1997), or online at econpapers.repec.org/paper/cwlcwldpp/1078. htm. Also see David Warsh, *Knowledge and the Wealth of Nations*, chapter 24, which describes Nordhaus's experiments.

219 Subsistence income: See Tim Harford, 'Cash 22,' *FT Magazine*, 31 March 2007, and Abhijit V. Banerjee and Esther Duflo, 'The Economic Lives of the Poor,' MIT working paper, October 2006, econ-www.mit.edu/files/530.

219 The halfway point: Maddison, data cited above.

219 For example, real wages: Gregory Clark, *Farewell to Alms* (Princeton, NJ: Princeton University Press, 2007), p. 42.

219 But by that measure: Kremer, 'Population Growth and Technological Change'. For modern population growth, see US Census Bureau, www.census.gov/ipc/www/idb.

220 Economic historian Robert Allen: Robert C. Allen, 'The British Industrial Revolution in Global Perspective: How Commerce Created the Industrial Revolution and Modern Economic Growth,' unpublished paper, 2006.

222 'In all countries': Smith, *The Wealth of Nations*, book II, chapter 30, paragraphs. 30–2, www.econlib.org/LIBRARY/Smith/smWN.html.

223 Twelve of Europe's fifty-six largest cities: J. Bradford DeLong and Andrei Shleifer, 'Princes and Merchants: City Growth before the Industrial Revolution,' *Journal of Law and Economics* 36 (October 1993): 671–702, econ161.berkeley.edu/pdf_files/Princes.pdf.

223 Europe started to become decisively richer: Daron Acemoglu, Simon Johnson and James Robinson, 'The Rise of Europe: Atlantic Trade, Institutional Change, and Economic Growth,' *American Economic Review* 95, no. 3 (June 2005): 546–79, econ-www.mit.edu/files/296.

225 Siaya District: Jeffrey Sachs, 'The End of Poverty,' *Time*, 14 March 2005. The article is an excerpt from Sachs's book of the same name.

226 Sachs and various colleagues: See especially John Luke Gallup, Jeffrey Sachs and Andrew Mellinger, 'Geography and Economic Development,' NBER Working Paper No. 6849, December 1998.

227 Around 1900, life expectancy: Matthew Kahn brought this to my attention (interview, November 2006). See also Michael Haines, 'The Urban Mortality Transition in the United States,' NBER Historical Paper No. 134, July 2001.

227 'by evill examples into extravagence': Wikipedia, 'Pilgrims,' en.wikipedia.org/w/index.php?title=Pilgrims#Decision_to_leave.

228 The Beauchamp Committee: Daron Acemoglu, Simon Johnson, and James A. Robinson, 'The Colonial Origins of Economic Development: An Empirical Investigation,' *American Economic Review* 91, no. 5 (December 2001): 1369–401.

229   As luck would have it: James Feyrer and Bruce Sacerdote, 'Colonialism and Modern Income: Islands as Natural Experiments' NBER Working Paper No. 12546, October 2006, www.nber.org /papers/w12546. A nice summary is Joel Waldfogel, 'Master of the Island: Which Country Is the Best Colonizer?' *Slate*, 19 October 2006, www.slate.com/id/2151852/. Another good popular account is 'Economics Focus: Winds of Change,' *The Economist*, 2 November 2006.

232   'Nobody ever saw a dog': Smith, *The Wealth of Nations*, book I, chapter 2, www.econlib.org/LIBRARY/Smith/smWN.html.

232   Computer-based simulations: See 'Homo Economicus?,' *The Economist*, 7 April 2005, and Richard D. Horan, Erwin Bulte and Jason F. Shogren, 'How Trade Saved Humanity from Biological Exclusion: An Economic Theory of Neanderthal Extinction,' *Journal of Economic Behavior and Organization* 58, no. 1 (September 2005): 1–29.

233   Neanderthals, apparently, did not: 'Mrs Adam Smith,' *The Economist*, 9 December 2006. Also Steven L. Kuhn and Mary C. Stiner, 'What's a Mother to Do? The Division of Labor among Neanderthals and Modern Humans in Eurasia,' *Current Anthropology* 47, no. 6 (December 2006): 953–80, www.journals .uchicago.edu/CA/journal/issues/v47n6/066001/066001.w eb.pdf.

233   'First, That food is necessary': Thomas Malthus, *An Essay on the Principle of Population*, 1798.

235   The end of the last ice age: Kremer, 'Population Growth and Technological Change'. Also see Clark, *Farewell to Alms*, chapter 7.

237   Most commodity prices: Julian Simon, *The State of Humanity* (Boston: Blackwell, 1995).

Index

About the author

Tim Harford is a member of the *Financial Times* editorial board. His column, 'The Undercover Economist', which reveals the economic ideas behind everyday experiences, is published in the *Financial Times* and *Slate*. He is also the only economist in the world to run a problem page, 'Dear Economist'; in it *Financial Times'* readers' personal problems are answered tongue-in-cheek with the latest economic theory. Tim presented the BBC television series *Trust Me, I'm an Economist* and now presents the BBC radio series *More or Less*. He is a regular contributor to *Marketplace* and the BBC World Service, and his writing has appeared in *Esquire*, *Forbes*, *New York* magazine, the *Washington Post*, and the *New York Times*. Tim won the 2006 Bastiat Prize for economic journalism. Before becoming a writer, Tim worked for Shell, the World Bank and as a tutor at Oxford University. He lives in London with his wife and two daughters. Visit his website at www.timharford.com.